Legitimacy and the State

Legitimacy and the State

Edited by WILLIAM CONNOLLY

New York University Press
New York 1984

First published in 1984 in the U.S.A. by
New York University Press, Washington Square,
New York N.Y. 10003

Library of Congress Cataloging in Publication Data
Main entry under title:
Legitimacy and the state.—(Readings in social and political
theory)
Includes bibliographies and index.
1. Legitimacy of governments—Addresses, essays, lectures.
I. Connolly, Willian E.   II. Series
JC328.2.L44   1984   320.2   84–91149

ISBN 0-8147-1394-7
ISBN 0-8147-1395-5 (pbk.)

Typeset by Katerprint Co. Ltd, Oxford
Printed and bound in Great Britain

Contents

Introduction:
Legitimacy and Modernity

WILLIAM CONNOLLY

The issue of legitimacy reaches into every corner of modernity and each claim to resolve it definitively eventually encounters a series of vocal counterclaims. Why do the search and the obstacles grow together? Is this a virtue or a defect of modernity? Is it a danger or a distinctive achievement? To answer these questions, consider two quotations from modern political thought. The first is from Jean-Jacques Rousseau in 1755:

> Man is born free, and everywhere he is in chains . . . How did this change occur? I do not know. What can make it legitimate? I believe I can answer this question . . . But the social order is a sacred right that serves as a basis for all others. However, this right does not come from nature; it is therefore based on convention. The problem is to know what these conventions are.[1]

The second is stated by Nietzsche in 1888:

> What I relate is the history of the next two centuries. I describe what is coming, what can no longer come differently: *the advent of nihilism*. This future speaks even now in a hundred signs; this destiny announces itself everywhere . . . For some time now, our whole European culture has been moving as toward a catastrophe, with a tortured tension that is growing from decade to decade: restlessly, violently, headlong like a river that wants to reach the end, that no longer reflects, that is afraid to reflect.[2]

Two statements separated by 130 years and a series of profound changes in the character of social and political life. And yet they are also linked. Each understands that modern life is governed by conventions rather than God or nature or immemorial tradition, and each perceives both danger and possibility in this development. Each too is guided by a sense of urgency, a sense that the author is confronting questions which others avoid or deny, and a feeling that denial here can come to no good. The issue of legitimacy blossoms when appreciation of the conventional character of social norms and institutions becomes widespread.

But these two texts, separated by merely a century, also express profound differences in mood and perspective. The two authors inhabit different worlds. While each is a radical critic of common-place assumptions governing thought in his own day, each shares more with his own age than either does with the other.

Rousseau stands at the inception of a new age, an age in which the decline of medieval institutions and understandings has pro-ceeded so far that it is imperative to find new bearings for political and moral life; just prior to the French Revolution, all the old foundations have rotted away and the answers available to the future have not yet been formulated clearly or subjected to the test of experience. The circumstances call for radical thought.

The question of legitimacy could be posed within the framework of medieval society, but compared to modernity, the space provided for such a question was cramped and confined. The common orientations to God, knowledge, nature, language and morality compressed, as it were, the understanding of the conventional character of social life; they squeezed, thereby, the space in which the question of legitimacy could be posed. The understanding by Crollius in 1624 of the relations among celestial bodies and earthbound plants would seem as strange to Rousseau in 1755 as it does to us today.

> The stars are the matrix of all the plants and every star in the sky is only the spiritual prefiguration of a plant, such that it represents that plant, and just as each herb or plant is a terrestrial star looking up at the sky, so also each star is a celestial plant in spiritual form, which differs from the terrestrial plants in matter alone . . . The celestial plants and herbs are turned toward the earth and look directly upon the plants they have procreated, imbuing them with some particu-lar virtue.[3]

In this world nature is alive with God's signature and purpose; by discerning resemblances residing in it (e.g. affinities between plants and stars, and between things and sacred words) we glimpse something of the purposeful order given to us by God. Words too are divine signs, given to us for a purpose. By studying sacred texts we participate, though darkly, in the purposeful world. To know, in this setting, is thus not to establish laws of nature experimentally or to collect facts which in themselves have no meaning. Knowledge assumes the form of commentary on meanings and affinities inscribed in the text of the world by God. In a world where things and words are filled with divine purpose, empiricism and the fact/value dichotomy make no sense. Authority resides within, or is expressed through, the words, things, events of the world. That's why dreams, madness and miracles could carry such different meanings in that world from those bestowed on them in ours.

In such a world convention is experienced lightly; custom is touched and circumscribed by divine purpose. The legitimacy of political authority might become a question, but it is a muted issue, confined within an understanding of divinely sanctioned hierarchies. Perhaps the church will occasionally charge the secular authority with overstepping its divinely established limits; maybe a maverick philosopher will justify tyrannicide. But the very grounding of political authority, the basic character of established custom, and the existence of finely drawn hierarchies are not treated as variable conventions in need of legitimation. They provide the settled and unquestioned matrix within which issues of politics and legitimacy are marginalized. As John Huizinga tells us, 'the idea of a proposed and continual reform . . . of society did not exist. Institutions in general are considered as good or as bad as they can be; having been ordained by God, they are intrinsically good, only the sins of men pervert them . . . Legislation . . . never aims . . . at creating a new organism . . . it only restores good old law . . . or mends special abuses.'[4]

By the time Rousseau wrote, the world was no long understandable as a meaningful order filled with divine purpose discernible to some degree by human beings. Changes in the understanding of God, nature, language, self, and knowledge forced the retreat of divine authority, enlarged the sense of the conventional, and, thereby, inflated the issue of legitimacy. After God's retreat from the world (he does not disappear altogether) nature becomes a deposit of objects to be understood through humanly constructed categories; words become human instruments of understanding and representation; knowledge is grounded in perception and logic; and agency, purpose, will, and intelligence migrate from a cosmos in which human beings are privileged participants to human beings alone. The accentuation of human will and agency goes together with the extension of the sense of the conventional. Established customs can now be understood to be the direct and indirect result of human will; they can therefore be revised through wilful action and validated by some standard endorsed by the will. The secularization of nature, the concentration of will and agency in human beings, the accentuation of the conventional, and the intensification of the question of legitimacy presuppose and engender one another. A clearing is thereby created in which the issue of legitimacy can receive its modern formulation.

Rousseau enters this clearing to pose the question of legitimacy in a radical, uncompromising manner. 'Man is born free', signifies that we are released from enclosure in a larger, meaningful cosmos. We are on our own, free to be, within very general limits, what we will to be. And yet 'everywhere he is in chains'. The experience of closure and confinement is magnified by the enhancement of human will. Unwilled limits are now chains, rather than customs touched by divine purpose. The chains have been created, not by God (as punishment, perhaps) or by nature; they emerge from the previous history of innocent and wilful beings, beings whose will has constantly outstripped their ability to anticipate its effects. We have chained ourselves and thus the remedy resides within us. Our unfree condition is the result of a series of 'different *accidents* that were able to perfect human reason, while deteriorating the species, make a being evil by making him sociable, and from such a distant origin finally bring man and the world to the point where we see them.'[5]

'What can make it legitimate?' What, that is, can render the conventions governing us valid by making them fully expressive of our will? Rousseau believes he can answer that question. By looking retrospectively at the process by which we have arrived at the current, ambiguous state of perfected reason and species deterioration, we can discern a possible set of conventions which merit our reflective allegiance.

The 'social order is a sacred right that serves as the basis for all others'. For without society, language, reason, and will could not develop, and without these achievements we are incapable of freedom, incapable, that is, of government by maxims that we will ourselves. Because we have developed language and reason, we are now capable of freedom, capable of living in an order which is legitimate because it expresses the moral will. But though the social order is a sacred right it is not given to us directly by God or nature: 'it is therefore based on convention.' The ideas of will, freedom, legitimacy, and convention complement one another in Rousseau's thought. Conventions are customs, habits, institutions which have their source in human will and could be otherwise. Therefore they are susceptible to the question of validation or legitimacy. Do existing conventions deserve our allegiance? If not, what set of conventions do?

Rousseau, while pessimistic about the prospects for realizing a truly legitimate order, is optimistic about the prospects for conceptualizing one. The problem is 'to know what these (legitimate) conventions are'; and Rousseau says, 'I believe I can answer that question.'

Yet the answer he gives is surprising. It requires of course that the laws governing the polity express the general will. But the preconditions for successful operation of the general will also place most spheres of the common life outside its reach. The relations between the sexes, for instance, are not products of that will; the authority of the male and his privileged role as citizen are rather preconditions *for* the operation of the general will. The economy is not a result of the general will; it is a community of self-subsistent, small farms which have evolved prior to its formation. The size of the polity, its isolation from foreign involvements, the patriarchal character and centrality of family life, the rough equality of material conditions, the values which communal censorship sustain – these are all *preserved* by the general will, but they are *established* before the general will itself emerges. They provide its conditions of existence. That is why Rousseau is so pessimistic about the prospects for achieving in history that which can be conceived abstractly: fortune seldom shines so bountifully on a people; most countries lack Rousseau's conditions for community.

We are wilful creatures capable of formulating and living in accordance with the general will. But our wilfulness requires the general will to be limited to a few simple laws; everything else is to be lived by the participants as a set of traditions insulated against the play of wilful change. Rousseau is, finally, a theorist of the minimal state (or, better, the minimal *polity*). He poses the issue of legitimacy in a modern way, but his solution expresses nostalgia for a pre-modern world which contained and tamed wilful politics.

Just as the Enlightenment theorists of will (and theorists of utility too) pierced through mystifications of medieval life, Nietzsche pierces through new mystifications spawned by the Enlightenment. But Nietzschean demystification is in one important respect unlike that of a Rousseau or a Hobbes. The earlier theorists demolished old standards to establish new ones; but the nihilism Nietzsche discerns at the centre of modernity devalues old standards without bringing any new and convincing ones into being.

Nietzsche thus relates 'the history of the next two centuries', one which will see determined efforts to ward off the self-destruction of Enlightenment understandings of self, will, truth, language, reason and legitimacy. The very tenacity of the defence is itself a sign of 'the advent of nihilism'. For 'passive nihilism', on Nietzsche's reading, is the struggle to remain innocent about the arbitrary character of modern ideas of agency, truth and legitimacy. It is, literally, the defence of nothing, of standards founded on nothing. Modernity moves toward acknowledgement of its own nihilism with a 'tortured tension'. It moves 'like a river . . . that no longer reflects, that is afraid to reflect'. As the capacity to detect the artificial and ungrounded character of established standards grows, the social and personal disciplines needed to protect those standards from such exposure grow too. Modern reflectiveness stops at the edge of this abyss; it 'is afraid to reflect' because it senses that there is no ground beneath its most basic constructions. It thereby heads 'toward a catastrophe'.

In Rousseau's world the state was minimally developed, bureaucracies were clumsy and limited in scope; commercialization was circumscribed; social tradition governed much of life. The sphere of legitimacy was still confined. Since 1888 the conventionalization of social life, the commercialization of life, bureaucratization, the celebration of the free individual, and the entanglement of the state in every sphere of life have advanced 'restlessly, violently, headlong like a river'. With these changes the issue of legitimacy has shifted and intensified. If Rousseau's definition of the issue remains pertinent to our world, his resolution has become hopelessly anachronistic. For today a very broad range of private activities and social practices must be co-ordinated by conscious means, and this extends indefinitely the range of practices and standards in need of legitimation. The conventionalization of social life thus simultaneously extends the scope of legitimation and shakes the ground upon which it seeks to stands. Contemporary radical, liberal, and conservative doctrines of legitimacy must constantly discount each other's specific theory of legitimacy, while collectively combatting the suspicion that they participate in a process whereby 'the highest values devaluate themselves?'[6]

The chapters in this volume might profitably be read, first, as a series of direct or indirect replies to the Nietzschean reading of the link between modernity and nihilism, and, second, as a series of debates over the proper meaning of legitimacy, the developments which threaten it, and the direction to pursue in securing it.

Echoes of Rousseau can be heard in Marx's essay on constitutional reform in Prussia, but there is a reaction as well against Rousseau's idea of political will. The embryo of a Marxist theory of the state – never fully developed by the mature Marx – is also apparent in this early text.

Citizens can construe themselves to be free if they can see the state as the vehicle of their common will. But in fact, Marx contends, the more *politics* in the existing civil society is seen as the medium through which to realize the collective will, the more the real social evils and their sources are occluded. To hold the state responsible for social evils such as pauperism is to pretend that its relation to civil society endows it with resources sufficient to resolve those evils. When that pretence is exposed through the failure of state programmes, the stage is set for reactionaries to blame the paupers themselves for their plight. The very wish to see the state as legitimate, to see it as the locus of the public will, obscures the true relation between the state and society.

> Insofar as the state acknowledges the evidence of social grievances it locates their origin either in the laws of nature over which no human agency has control, or in private life which is independent of the state, or else in a malfunction of the administration which is dependent on it.

Control of the state oscillates between a conservative party which construes paupers to be in need of punishment and a liberal party which recurrently reforms state assistance programmes in the vain hope of eliminating pauperism. The source of this oscillation resides in the character of political understanding itself.

> Political understanding is just political understanding because its thought does not transcend the limits of politics. The sharper and livelier it is, the more completely it puts its faith in the omnipotence of the *will*, the more incapable it becomes of discovering the real sources of evil in society.

Marx understands the accentuation of political will to flow from the conventionalization of social life. And he criticizes the wilful character of capitalist politics. But he does so in anticipation of a world in which the collective will can be realized truly. He anticipates a future condition in which ideology and mystification disappear and the collectivity assumes control of its own fate. The state, which by definition is linked to mystification, thus withers away as mystification is lifted. The conventions will become transparent to the participants, reflecting the rational will of the collectivity which gives its informed allegiance to them. This hope to dissolve the issue of legitimacy into the solution of a transparent order is central not only to the 'young Marx' but to mature Marxism. It is explicitly articulated in *Das Kapital*:

> The religious reflex of the real world can, in any case, only vanish when the practical relations of everyday life offer to man none but perfectly intelligible relations with his fellows and to nature. The life process of society, which is based on the process of material production, does not strip off its mystical veil until it is treated as production by freely associated men, and is consciously regulated by them in accordance with a settled plan.[7]

It is this faith which allows Marxism to locate the riddle of legitimacy, not in the character of modernity itself, but in the particular structure of modern capitalism.

Weber's definition of legitimacy provides the starting point for contemporary discussion; it is adopted by some writers in this text and challenged at central points by others. Weber discerns three alternative claims to legitimacy. A claim might appeal to rational procedures, to 'a belief in the legality of enacted rules and the right of those elevated to authority under such rules to issue commands (legal authority)'. It might appeal to tradition, – 'an established belief in the sanctity of immemorial traditions and the legitimacy of those exercising authority under them (traditional authority)'. Or it might be founded on charisma, 'on devotion to the exceptional sanctity, heroism or exemplary character of an individual person and of the normative patterns of order revealed or ordained by him (charismatic authority)'.[89]

The disenchantment of the world – the withdrawal of God's will from the things, events, words and standards which surround a people – conventionalizes social life. Since conventionalization is incompatible with traditional authority, modern order and legitimacy assume a bureaucratic face. 'Everywhere the modern state is undergoing bureaucratization. But whether the *power* of bureaucracy within the polity is universally increasing must remain an open question.'

A bureaucratic state achieves legitimacy through following impersonal and rational procedures of decision making. The bureaucratic method legitimizes the conventions emanating from it, but it also generates 'discipline, the consistently rationalized, methodically trained and exact execution of received orders'. The extension of discipline into new areas of life – into the army, the factory, the public agencies – fosters a new kind of self:

> The individual is shorn of his natural rhythm as determined by the structure of his organism; his psycho-physical apparatus is attuned to a new rhythm through a methodical specialization of separately functioning muscles, and an optimal economy of forces is established corresponding to the conditions of work.

There are various readings of Weber's theory of modern legitimacy. Wolin offers one reading in this text, while Lipset, Schaar, Habermas and Foucault draw selective sustenance from Weber in developing divergent theories of their own.

Sheldon Wolin understands Weber to be a theorist troubled by the Nietzschean thesis that modernity progressively fosters nihilism. Weber seeks to establish a veneer of legitimacy in a world haunted by its own nihilistic tendencies. The scientific method, bureaucratic rationality, and legal procedures become the vehicles through which disorder can be avoided, overt force minimized, and modern legitimacy secured. Weber's 'iron cage' – the view that even attempts to contain bureaucracy foster its expansion – 'is a symbol with many meanings'. It symbolizes at once the displacement of the enchanted, medieval world by the grid of rational procedures governing modernity, 'our helplessness before "the tremendous cosmos of the economic order . . . which today determines the lives of all who are born into this mechanism"'; and the sense that the triumph of 'science, capitalism and bureaucratic organization' are so complete that, even though they do not exhaust the possible orientations to world and life, 'the mind has no purchase to attack them'.

'The fundamental political riddle' governing Western political thought, asserts Wolin, has been 'how to combine vast power with perfect right'. It is this search which drives theorists to contrast mundane being with a more ultimate being which grounds power in truth. But the riddle's centre of gravity is shifted in Weber's thought, since he believes there is no demonstrable answer to it. It now becomes, How is belief in the legitimacy of the modern state to be secured? The solution to this riddle is lodged in the relation between modern scientific *method* and the bureaucratic mode of legitimation. The Weberian strategy to legitimate method is part of the strategy to legitimate bureaucratic politics. The example of

Weber allows us to ponder this connection more closely: 'methodology is mind engaged in the legitimation of its own political activity'.

Wolin's account of Weber opens a series of questions. Does the modern mode of legitimation constantly open the door to corollary processes of delegitimation? Does the proliferation of rules, penalties, incentives and monitoring devices (e.g. disciplines) which accompany modern bureaucracy help to foster the spirit of evasion, litigiousness and resistance? Does the emergence of the latter in a bureaucratic world, encourage self-depoliticization?

The relation between method, bureaucracy and legitimacy is a fascinating one susceptible to alternative readings. Perhaps it is an affirmative relation in that the scientific method provides citizens with knowledge about nature and society while bureaucracies allow citizens to translate this knowledge into public action. Or perhaps these forms are the smile on the face of 'disciplinary society', as Foucault characterizes modernity, and the disciplines press the individual to 'inscribe in *himself* the power relation and become the principle of his own subjection'.[9] The ways in which conventionalization, democratization, bureaucratization, the formation of the modern self as an agent or self-discipline, and the modern state all simultaneously constitute one another and delimit the form the question of legitimacy assumes today – these ways are still in need of illumination. Though Foucault and Weber interpret these relations differently, there is also an uncanny affinity between them which revolves around their understandings of method and discipline. Wolin's essay enables one to probe these differences and affinities more deeply and helps one to plumb the connection between two modern principles: the primacy of method in inquiry and the primacy of procedural legitimacy in politics.

Seymour Martin Lipset endorses Weber's theory of legitimacy in modern democracies while stilling the Nietzschean undercurrents discernible in Weber's thought. Writing just before the dislocations and disaffection of the 1960s Lipset expresses confidence in the stabilizing effects of democratic accountability and bureaucratic rationality. Legitimacy and popular belief in the legitimacy of established institutions are treated as equivalents by Lipset. 'Legitimacy involves the capacity of the system to engender and maintain the belief that the existing political institutions are the most appropriate ones for the society.' The genius of democracy is that it allows social conflicts to find open expression, moderates the intensity of those conflicts, and provides procedures by which to legitimize their public resolution.

Legitimacy and tolerance flourish when people identify with a plurality of groups and principles; these 'cross-cutting' pressures moderate the intensity of particular interests and modulate social conflicts. Successful economic development is also essential to legitimacy, since it generates a surplus to relieve felt injustices and dampens the class struggle over income shares. It is perhaps the key to modern democratic legitimacy: 'the factors involved in modernization or economic development are linked to those which establish legitimacy and tolerance.'

John Schaar identifies Lipset's definition of legitimacy as part of a larger failure of publicists to understand the 'crisis of legitimacy' which has been brewing for some time in modern societies. 'The new definitions all dissolve legitimacy into belief or opinion.' They overlook the fact that these beliefs might be ungrounded or sustained by institutional arrangements whose real principles of operation are misunderstood by participants. The erosion of traditional authority has not been acknowledged as a loss by most moderns, but its absence helps to account for pressures to 'rationalize' modern life. Rousseau, Schaar agrees, 'was the first to understand fully . . . that ours is the task of the development of the theory and institution of a community in which men can be both conscious and individual and share the moral bends and limits of the group'. Rousseau understood, then, the distinctive challenge facing an age in which tradition has been devalued.

The insurrections of the 1960s were not marginal phenomena to be forgotten after their disappearance; these were 'the cries of people who feel that the processes and powers which control their lives are inhuman and destructive'. The celebration of will, central to the self-definition of modernity, helps to generate these cries, but it also thins out the epistemic and moral ground available to respond to them.

Schaar is, perhaps, nostalgic for a world we have lost, even though he realizes it possessed its own drudgery and brutality, and even though he knows that it cannot return to us. This trace of nostalgia may be ambiguous in its implications. It both encourages a wistful yearning for a world *we* could no longer endow with legitimacy and it helps us to discern presuppositions, limits, and dangers in our own world which remain hidden when we appraise it only through the standards and categories authorized by that world.

Jürgen Habermas has given an account of the potential for legitimacy crisis in advanced capitalist societies which now stands at the centre of contemporary debates. Habermas does not claim that we are in a crisis — as many have falsely interpreted him to say — or that a crisis is inevitable in the future. He does argue that a variety of institutional developments press toward the formation of a legitimacy crisis, a crisis in which the allegiance needed if dominant institutions are to function effectively is well below the level they actually receive.

Habermas's theory can be seen as a synthesis of themes drawn from Marx and Weber, applied to the particular conditions facing advanced capitalist societies in the last quarter of the twentieth century. Drawing from Marx, Habermas perceives the state to be caught within a set of contradictory institutional imperatives: if it responds to one set, it undermines the rationality of the economy, and if it responds to others, it depletes the legitimacy the state itself needs to steer the economy and the motivations people require to carry out the roles available to them in the political economy.

Habermas is indebted to Weber's account of the sources and effects of modern bureaucratization, but he rejects Weber's theory of legitimacy. Weber, Habermas says, was concerned with the ability of an order to generate belief in its legitimacy, not in the truth or falsity of the beliefs themselves. Why does Weber shy away from the latter question? Because of his 'view of the rationally irresolvable pluralism of competing value systems and beliefs'.[10] To demand that the belief in legitimacy be true is thus to impose an impossible requirement on social systems. However, as Habermas sees it, to fail to make that demand is tantamount to saying that every legitimate order must be grounded in mystification, manipulation, and ideology. In Habermas's alternative view, 'every effective belief in legitimacy is assumed to have an immanent relation to truth ... that can be tested and criticized.'[11] The relation is 'immanent' in that the most basic presuppositions of modern discourse provide a standard against which specific doctrines of value and legitimacy can be assessed.

The task of critical theory is to clarify and vindicate rational standards against which beliefs in legitimacy (or illegitimacy) can be tested and to conceptualize a modern form of life which deserves and receives the reflective allegiance of its members. The standard Habermas sets is very demanding:

> How would members of a social system, at a given stage in the development of productive forces, have collectively and bindingly interpreted their needs (and which norms would they have accepted as justified) if they could and would have decided on the organization of social intercourse through

discursive will-formation, with adequate knowledge of the limiting conditions and functional imperatives of the society?[12]

This is an audacious question. But it is the sort of question we implicitly pose when we ask not merely whether people *believe* existing arrangements are legitimate, but whether their beliefs are well grounded or rest upon mystification of some sort. People may, for instance, believe falsely that their current activities are building a brighter future for future generations or that existing inequalities are necessary to generate the productivity levels needed by society. Or the standards they explicitly endorse may contradict those immanent in the very conditions of social communication. The question of legitimacy, on the Habermas reading, must pose these issues, even though he acknowledges that it is difficult to achieve confident answers to them. Such questions are important, first, because our view of democracy and freedom involves the idea that rational persuasion is preferable to manipulation or mystification and, second, because mystifications which stabilize an order at one moment may veil existing injustices and prepare the stage for later decay or crisis. It is one thing, though, to discern the link between this question and cherished ideals of private and public freedom; it is another to show if and how to answer it.[13]

Habermas believes that the extension of the state into more and more areas of economic and social life – an extension required to maintain the performance of the economy and to protect the natural and social environment damaged by the history of its operation – helps to render the conventional character of existing rules and norms more visible, and thereby amplifies pressure on the state to legitimate the specific rules and policies it enacts. Such questions emerge with respect to the distribution of income, closure of opportunities for democratic participation, economic practices which damage self-purifying systems in nature, gender-specific roles, the composition of the school curriculum, and the treatment of old people. The expansion of the state enhances the visibility of the conventional and political dimension of social life and encourages citizens to ask the state to legitimize the particular conventions supported by its action. This new visibility politicizes established conventions. The introduction of bureaucratic procedures of decision making can veil the political character of state activities to some degree, but the enlarged role of the state extends questions of legitimacy to areas previously left to the authority of tradition or to the apparent play of the impersonal market.

If a legitimacy crisis unfolds in its pure form it will reflect the inability of the state, given the economic imperatives facing it, to legitimize the actions it must take in the eyes of those holding it to rational standards of legitimacy.

Habermas insists that in a rationally formed society it is possible to elaborate valid criteria of legitimacy and for the public authority to act in ways which correspond to those standards. But his theory of rational discourse is still incomplete and contestable. Behind the effort to construct such a theory is the spectre of Nietzsche and nihilism. For, as Habermas expressed it in an earlier work, the disenchantment of the medieval world created space for science to constitute nature as an object of human explanation and control while displacing it as a normative guide. It thereby impressively increased both the potential for freedom and for nihilism. Nietzsche, according to Habermas, saw that 'the critical dissolution of dogmas' threatened to be 'not emancipatory but nihilistic'.[14]

As a child of the Enlightenment and as one who lived as a young boy through the final years of German Nazism, Habermas seeks to see the modern dissolution of dogma become the realization of emancipation. A theory of legitimacy appropriate to the conditions of modern life is a crucial ingredient in that aspiration.

Not all aspects of Habermas's work are readily comprehensible to Anglo-American readers unfamiliar with the philosophical context in which it is written. Thomas McCarthy's essay admirably clarifies the themes and arguments advanced by Habermas and poses critical questions which Habermas, he thinks, has not yet answered. In his summary, McCarthy shows why Habermas believes a 'universalist morality' has emerged in modern capitalism, why advanced capitalism contravenes that morality, and why Habermas believes this morality calls for a theory of 'communicative ethics' which can sustain it. In his critique he concludes that the Habermas version of critical theory 'finds itself in a familiar embarrassment: there is no organized social movement whose interests it might seek to articulate'. The Habermas critique, in contrast to a Marxian theory addressed to the proletariat, is addressed to 'mankind as such and thus to no group in particular'.

George Kateb is less gentle with Habermas, and, by implication, with Schaar and Connolly as well. He finds America to be a unique society, expressive of a sense of individuality and scepticism toward authority, which gives its politics a certain volatility and resistance to regimentation. There is no 'legitimacy crisis' today, nor is one likely to occur; but there is a recurrent pattern of creative turmoil in American politics which theorists committed to the idea of a tight, smooth-running order mistake as a preamble to a legitimacy crisis. A legitimation crisis, on Kateb's reading, would involve deep disaffection from the constitutional principles governing the democracy. There are no signs that such a development is about to occur; there are no 'deep and widespread feelings and opinions marked by disaffection from . . . constitutional representative democracy'.

Kateb seeks to return to a conception of legitimacy in which the orientation of citizens to the constitutional principles of the state are definitive. He is unimpressed, apparently, with the claim that the politicization of broad areas of life, the extension of conscious coordination of social life, and the entanglement of the state in all corners of life, enlarges the scope of legitimacy. Kateb does not, however, ignore economic matters completely. A legitimate government (there is no 'state' in America in Kateb's view) today requires democratic principles, and a democratic polity requires capitalism. While democracy and capitalism remain in constant tension, it is a creative tension; and other forms of economic organization, most notably socialism, are incompatible with democracy. They resolve the tension in the wrong way.

Radical theorists of legitimacy crisis fail to appreciate this creative tension between capitalism and democracy; they pander to an ideal of community unrealizable in modern life and destructive of democratic citizenship. Though 'corporate capitalism gravely wounds equal citizenship . . . the socialist alternative, in either of its main types, kills it'.

Foucault poses a challenge to every other essay in this text. He is best and most briefly characterized, perhaps, as a 'left Nietzschean'. His work is on the left in its relentless effort to expose the ways in which modern forms of observation, organization, architecture, therapy and normalization work to discipline and subjugate the self, to produce the modern 'subject' whose visibility subjects it to normalization. His work is on the left too in its concentration on those pushed to the margins of the order – the insane, the perverse, the criminal, the delinquent, the unstable, and the sick. The disciplines applied to the extremities of the social order reveal much about the forms of self-discipline absorbed by those who behave according to the norm.

Foucault is Nietzschean in his refusal to adopt a theory of self, truth, reason, or legitimacy against which to appraise these disciplines. For Foucault finds the deepest standards and norms of modernity to be arbitrary constructions. They are not expressive of being, but are artefacts of power. In attacking modern conceptions of self, knowledge, and reason, he attacks the problematic of legitimacy itself. His thought disturbs and unsettles because it refuses either to endorse this order or to contrast evils in it to an ideal of a legitimate order. In theorizing order itself as imposition, he incites disorder; he supports 'the insurrection of subjugated knowledges'.

In *The Order of Things* Foucault contended that the very structure of modern discourse, its very attempt to build transcendental standards out of the understandings of a historically specific way of life, guaranteed that every enunciated social theory or moral code would generate its own counter-enunciations. None of these competitors has the capacity to sustain its legitimacy, except through imposition.

> For modern thought, no morality is possible . . . As soon as it functions it offends or reconciles, attracts or repels, breaks, dissociates, unites or reunites; it cannot help but liberate and enslave. Sade, Nietzsche, Artaud and Bataille have understood this on behalf of all who tried to ignore it.[15]

To oppose, as Foucault does, the problematic of legitimacy is to identify power as the basis of order. Foucault, in fact, identifies two complementary loci of power in modernity. There are, first, those overt forms of coercion, force, incentives, regulations, penalties which regulate behaviour in so many areas of life. And there are, second, the more insidious mechanisms of normalization which draw people into the sticky web of self-discipline. The spread of the Church confessional into secular fields of sexuality and mental health constitutes one example of this latter phenomenon. Indeed on Foucault's reading, humanists and technocrats, while often opposing each other politically, complement each other in extending the tentacles of social discipline. Each depends upon the institutional support provided by its adversary.

Foucault would sympathize, then, with some of the critical themes developed by Schaar and Habermas in this volume, but he would not endorse their quest for an affirmative theory of legitimacy. Any such effort sanctions the imposition of arbitrary disciplines; it participates ultimately in the cover-up it has promised to expose. They will reply that a theory which attacks every conception of order must lose, in a world where human life requires social form to be, its ability to differentiate oppression from the enforcement of justifiable limits.

The Connolly essay seeks to profit from the work of both Habermas and Foucault while offering criticisms of each. It does not identify an actual or incipient crisis of legitimacy but it discerns seeds of a dilemma of legitimacy in which the 'civilization of productivity' is pressed either to compromise democratic standards to fulfil the growth imperative or to compromise them through the consequences of failing to meet this imperative. The order might sustain itself if this dilemma tightens but its democratic character would be weakened. After delineating elements in this condition, emphasizing tacit shifts in contemporary orientations to the future and binds facing the welfare state, I explore theoretical perspectives which can be understood to be symptoms of it.

The contemporary bifurcation of liberalism into the soulless liberal, who devises new techniques to bring conduct into closer proximity to imperatives of the system, and the soulful liberal who concentrates on principles of right, justice, and legitimacy abstracted from the operation of the established political economy, provides one manifestation of this emerging dilemma. By examining this bifurcation we can better comprehend the political and rhetorical strategies by which the dilemma of legitimacy is evaded. Habermas and Foucault also delineate some features of this condition while evading others.

The Ricoeur essay was sparked by events in Hungary in 1956, but it could just as easily have been written in the aftermath of the late 1970s Solidarity movement in Poland. The state, on Ricoeur's reading, must be an abstract institution which lacks the familiarity and intimacy of a community. Relations between the citizen and the state are mediated by representation, and the experiences of everyday life do not mesh neatly with those facing political leaders. The abstract state cannot be eliminated in Ricoeur's view; neither the Rousseauian ideal of the general will, nor the Marxist ideal of communal freedom and transparency, are appropriate to the conditions of the modern state.

Our relation to the state creates a paradox which we must try to ameliorate rather than remove: the modern state must have ample power to foster the common good recognized by its members, whilst this very mobilization of power endows it with awesome potential for evil. Constitutionalism is the best way to cope with this paradox. In this respect Ricoeur anticipates Kateb. But Ricoeur refuses to restrict the question of legitimacy to the constitutional principles of the state, or to conclude that the capitalist state supports democracy while the socialist state cannot. He seeks reforms in the socialist state which would enhance its legitimacy while relieving some of the injustices historically attached to the capitalist state.

Unlike Marx, Ricoeur acknowledges the necessity for the abstract state in modernity and thus he recognizes the persistence of the issue of legitimacy; unlike Habermas he articulates a paradox in the character of modern politics itself, linked to the very ideal of freedom celebrated by Habermas, which transcends the relation between the state and the economy in advanced capitalism; unlike Foucault he vindicates norms of legitimacy, despite the paradox of politics; unlike Kateb he explores virtues in a Socialist state endowed with constitutional principles; and (perhaps) unlike Schaar his indictment of the potential for evil in modernity is tempered by appreciation of the new forms of mystification and control which would be required to reinstall the authority of tradition at the centre of modernity. When one reads Ricoeur on the paradox of politics, one is moved to reread these other pieces to ascertain what questions and rejoinders they might pose to him.

NOTES

1 Rousseau, *On the Social Contract* (ed.) Roger Masters and (tr.) Judith Masters (New York: St. Martins Press, 1978).

2 Nietzsche, *The Will to Power* (ed.) Walter Kaufman and (tr.) Walter Kaufman and R. J. Hollingdale (New York: Random House, 1967), p. 4.

3 Quoted in Michel Foucault, *The Order of Things* (London: Tavistock Press, 1970), p. 20.

4 John Huizinga, *The Waning of the Middle Ages* (New York: Double-day Anchor Books, 1954), p. 38.

5 Rousseau, *Discourse on the Origin of Inequality* in Roger Masters (ed.) *The First and Second Discourse* (New York: St. Martin's Press), p. 140.

6 Nietzsche, *The Will To Power*, p. 9.

7 Marx *Das Kapital*, vol. 1 (New York: International Publishers, 1961), pp. 78–9.

8 Max Weber, *Economy and Society*, vol. 1 (eds) Guenther Roth and Claus Wittich (Berkeley: University of California Press, 1978), p. 215.

9 Michel Foucault, *Discipline and Punish* (New York: Pantheon Books, 1977), p. 203.

10 *Legitimation Crisis* (tr.) Thomas McCarthy (Boston: Beacon Press, 1973), p. 100.

11 Ibid., p. 97.

12 Ibid., p. 113.

13 Steven Lukes 'Of gods and demons: Habermas and practical reason', in David Held and John B. Thompson (eds) *Habermas: Critical Debates* (London: Macmillan, 1982), pp. 134–48, gives a thoughtful, Weberian

response to Habermas. Habermas replies to this argument, and to the other pieces in this excellent volume, in 'A reply to my critics', pp. 219–83.

14 Habermas, *Knowledge and Human Interests* (tr.) Jeremy Shapiro (Boston: Beacon Press, 1968), p. 292.
15 *The Order of Things* (London: Tavistock Publications, 1970), p. 328.

1
Critical . . . Notes on . . . Social Reform

KARL MARX

No. 60 of *Vorwärts* contains an article headed '*Der König von Preussen und die Sozialreform*', signed 'A Prussian'.

First of all this alleged Prussian sets out the content of the royal Prussian Cabinet order on the uprising of the Silesian workers and the opinion of the French newspaper *La Réforme* on the Prussian Cabinet order. The *Réforme*, he writes, considers that the King's 'alarm and religious feeling' are the source of the Cabinet order. It even sees in this document a presentiment of the great reforms which are in prospect for bourgeois society. The 'Prussian' lectures the *Réforme* as follows:

> The King and German society has not yet arrived at the 'presentiment of their reform',[2] even the Silesian and Bohemian uprisings have not aroused this feeling. It is impossible to make such an unpolitical country as Germany regard the partial distress of the factory districts as a matter of general concern, let alone as an affliction of the whole civilised world. The Germans regard this event as if it were of the same nature as any local distress due to flood or famine. Hence the King regards it as due to deficiencies in the administration or in charitable activity. For this reason, and because a few soldiers sufficed to cope with the feeble weavers, the destruction of factories and machinery, too, did not inspire any 'alarm' either in the King or the authorities. Indeed, the Cabinet order was not prompted even by religious feeling: it is a very sober expression of the Christian art of statesmanship and of a doctrine which considers that no difficulties can withstand its

Source: Karl Marx, 'Critical notes on the article, The King of Prussia and Social Reform', in *The Collected Works of Marx and Engels* (New York: International Publishers, 1975), pp. 189–91, 192–5, 197–9, 203–6, reprinted with permission of International Publishers.

sole medicine — 'the well-disposed Christian hearts'. Poverty and crime are two great evils; who can cure them? The state and the authorities? No, but the union of all Christian hearts can.

The alleged Prussian denies the King's 'alarm' on the grounds among others, that a few soldiers sufficed to cope with the feeble weavers.

Therefore, in a country where ceremonial dinners with liberal toasts and liberally foaming champagne — recall the Düsseldorf festival — inspired a royal Cabinet order; where not a single soldier was needed to shatter the desires of the entire liberal bourgeoisie for freedom of the press and a constitution; in a country where passive obedience is the order of the day — can it be that in such a country the necessity to employ armed force against feeble weavers is not an event, and not an alarming event? Moreover, at the first encounter the feeble weavers were victorious. They were suppressed only by subsequent troop reinforcements. Is the uprising of a body of workers less dangerous because it did not require a whole army to suppress it? Let the wise Prussian compare the uprising of the Silesian weavers with the revolts of the English workers, and the Silesian weavers will be seen by him to be strong weavers.

Starting out from the general relation of politics to social ills, we shall show why the uprising of the weavers could not cause the King any special 'alarm'. For the time being we shall say only the following: the uprising was not aimed directly against the King of Prussia, but against the bourgeoisie. As an aristocrat and absolute monarch, the King of Prussia cannot love the bourgeoisie; still less can he be alarmed if the submissiveness and impotence of the bourgeoisie is increased because of a tense and difficult relationship between it and the proletariat. Further: the orthodox Catholic is more hostile to the orthodox Protestant than to the atheist, just as the Legitimist is more hostile to the liberal than to the Communist. This is not because the atheist and the Communist are more akin to the Catholic or Legitimist, but because they are more foreign to him than are the Protestant and the liberal, being outside his circle. In the sphere of politics, the King of Prussia, as a politician, has his direct opposite in liberalism. For the King, the proletariat is as little an antithesis as the King is for the proletariat. The proletariat would have to have already attained considerable power for it to stifle the other antipathies and political antitheses and to divert to itself all political enmity. Finally: in view of the well-known character of the King, avid for anything interesting and significant, it must have been a joyful surprise for him to discover this 'interesting' and 'much discussed' pauperism in his own territory and consequently a new opportunity for making people talk about him. How pleasant for him must have been the news that henceforth he possesses his 'own', royal Prussian pauperism! Our 'Prussian' is still more unlucky when he seeks to deny that 'religious feeling' is the source of the royal Cabinet order . . .

Why does German society lack this [reform] instinct?

'It is impossible to make such an unpolitical country as Germany' replies the Prussian, 'regard the partial distress of the factory districts as a matter of general concern, let alone as an affliction of the whole civilised world. The Germans regard this event as if it were of the same nature as any local distress due to flood or famine. Hence the King regards it as due to deficiencies in the administration and in charitable activity.'

Thus the 'Prussian' explains this misinterpretation of the distressed state of the workers as due to the special character of an unpolitical country.

It will be admitted that England is a political country. It will be admitted also that England is the country of pauperism, even the word itself is of English origin. Observing the state of things in England, therefore, is the surest means of learning the attitude of a political country to pauperism. In England, the distress of the workers is not partial but universal; it is not restricted to the factory districts, but extends to the rural districts. The movements here are not just beginning to arise, for almost a century they have periodically recurred.

What then is the view about pauperism held by the English bourgeoisie and the government and press connected with it?

Insofar as the English bourgeoisie acknowledges that politics are to blame for pauperism, the Whig regards the Tory, and the Tory regards the Whig, as the cause of pauperism. According to the Whig, the main source of pauperism is the monopoly of big landownership and the prohibitive legislation against the import of corn. According to the Tory, the whole evil lies in liberalism, in competition, and in the excessive development of the factory system. Neither of the parties sees the cause in politics in general, but each sees it only in the politics of the opposing party; neither party even dreams of a reform of society.

The most definite expression of the English view of pauperism — we are speaking always of the view of the English bourgeoisie and government — is English political economy, i.e. the scientific reflection of English economic conditions.

One of the best and most famous English economists, McCulloch — a pupil of the cynical Ricardo — who is familiar with present-day conditions and ought to have a comprehensive view of the movement of bourgeois society, still dares in a public lecture, and with applause from the audience, to apply to political economy what Bacon says about philosophy:

> The man who, with true and untiring wisdom, suspends his judgement, who goes forward step by step, surmounting one after the other the obstacles which, like mountains, hinder the course of study, will eventually reach the summit of science, where peace and pure air may be enjoyed, where nature presents itself to the eye in all its beauty, and from where it is possible to descend by a comfortably sloping path to the last details of practice.

Good pure air — the pestilential atmosphere of English cellar dwellings! Great beauty of nature — the fantastic rags worn by the English poor, and the flabby, shrunken flesh of the women, undermined by labour and poverty; children crawling about in the dirt; deformity resulting from excessive labour in the monotonous mechanical operations of the factories! The most delightful last details of practice: prostitution, murder and the gallows!

Even that part of the English bourgeoisie which is impressed by the danger of pauperism conceives this danger, as also the means to remedy it, not merely in a partial way, but also, frankly speaking, in a childish and stupid way.

Thus Dr Kay, for example, in his pamphlet *Recent Measures for the Promotion of Education in England* reduces everything to neglected education. Guess why! Owing to lack of education, the worker does not understand the 'natural laws of trade', laws which necessarily reduce him to pauperism. That is why he rebels. This could

> affect the prosperity of English manufactures and English commerce, shake the mutual confidence of mercantile men, and diminish the stability of political and social institutions.

So great is the mental vacuity of the English bourgeoisie and its press on the subject of pauperism, this national epidemic of England

Let us suppose then that the reproaches our 'Prussian' levels

against German society are well founded. Does the reason lie in the
unpolitical condition of Germany? But if the bourgeoisie of
unpolitical Germany is unable to see that a partial distress is a
matter of general significance, the bourgeoisie of political England,
on the other hand, manages to misunderstand the general significance of a universal state of distress – a distress the general
significance of which has been made evident partly by its periodical
recurrence in time, partly by its extension in space, and partly by
the failure of all attempts to remedy it.

Further, the 'Prussian' makes the unpolitical condition of Germany responsible for the fact that the King of Prussia finds the
cause of pauperism in deficiencies in the administration and in
charitable activity and therefore seeks the means to counter
pauperism in administrative and charitable measures.

Is this kind of view peculiar to the King of Prussia? Let us take a
quick look at England, the only country where large-scale political
action against pauperism can be said to have taken place.

The present English legislation on the poor dates from the Poor
Law enacted in the 43rd year of the reign of Elizabeth.[3] What are
the means adopted in this legislation? They consist in the
obligation of the parishes to support their poor labourers, in the
poor rate, and in legal charity. This legislation – charity carried out
by administrative means – has lasted for two centuries. What
attitude do we find adopted by Parliament, after long and painful
experience, in its Amendment Bill of 1834?

First of all, it explains the frightful increase of pauperism by
'deficiencies in the administration'.

Consequently, the administration of the poor rate, which was in
the hands of officials of each of the parishes, is reformed. Unions
are formed of about 20 parishes which are united in a single
administration. A committee of officials, a Board of Guardians,[4]
consisting of officials elected by the taxpayers, meets on an
appointed day in the administrative centre of the Union and decides
on the admissibility of relief. These Boards of Guardians are
directed and supervised by government representatives sitting in a
Central Commission at Somerset House, the Ministry of Pauperism, as a Frenchman[5] aptly calls it. The capital supervised by this
administration is almost equal to the amount which the military
administration in France costs. It employs 500 local administrative
bodies, and each of these in its turn has at least 12 officials working
for it.

The English Parliament did not restrict itself to a formal reform
of the administration.

It found the main source of the acute state of English pauperism in the Poor Law itself. Charity, the means prescribed by law against the social malady, is alleged to promote the social malady. As far as pauperism in general is concerned, it is said to be an eternal law of nature, according to the theory of Malthus:

> Since population is constantly tending to overtake the means of subsistence, charity is folly, a public encouragement of poverty. The state can therefore do nothing but leave the poor to their fate and, at the most, make death easy for them.

With this philanthropic theory the English Parliament combines the view that pauperism is poverty which the workers have brought upon themselves by their own fault, and therefore it is not a misfortune which must be prevented, but rather a crime which has to be suppressed and punished.

Thus there arose the system of workhouses,[6] i.e. houses for the poor, the internal organisation of which tends to deter the poor wretches from seeking refuge in them from death by starvation. In the workhouses, charity is cunningly combined with revenge of the bourgeoisie on the poor who appeal to its charity.

At first, therefore, England tried to abolish pauperism by charity and administrative measures. Then it came to see in the progressive advance of pauperism not the inevitable consequence of modern industry but, on the contrary, the consequence of the English poor rate. It regarded the universal distress merely as a specific feature of English legislation. What was previously ascribed to a lack of charity now began to be attributed to an excess of charity. Finally, poverty came to be regarded as the fault of the poor themselves, and consequently they were punished for it.

The general significance which pauperism has acquired in political England is restricted to the fact that in the course of its development, in spite of all the administrative measures, pauperism has become a national institution and has therefore inevitably become the object of a ramified and widely extended administration, but an administration which no longer has the task of abolishing pauperism but of disciplining it, of perpetuating it. This administration has given up trying to stop pauperism at its source by positive methods; it is satisfied to dig a grave for it with policeman-like gentleness whenever it wells up to the surface of the official world. Far from going beyond administrative and charitable measures, the English state has taken a big step backwards from them. Its administration now extends only to that pauperism which is so desperate as to allow itself to be caught and locked up . . .

No government in the world has issued regulations regarding pauperism at once, without reaching agreement with the authorities. The English Parliament even sent representatives to all the countries of Europe to learn about the various administrative remedies for pauperism. But insofar as the states have occupied themselves with pauperism, they have either confined themselves to administrative and charitable measures, or they have retreated to less than administrative action and charity.

Can the state act in any other way?

The state — contrary to what the Prussian demands of his King — will never see in 'the state and the system of society' the source of social maladies. Where political parties exist, each party sees the root of every evil in the fact that, instead of itself, an opposing party stands at the helm of the state. Even radical and revolutionary politicians seek the root of the evil not in the essential nature of the state, but in a definite state form, which they wish to replace by a different state form.

From the political point of view, the state and the system of society are not two different things. The state is the system of society. Insofar as the state admits the existence of social defects, it sees their cause either in the laws of nature, which no human power can command, or in private life, which does not depend on the state, or in the inexpedient activity of the administration, which does not depend on it. Thus England sees the cause of poverty in the law of nature by which the population must always be in excess of the means of subsistence. On the other hand, England explains pauperism as due to the bad will of the poor, just as the King of Prussia explains it by the un-Christian feelings of the rich, and just as the Convention explained it by the suspect counter-revolutionary mentality of the property owners. Therefore England punishes the poor, the King of Prussia admonishes the rich, and the Convention cuts off the heads of the property owners.

Finally, every state seeks the cause in accidental or deliberate shortcomings of the administration, and therefore it seeks the remedy for its ills in measures of the administration. Why? Precisely because administration is the organizing activity of the state.

The contradiction between the purpose and goodwill of the administration, on the one hand, and its means and possibilities, on the other hand, cannot be abolished by the state without the latter abolishing itself, for it is based on this contradiction. The state is based on the contradiction between public and private life, on the contradiction between general interests and private interests. Hence the administration has to confine itself to a formal and negative activity, for where civil life and its labour begin, there the power of the administration ends. Indeed, confronted by the consequences which arise from the unsocial nature of this civil life, this private ownership, this trade, this industry, this mutual plundering of the various circles of citizens, confronted by all these consequences, impotence is the law of nature of the administration. For this fragmentation, this baseness, this slavery of civil society is the natural foundation on which the modern state rests, just as the civil society of slavery was the natural foundation on which the ancient state rested. The existence of the state and the existence of slavery are inseparable. The ancient state and ancient slavery – these straightforward classic opposites – were not more intimately riveted to each other than are the modern state and the modern commercial world, these hypocritical Christian opposites. If the modern state wanted to abolish the impotence of its administration, it would have to abolish the private life of today. But if it wanted to abolish private life, it would have to abolish itself, for it exists only in the contradiction to private life. But no living being believes that the shortcomings of his existence have their basis in the principle of his life, in the essence of his life; everyone believes that their basis lies in circumstances external to his life. Suicide is against nature. Therefore the state cannot believe in the inherent impotence of its administration, i.e. in its own impotence. It can perceive only formal, accidental deficiencies in its administration and try to remedy them. And if these modifications prove fruitless, the conclusion is drawn that social ills are a natural imperfection independent of man, a law of God or – that the will of private individuals is too spoilt to be able to respond to the good intentions of the administration. And how preposterous these private individuals are! They grumble at the government whenever it restricts their freedom, and at the same time they demand that the government prevent the inevitable results of this freedom!

The mightier the state, and the more political therefore a country is, the less is it inclined to grasp the general principle of social maladies and to seek their basis in the principle of the state, hence in the present structure of society, the active, conscious and official expression of which is the state. The political mind is a political mind precisely because it thinks within the framework of politics. The keener and more lively it is, the more incapable is it of understanding social ills. The classic period of political intellect is the French Revolution. Far from seeing the source of social shortcomings in the principle of the state, the heroes of the French Revolution instead saw in social defects the source of political evils. Thus, Robespierre saw in great poverty and great wealth only an obstacle to pure democracy. Therefore he wished to establish a universal Spartan frugality. The principle of politics is the will. The more one-sided and, therefore, the more perfected the political mind is, the more does it believe in the omnipotence of the will, the more is it blind to the natural and spiritual limits of the will, and the more incapable is it therefore of discovering the source of social ills. There is no need of further argument against the 'Prussian's' silly hope that 'political understanding' is destined 'to discover the roots of social distress in Germany'.

That social distress produces political understanding is so incorrect that, on the contrary, what is correct is the opposite: social well-being produces political understanding. Political under-standing is a spiritualist, and is given to him who already has, to him who is already comfortably situated. Let our 'Prussian' listen to a French economist, M. Michel Chevalier, on this subject:

> When the bourgeoisie rose up in 1789, it lacked – in order to be free – only participation in governing the country. Emancipation consisted for it in wresting the control of public affairs, the principal civil, military and religious functions, from the hands of the privileged who had the monopoly of these functions. Rich and enlightened, capable of being self-sufficient and of managing its own affairs, it wanted to escape from the system of arbitrary rule.[7]

We have already shown the 'Prussian' how incapable political understanding is of discovering the source of social distress. Just one word more on this view of his. The more developed and universal the political understanding of a people, the more does the proletariat – at any rate at the beginning of the movement – squander its forces in senseless, useless revolts, which are drowned in blood. Because it thinks in the framework of politics, the proletariat sees the cause of all evils in the will, and all means of remedy in violence and in the overthrow of a particular form of state. The proof: the first uprising of the French proletariat. The Lyons workers believed that they were pursuing only political aims, that they were only soldiers of the republic, whereas actually they were soldiers of socialism. Thus their political understanding concealed from them the roots of social distress, thus it falsified their insight into their real aim, thus their *political understanding deceived* their *social instinct.*

But if the 'Prussian' expects understanding to be produced by distress, why does he lump together 'smothering in blood' and 'smothering in incomprehension'? If distress is in general a means of producing understanding, then bloody distress is even a very acute means to this end. The 'Prussian' therefore should have said that smothering in blood will smother incomprehension and procure a proper current of air for the understanding.

The 'Prussian' prophesies the smothering of uprisings which break out in 'disastrous isolation of people from the community, and in the separation of their thoughts from social principles'.

We have shown that the Silesian uprising occurred by no means in circumstances of the separation of thoughts from social principles. It only remains for us to deal with the 'disastrous isolation of people from the community'. By community here is meant the political community, the state. This is the old story about unpolitical Germany.

But do not all uprisings, without exception, break out in a disastrous isolation of man from the community? Does not every uprising necessarily presuppose isolation? Would the 1789 revolution have taken place without the disastrous isolation of French citizens from the community? It was intended precisely to abolish this isolation.

But the community from which the worker is isolated is a community the real character and scope of which is quite different from that of the political community. The community from which the worker is isolated by his own labour is life itself, physical and mental life, human morality, human activity, human enjoyment, human nature. Human nature is the true community of men. The disastrous isolation from this essential nature is incomparably more universal, more intolerable, more dreadful, and more contradictory, than isolation from the political community. Hence, too, the abolition of his isolation – and even a partial reaction to it, an uprising against it – is just as much more infinite as man is more infinite than the citizen, and human life more infinite than political life. Therefore, however partial the uprising of the industrial workers may be, it contains within itself a universal soul; however universal a political uprising may be, it conceals even in its most grandiose form a narrow-minded spirit.

The 'Prussian' worthily concludes his article with the following sentence: 'A social revolution without a political soul (i.e. without an organising idea from the point of view of the whole) is impossible.'

We have already seen that a social revolution is found to have the point of view of the whole because – even if it were to occur in only one factory district – it represents man's protest against a dehumanized life, because it starts out from the point of view of a separate real individual, because the community, against the separation of which from himself the individual reacts, is man's true community, human nature. The political soul of revolution, on the other hand, consists in the tendency of classes having no political influence to abolish their isolation from statehood and rule. Its point of view is that of the state, of an abstract whole, which exists only through separation from real life, and which is inconceivable without the organized contradiction between the universal idea of man and the individual existence of man. Hence, too, a revolution with a political soul, in accordance with the limited and dichotomous nature of this soul, organizes a ruling stratum in society at the expense of society itself.

We want to divulge to the 'Prussian' what a 'social revolution with a political soul' actually is; we shall thereby at the same time confide the secret to him that he himself is unable, even in words, to rise above the narrow-minded political point of view.

A 'social' revolution with a political soul is either a nonsensical concoction, if by 'social' revolution the 'Prussian' means a 'social' as opposed to a political revolution, and nevertheless endows the social revolution with a political soul instead of a social one; or else a 'social revolution with a political soul' is only a paraphrase for what was usually called a 'political revolution', or 'simply a revolution'. Every revolution dissolves the old society and to that extent it is social. Every revolution overthrows the old power and to that extent it is political.

Let the 'Prussian' choose between the paraphrase and the nonsense! But whereas a social revolution with a political soul is a paraphrase or nonsense, a political revolution with a social soul has a rational meaning. Revolution in general – the overthrow of the existing power and dissolution of the old relationships – is a political act. But socialism cannot be realised without revolution. It needs this political act insofar as it needs destruction and dissolution. But where its organizing activity begins, where its proper object, its soul, comes to the fore – there socialism throws off the political cloak.

How much detailed argument has been necessary to tear to pieces the tissue of errors concealed on a single newspaper column. Not all readers can have the education and time to get to the bottom of such literary charlatanism. Is it therefore not the anonymous 'Prussian's' duty to the reading public to refrain for the time being from all writing on political and social matters, such as the declamations about conditions in Germany, and instead sincerely try to come to an understanding of his own condition?

NOTES

1 Special reasons prompt me to state that the present article is the first which I have contributed to Vorwärts.
2 Note the stylistic and grammatical lack of sense. 'The King of Prussia and society has not yet arrived at the presentiment of their (to whom does this 'their' relate?) reform'.
3 For our purpose it is not necessary to go back to the Statute of Labourers under Edward III.
4 The words 'Board of Guardians' are in English in the manuscript.
5 Eugène Buret.
6 This word is here and further on given in English in the original.
7 M. Chevalier, *Des intérêts matériels en France*, p. 3 (Marx gives a free translation).

2

Legitimacy, Politics and the State

MAX WEBER

POLITICS AS A VOCATION

This lecture, which I give at your request, will necessarily disappoint you in a number of ways. You will naturally expect me to take a position on actual problems of the day. But that will be the case only in a purely formal way and toward the end, when I shall raise certain questions concerning the significance of political action in the whole way of life. In today's lecture, all questions that refer to what policy and what content one should give one's political activity must be eliminated. For such questions have nothing to do with the general question of what politics as a vocation means and what it can mean. Now to our subject matter.

What do we understand by politics? The concept is extremely broad and comprises any kind of independent leadership in action. One speaks of the currency policy of the banks, of the discounting policy of the Reichsbank, of the strike policy of a trade union; one may speak of the educational policy of a municipality or a township, of the policy of the president of a voluntary association, and, finally, even of the policy of a prudent wife who seeks to guide her husband. Tonight, our reflections are, of course, not based upon such a broad concept. We wish to understand by politics only the leadership, or the influencing of the leadership, of a political association, hence today, of a state.

But what is a 'political' association from the sociological point of view? What is a 'state'? Sociologically, the state cannot be defined in terms of its ends. There is scarcely any task that some political association has not taken in hand, and there is no task that one could say has always been exclusive and peculiar to those associations which are designated as political ones: today the state, or historically, those associations which have been the predecessors of

Source: Hans Gerth and C. W. Mills (eds) From Max Weber: Essays in Sociology (New York: Oxford University Press, 1958), pp. 77–83, 95–5, 196–201, 230–5, 253–5, 261–4, reprinted with permission of Oxford University Press.

the modern state. Ultimately, one can define the modern state sociologically only in terms of the specific means peculiar to it, as to every political association, namely, the use of physical force.

'Every state is founded on force,' said Trotsky at Brest-Litovsk. That is indeed right. If no social institutions existed which knew the use of violence, then the concept of 'state' would be eliminated, and a condition would emerge that could be designated as 'anarchy', in the specific sense of this word. Of course, force is certainly not the normal or the only means of the state – nobody says that – but force is a means specific to the state. Today the relation between the state and violence is an especially intimate one. In the past, the most varied institutions – beginning with the sib – have known the use of physical force as quite normal. Today, however, we have to say that a state is a human community that (successfully) claims the monopoly of the legitimate use of physical force within a given territory. Note that 'territory' is one of the characteristics of the state. Specifically, at the present time, the right to use physical force is ascribed to other institutions or to individuals only to the extent to which the state permits it. The state is considered the sole source of the 'right' to use violence. Hence, 'politics' for us means striving to share power or striving to influence the distribution of power, either among states or among groups within a state.

This corresponds essentially to ordinary usage. When a question is said to be a 'political' question, when a cabinet minister or an official is said to be a 'political' official, or when a decision is said to be 'politically' determined, what is always meant is that interests in the distribution, maintenance, or transfer of power are decisive for answering the questions and determining the decision or the official's sphere of activity. He who is active in politics strives for power either as a means in serving other aims, ideal or egoistic, or as 'power for power's sake,' that is, in order to enjoy the prestige-feeling that power gives.

Like the political institutions historically preceding it, the state is a relation of men dominating men, a relation supported by means of legitimate (i.e. considered to be legitimate) violence. If the state is to exist, the dominated must obey the authority claimed by the powers that be. When and why do men obey? Upon what inner justifications and upon what external means does this domination rest?

To begin with, in principle, there are three inner justifications, hence basic legitimations of domination.

First, the authority of the 'eternal yesterday', i.e. of the mores sanctified through the unimaginably ancient recognition and habitual orientation to conform. This is 'traditional' domination exercised by the patriarch and the patrimonial prince of yore.

There is the authority of the extraordinary and personal gift of grace (charisma), the absolutely personal devotion and personal confidence in revelation, heroism, or other qualities of individual leadership. This is 'charismatic' domination, as exercised by the prophet or − in the field of politics − by the elected war lord, the plebiscitarian ruler, the great demagogue, or the political party leader.

Finally, there is domination by virtue of 'legality', by virtue of the belief in the validity of legal statute and functional 'competence' based on rationally created rules. In this case, obedience is expected in discharging statutory obligations. This is domination as exercised by the modern 'servant of the state' and by all those bearers of power who in this respect resemble him.

It is understood that, in reality, obedience is determined by highly robust motives of fear and hope − fear of the vengeance of magical powers or of the power-holder, hope for reward in this world or in the beyond − and besides all this, by interests of the most varied sort. Of this we shall speak presently. However, in asking for the 'legitimations' of this obedience, one meets with these three 'pure' types: 'traditional', 'charismatic', and 'legal'.

These conceptions of legitimacy and their inner justifications are of very great significance for the structure of domination. To be sure, the pure types are rarely found in reality. But today we cannot deal with the highly complex variants, transitions, and combinations of these pure types, which problems belong to 'political science'. Here we are interested above all in the second of these types: domination by virtue of the devotion of those who obey the purely personal 'charisma' of the 'leader'. For this is the root of the idea of a calling in its highest expression.

Devotion to the charisma of the prophet, or the leader in war, or to the great demagogue in the ecclesia or in parliament, means that the leader is personally recognized as the innerly 'called' leader of men. Men do not obey him by virtue of tradition or statute, but because they believe in him. If he is more than a narrow and vain upstart of the moment, the leader lives for his cause and 'strives for his work'.[1] The devotion of his disciples, his followers, his personal party friends is oriented to his person and to its qualities.

Charismatic leadership has emerged in all places and in all historical epochs. Most importantly in the past, it has emerged in the two figures of the magician and the prophet on the one hand, and in the elected war lord, the gang leader and *condotierre* on the other hand. Political leadership in the form of the free 'demagogue' who grew from the soil of the city state is of greater concern to us; like the city state, the demagogue is peculiar to the Occident and especially to Mediterranean culture. Furthermore, political leadership in the form of the parliamentary 'party leader' has grown on the soil of the constitutional state, which is also indigenous only to the Occident.

These politicians by virtue of a 'calling', in the most genuine sense of the word, are of course nowhere the only decisive figures in the cross-currents of the political struggle for power. The sort of auxiliary means that are at their disposal is also highly decisive. How do the politically dominant powers manage to maintain their domination? The question pertains to any kind of domination, hence also to political domination in all its forms, traditional as well as legal and charismatic.

Organized domination, which calls for continuous administration, requires that human conduct be conditioned to obedience towards those masters who claim to be the bearers of legitimate power. On the other hand, by virtue of this obedience, organized domination requires the control of those material goods which in a given case are necessary for the use of physical violence. Thus, organized domination requires control of the personal executive staff and the material implements of administration.

The administrative staff, which externally represents the organization of political domination, is, of course, like any other organization, bound by obedience to the power-holder and not alone by the concept of legitimacy, of which we have just spoken. There are two other means, both of which appeal to personal interests: material reward and social honour. The fiefs of vassals, the prebends of patrimonial officials, the salaries of modern civil servants, the honour of knights, the privileges of estates, and the honour of the civil servant comprise their respective wages. The fear of losing them is the final and decisive basis for solidarity between the executive staff and the power-holder. There is honour and booty for the followers in war; for the demagogue's following, there are 'spoils' – that is, exploitation of the dominated through the monopolization of office – and there are politically determined profits and premiums of vanity. All of these rewards are also derived from the domination exercised by a charismatic leader.

To maintain a dominion by force, certain material goods are required, just as with an economic organization. All states may be classified according to whether they rest on the principle that the staff of men themselves own the administrative means, or whether the staff is 'separated' from these means of administration. This distinction holds in the same sense in which today we say that the salaried employee and the proletarian in the capitalistic enterprise are 'separated' from the material means of production. The power-holder must be able to count on the obedience of the staff members, officials, or whoever else they may be. The administrative means may consist of money, building, war material, vehicles, horses, or whatnot. The question is whether or not the power-holder himself directs and organizes the administration while delegating executive power to personal servants, hired officials, or personal favourites and confidants, who are non-owners, i.e. who do not use the material means of administration in their own right but are directed by the lord. The distinction runs through all administrative organizations of the past.

These political associations in which the material means of administration are autonomously controlled, wholly or partly, by the dependent administrative staff may be called associations organized in 'estates'. The vassal in the feudal association, for instance, paid out of his own pocket for the administration and judicature of the district enfeoffed to him. He supplied his own equipment and provisions for war, and his sub-vassals did likewise. Of course, this had consequences for the lord's position of power, which only rested upon a relation of personal faith and upon the fact that the legitimacy of his possession of the fief and the social honour of the vassal were derived from the overlord.

However, everywhere, reaching back to the earliest political formations, we also find the lord himself directing the administration. He seeks to take the administration into his own hands by having men personally dependent upon him: slaves, household officials, attendants, personal 'favourites', and prebendaries enfeoffed in kind or in money from his magazines. He seeks to defray the expenses from his own pocket, from the revenues of his patrimonium; and he seeks to create an army which is dependent upon him personally because it is equipped and provisioned out of his granaries, magazines, and armouries. In the association of 'estates', the lord rules with the aid of an autonomous 'aristocracy' and hence shares his domination with it; the lord who personally administers is supported either by members of his household or by plebeians. These are propertyless strata having no social honour of their own; materially, they are completely chained to him and are not backed up by any competing power of their own. All forms of patriarchal and patrimonial domination, Sultanist despotism, and bureaucratic states belong to this latter type. The bureaucratic state order is especially important; in its most rational development, it is precisely characteristic of the modern state.

Everywhere the development of the modern state is initiated through the action of the prince. He paves the way for the expropriation of the autonomous and 'private' bearers of executive power who stand beside him, of those who in their own right possess the means of administration, warfare, and financial organization, as well as politically usable goods of all sorts. The whole process is a complete parallel to the development of the capitalist enterprise through gradual expropriation of the independent producers. In the end, the modern state controls the total means of political organization, which actually come together under a single head. No single official personally owns the money he pays out, or the buildings, stores, tools, and war machines he controls. In the contemporary 'state' – and this is essential for the concept of state – the 'separation' of the administrative staff, of the administrative officials, and of the workers from the material means of administrative organization is completed. Here the most modern development begins, and we see with our own eyes the attempt to inaugurate the expropriation of this expropriator of the political means, and therewith of political power.

The revolution [of Germany, 1918] has accomplished, at least insofar as leaders have taken the place of the statutory authorities, this much: the leaders, through usurpation or election, have attained control over the political staff and the apparatus of material goods; and they deduce their legitimacy – no matter with what right – from the will of the governed. Whether the leaders, on the basis of this at least apparent success, can rightfully entertain the hope of also carrying through the expropriation within the capitalist enterprises is a different question. The direction of capitalist enterprises, despite far-reaching analogies, follows quite different laws than those of political administration.

Today we do not take a stand on this question. I state only the purely conceptual aspect for our consideration: the modern state is a compulsory association which organizes domination. It has been successful in seeking to monopolize the legitimate use of physical force as a means of domination within a territory. To this end the state has combined the material means of organization in the hands of its leaders, and it has expropriated all autonomous functionaries of estates who formerly controlled these means in their own right. The state has taken their positions and now stands in the top place.

During this process of political expropriation, which has occurred with varying success in all countries on earth, 'professional politicians' in another sense have emerged. They arose first in the service of a prince. They have been men who, unlike the charismatic leader, have not wished to be lords themselves, but who have entered the service of political lords. In the struggle of expropriation, they placed themselves at the princes' disposal and by managing the princes' politics they earned, on the one hand, a living and, on the other hand, an ideal content of life. Again, it is only in the Occident that we find this kind of professional politician in the service of powers other than the princes. In the past, they have been the most important power instrument of the prince and his instrument of political expropriation . . .

To take a stand, to be passionate – *ira et studium* – is the politician's element, and above all the element of the political leader. His conduct is subject to quite a different, indeed, exactly the opposite, principle of responsibility from that of the civil servant. The honour of the civil servant is vested in his ability to execute conscientiously the order of the superior authorities, exactly as if the order agreed with his own conviction. This holds even if the order appears wrong to him and if, despite the civil servant's remonstrances, the authority insists on the order. Without this moral discipline and self-denial, in the highest sense, the whole apparatus would fall to pieces. The honour of the political leader, of the leading statesman, however, lies precisely in an exclusive personal responsibility for what he does, a responsibility he cannot and must not reject or transfer. It is in the nature of officials of high moral standing to be poor politicians, and above all, in the political sense of the word, to be irresponsible politicians. In this sense, they are politicians of low moral standing, such as we unfortunately have had again and again in leading positions. This is what we have called *Beamtenherrschaft* [civil-service rule], and truly no spot soils the honour of our officialdom if we reveal what is politically wrong with the system from the standpoint of success. But let us return once more to the types of political figures.

Since the time of the constitutional state, and definitely since democracy has been established, the 'demagogue' has been the typical political leader in the Occident. The distasteful flavour of the word must not make us forget that not Cleon but Pericles was the first to bear the name of demagogue. In contrast to the offices of ancient democracy that were filled by lot, Pericles led the sovereign ecclesia of the demos of Athens as a supreme strategist holding the only elective office or without holding any office at all. Modern demagoguery also makes use of oratory, even to a tremendous extent, if one considers the election speeches a modern candidate has to deliver. But the use of the printed word is more enduring. The political publicist, and above all the journalist, is nowadays the most important representative of the demagogic species.

Within the limits of this lecture, it is quite impossible even to sketch the sociology of modern political journalism, which in every respect constitutes a chapter in itself. Certainly, only a few things concerning it are in place here. In common with all demagogues and, by the way, with the lawyer (and the artist), the journalist shares the fate of lacking a fixed social classification. At least, this is the case on the Continent, in contrast to the English, and, by the way, also to former conditions in Prussia. The journalist belongs to a sort of pariah caste, which is always estimated by 'society' in terms of its ethically lowest representative. Hence, the strangest notions about journalists and their work are abroad. Not everybody realizes that a really good journalistic accomplishment requires at least as much 'genius'[2] as any scholarly accomplishment, especially because of the necessity of producing at once and 'on order', and because of the necessity of being effective, to be sure, under quite different conditions of production. It is almost never acknowledged that the responsibility of the journalist is far greater, and that the sense of responsibility of every honourable journalist is, on the average, not a bit lower than that of the scholar, but rather, as the war has shown, higher. This is because, in the very nature of the case, irresponsible journalistic accomplishments and their often terrible effects are remembered . . .

BUREAUCRACY

Characteristics of Bureaucracy

Modern officialdom functions in the following specific manner:

1 There is the principle of fixed and official jurisdictional areas, which are generally ordered by rules, that is, by laws or administrative regulations.

   (a) The regular activities required for the purposes of the bureaucratically governed structure are distributed in a fixed way as official duties.

   (b) The authority to give the commands required for the discharge of these duties is distributed in a stable way and is strictly delimited by rules concerning the coercive means, physical, sacerdotal, or otherwise, which may be placed at the disposal of officials.

(c) Methodical provision is made for the regular and continuous fulfilment of these duties and for the execution of
the corresponding rights; only persons who have the
generally regulated qualifications to serve are employed.

In public and lawful government these three elements
constitute 'bureaucratic authority'. In private economic
domination, they constitute bureaucratic 'management.'
Bureaucracy, thus understood, is fully developed in political and ecclesiastical communities only in the modern
state, and, in the private economy, only in the most
advanced institutions of capitalism. Permanent and public
office authority, with fixed jurisdiction, is not the historical rule but rather the exception. This is so even in large
political structures such as those of the ancient Orient, the
Germanic and Mongolian empires of conquest, or of
many feudal structures of state. In all these cases, the ruler
executes the most important measures through personal
trustees, table companions, or court servants. Their com-
missions and authority are not precisely delimited and are
temporarily called into being for each case.

2 The principles of office hierarchy and of levels of graded
authority mean a firmly ordered system of super- and subordination in which there is a supervision of the lower offices by the
higher ones. Such a system offers the governed the possibility of
appealing the decision of a lower office to its higher authority, in
a definitely regulated manner. With the full development of the
bureaucratic type, the office hierarchy is monocratically organized. The principle of hierarchical office authority is found in all
bureaucratic structures: in state and ecclesiastical structures as
well as in large party organizations and private enterprises. It
does not matter for the character of bureaucracy whether its
authority is called 'private' or 'public'.

When the principle of jurisdictional 'competency' is fully
carried through, hierarchical subordination − at least in public
office − does not mean that the 'higher' authority is simply
authorized to take over the business of the 'lower'. Indeed, the
opposite is the rule. Once established and having fulfilled its
task, an office tends to continue in existence and be held by
another incumbent.

3 The management of the modern office is based upon written
documents ('the files'), which are preserved in their original or

draft form. There is, therefore, a staff of subaltern officials and scribes of all sorts. The body of officials actively engaged in a 'public' office, along with the respective apparatus of material implements and the files, make up a 'bureau'. In private enterprise, 'the bureau' is often called 'the office'.

In principle, the modern organization of the civil service separates the bureau from the private domicile of the official, and, in general, bureaucracy segregates official activity as something distinct from the sphere of private life. Public monies and equipment are divorced from the private property of the official. This condition is everywhere the product of a long development. Nowadays, it is found in public as well as in private enterprises; in the latter, the principle extends even to the leading entrepreneur. In principle, the executive office is separated from the household, business from private correspondence, and business assets from private fortunes. The more consistently the modern type of business management has been carried through, the more are these separations the case. The beginnings of this process are to be found as early as the Middle Ages.

It is the peculiarity of the modern entrepreneur that he conducts himself as the 'first official' of his enterprise, in the very same way in which the ruler of a specifically modern bureaucratic state spoke of himself as 'the first servant' of the state.[3] The idea that the bureau activities of the state are intrinsically different in character from the management of private economic offices is a continental European notion and, by way of contrast, is totally foreign to the American way.

4 Office management, at least all specialized office management – and such management is distinctly modern – usually presupposes thorough and expert training. This increasingly holds for the modern executive and employee of private enterprises, in the same manner as it holds for the state official.

5 When the office is fully developed, official activity demands the full working capacity of the official, irrespective of the fact that his obligatory time in the bureau may be firmly delimited. In the normal case, this is only the product of a long development, in the public as well as in the private office. Formerly, in all cases, the normal state of affairs was reversed: official business was discharged as a secondary activity.

6 The management of the office follows general rules, which are more or less stable, more or less exhaustive, and which can be

learned. Knowledge of these rules represents a special technical learning which the officials possess. It involves jurisprudence, or administrative or business management.

The reduction of modern office management to rules is deeply embedded in its very nature. The theory of modern public administration, for instance, assumes that the authority to order certain matters by decree – which has been legally granted to public authorities – does not entitle the bureau to regulate the matter by commands given for each case, but only to regulate the matter abstractly. This stands in extreme contrast to the regulation of all relationships through individual privileges and bestowals of favour, which is absolutely dominant in patrimonialism, at least insofar as such relationships are not fixed by sacred tradition.

The Position of the Official

All this results in the following for the internal and external position of the official:

1 Office holding is a 'vocation'. This is shown, first, in the requirement of a firmly prescribed course of training, which demands the entire capacity for work for a long period of time, and in the generally prescribed and special examinations which are prerequisites of employment. Furthermore, the position of the official is in the nature of a duty. This determines the internal structure of his relations, in the following manner: legally and actually, office holding is not considered a source to be exploited for rents or emoluments, as was normally the case during the Middle Ages and frequently up to the threshold of recent times. Nor is office holding considered a usual exchange of services for equivalents, as is the case with free labour contracts. Entrance into an office, including one in the private economy, is considered an acceptance of a specific obligation of faithful management in return for a secure existence. It is decisive for the specific nature of modern loyalty to an office that, in the pure type, it does not establish a relationship to a person, like the vassal's or disciple's faith in feudal or in patrimonial relations of authority. Modern loyalty is devoted to impersonal and functional purposes. Behind the functional purposes, of course, 'ideas of culture-values' usually stand. These are *ersatz* for the earthly or supra-mundane personal master: ideas such as 'state', 'church', 'community', 'party', or 'enterprise' are thought of as being realized in a community; they provide an ideological halo for the master.

The political official – at least in the fully developed modern state – is not considered the personal servant of a ruler. Today, the bishop, the priest, and the preacher are in fact no longer, as in early Christian times, holders of purely personal charisma. The supra-mundane and sacred values which they offer are given to everybody who seems to be worthy of them and who asks for them. In former times, such leaders acted upon the personal command of their master; in principle, they were responsible only to him. Nowadays, in spite of the partial survival of the old theory, such religious leaders are officials in the service of a functional purpose, which in the present-day 'church' has become routinized and, in turn, ideologically hallowed.

2 The personal position of the official is patterned in the following way:

(a) Whether he is in private office or a public bureau, the modern official always strives and usually enjoys a distinct social esteem as compared with the governed. His social position is guaranteed by the prescriptive rules of rank order and, for the political official, by special definitions of the criminal code against 'insults of officials' and 'contempt' of state and church authorities.

The actual social position of the official is normally highest where, as in old civilized countries, the following conditions prevail: a strong demand for administration by trained experts; a strong and stable social differentiation, where the official predominantly derives from socially and economically privileged strata because of the social distribution of power; or where the costliness of the required training and status conventions are binding upon him. The possession of educational certificates – to be discussed elsewhere[4] – are usually linked with qualification for office. Naturally, such certificates or patents enhance the 'status element' in the social position of the official. For the rest this status factor in individual cases is explicitly and impassively acknowledged; for example, in the prescription that the acceptance or rejection of an aspirant to an official career depends upon the consent ('election') of the members of the official body. This is the case in the German army with the officer corps. Similar phenomena, which promote this guild-like closure of officialdom, are typically found in patrimonial and, particularly, in prebendal officialdoms of the past. The desire to resurrect such phenomena in changed forms is by no means infrequent among modern bureaucrats. For instance, they have played a role among the demands of the quite proletarian and expert officials (the *tretyj* element) during the Russian Revolution.

Usually the social esteem of the officials as such is especially low where the demand for expert administration and the dominance of status conventions are weak. This is especially the case in the United States; it is often the case in new settlements by virtue of their wide fields for profit-making and the great instability of their social stratification.

(b) The pure type of bureaucratic official is appointed by a superior authority. An official elected by the governed is not a purely bureaucratic figure. Of course, the formal existence of an election does not by itself mean that no appointment hides behind the election – in the state, especially, appointment by party chiefs. Whether or not this is the case does not depend upon legal statutes, but upon the way in which the party mechanism functions. Once firmly organized, the parties can turn a formally free election into the mere acclamation of a candidate designated by the party chief. As a rule, however, a formally free election is turned into a fight, conducted according to definite rules, for votes in favour of one of two designated candidates.

In all circumstances, the designation of officials by means of an election among the governed modifies the strictness of hierarchical subordination. In principle, an official who is so elected has an autonomous position opposite the superordinate official. The elected official does not derive his position 'from above' but 'from below', or at least not from a superior authority of the official hierarchy but from powerful party men ('bosses'), who also determine his further career. The career of the elected official is not, or at least not primarily, dependent upon his chief in the administration. The official who is not elected but appointed by a chief normally functions more exactly, from a technical point of view, because, all other circumstances being equal, it is more likely that purely functional points of consideration and qualities will determine his selection and career. As laymen, the governed can become acquainted with the extent to which a candidate is expertly qualified for office only in terms of experience, and hence only after his service. Moreover, in every sort of selection of officials by election, parties quite naturally give decisive weight not to expert considerations but to the services a follower renders to the party boss. This holds for all kinds of procurement of officials by elections, for the designation of formally free, elected officials by party bosses when they determine the slate of candidates, or the free appointment by a chief who has himself been elected. The contrast, however, is relative: substantially similar conditions hold where legitimate monarchs and their subordinates appoint officials, except that the influence of the followings are then less controllable.

Where the demand for administration by trained experts is considerable, and the party followings have to recognize an intellectually developed, educated, and freely moving 'public opinion,' the use of unqualified officials falls back upon the party in power at the next election. Naturally, this is more likely to happen when the officials are appointed by the chief. The demand for a trained administration now exists in the United States, but in the large cities, where immigrant votes are 'corraled', there is, of course, no educated public opinion. Therefore, popular elections of the administrative chief and also of his subordinate officials usually endanger the expert qualification of the official as well as the precise functioning of the bureaucratic mechanism. It also weakens the dependence of the officials upon the hierarchy . . .

Economic and Social Consequences of Bureaucracy

It is clear that the bureaucratic organization of a social structure, and especially of a political one, can and regularly does have far-reaching economic consequences. But what sort of consequences? Of course in any individual case it depends upon the distribution of economic and social power, and especially upon the sphere that is occupied by the emerging bureaucratic mechanism. The consequences of bureaucracy depend therefore upon the direction which the powers using the apparatus give to it. And very frequently a crypto-plutocratic distribution of power has been the result.

In England, but especially in the United States, party donors regularly stand behind the bureaucratic party organizations. They have financed these parties and have been able to influence them to a large extent. The breweries in England, the so-called 'heavy industry,' and in Germany the Hansa League with their voting funds are well enough known as political donors to parties. In modern times bureaucratization and social levelling within political, and particularly within state organizations in connection with the destruction of feudal and local privileges, have very frequently benefited the interests of capitalism. Often bureaucratization has been carried out in direct alliance with capitalist interests, for example, the great historical alliance of the power of the absolute prince with capitalist interests. In general, a legal levelling and destruction of firmly established local structures ruled by notables has usually made for a wider range of capitalist activity. Yet one may expect as an effect of bureaucratization, a policy that meets the petty bourgeois interest in a secured traditional 'subsistence', or even a state socialist policy that strangles opportunities for private profit. This has occurred in several cases of historical and far-reaching importance, specifically during antiquity; it is undoubtedly to be expected as a future development. Perhaps it will occur in Germany.

The very different effects of political organizations which were, at least in principle, quite similar – in Egypt under the Pharaohs and in Hellenic and Roman times – show the very different economic significances of bureaucratization which are possible according to the direction of other factors. The mere fact of bureaucratic organization does not unambiguously tell us about the concrete direction of its economic effects, which are always in some manner present. At least it does not tell us as much as can be told about its relatively levelling effect socially. In this respect, one has to remember that bureaucracy as such is a precision instrument which can put itself at the disposal of quite varied – purely political as well as purely economic, or any other sort – interests in domination. Therefore, the measure of its parallelism with democratization must not be exaggerated, however typical it may be. Under certain conditions, strata of feudal lords have also put bureaucracy into their service. There is also the possibility – and often it has become a fact, for instance, in the Roman principate and in some forms of absolutist state structures – that a bureaucratization of administration is deliberately connected with the formation of estates, or is entangled with them by the force of the existing groupings of social power. The express reservation of offices for certain status groups is very frequent, and actual reservations are even more frequent. The democratization of society in its totality, and in the modern sense of the term, whether actual or perhaps merely formal, is an especially favourable basis of bureaucratization, but by no means the only possible one. After all, bureaucracy strives merely to level those powers that stand in its way and in those areas that, in the individual case, it seeks to occupy. We must remember this fact – which we have encountered several times and which we shall have to discuss repeatedly: that 'democracy' as such is opposed to the 'rule' of bureaucracy, in spite and perhaps because of its unavoidable yet unintended promotion of bureaucratization. Under certain conditions, democracy creates obvious ruptures and blockages to bureaucratic organization. Hence, in every individual historical case, one must observe in what special direction bureaucratization has developed.

The Power Position of Bureaucracy

Everywhere the modern state is undergoing bureaucratization. But whether the power of bureaucracy within the polity is universally increasing must here remain an open question.

The fact that bureaucratic organization is technically the most highly developed means of power in the hands of the man who controls it does not determine the weight that bureaucracy as such is capable of having in a particular social structure. The ever-increasing 'indispensability' of the officialdom, swollen to millions, is no more decisive for this question than is the view of some representatives of the proletarian movement that the economic indispensability of the proletarians is decisive for the measure of their social and political power position. If 'indispensability' were decisive, then where slave labour prevailed and where freemen usually abhor work as a dishonour, the 'indispensable' slaves ought to have held the positions of power, for they were at least as indispensable as officials and proletarians are today. Whether the power of bureaucracy as such increases cannot be decided *a priori* from such reasons. The drawing in of economic interest groups or other non-official experts, or the drawing in of non-expert lay representatives, the establishment of local, inter-local, or central parliamentary or other representative bodies, or of occupational associations – these seem to run directly against the bureaucratic tendency. How far this appearance is the truth must be discussed in another chapter rather than in this purely formal and typological discussion. In general, only the following can be said here:

Under normal conditions, the power position of a fully developed bureaucracy is always overtowering. The 'political master' finds himself in the position of the 'dilettante' who stands opposite the 'expert', facing the trained official who stands within the management of administration. This holds whether the 'master' whom the bureaucracy serves is a 'people', equipped with the weapons of 'legislative initiative', the 'referendum', and the right to remove officials, or a parliament, elected on a more aristocratic or more 'democratic' basis and equipped with the right to vote a lack of confidence, or with the actual authority to vote it. It holds whether the master is an aristocratic, collegiate body, legally or actually based on self-recruitment, or whether he is a popularly elected president, an hereditary and 'absolute', or a 'constitutional' monarch.

Every bureaucracy seeks to increase the superiority of the professionally informed by keeping their knowledge and intentions secret. Bureaucratic administration always tends to be an administration of 'secret sessions': insofar as it can, it hides its knowledge and action from criticism. Prussian church authorities now threaten to use disciplinary measures against pastors who make reprimands or other admonitory measures in any way accessible to third parties. They do this because the pastor, in making such criticism available, is 'guilty' of facilitating a possible criticism of the church authorities. The treasury officials of the Persian shah have made a secret doctrine of their budgetary art and even use secret script. The official statistics of Prussia, in general, make public only what cannot do any harm to the intentions of the power-wielding bureaucracy. The tendency toward secrecy in certain administrative fields follows their material nature: everywhere that the power interests of the domination structure toward the outside are at stake, whether it is an economic competitor of a private enterprise, or a foreign, potentially hostile polity, we find secrecy. If it is to be successful, the management of diplomacy can only be publicly controlled to a very limited extent. The military administration must insist on the concealment of its most important measures; with the increasing significance of purely technical aspects, this is all the more the case. Political parties do not proceed differently, in spite of all the ostensible publicity of Catholic congresses and party conventions. With the increasing bureaucratization of party organizations, this secrecy will prevail even more. Commercial policy, in Germany for instance, brings about a concealment of production statistics. Every fighting posture of a social structure toward the outside tends to buttress the position of the group in power.

The pure interest of the bureaucracy in power, however, is efficacious far beyond those areas where purely functional interests make for secrecy. The concept of the 'official secret' is the specific invention of bureaucracy, and nothing is so fanatically defended by the bureaucracy as this attitude, which cannot be substantially justified beyond these specifically qualified areas. In facing a parliament, the bureaucracy, out of a sure power instinct, fights every attempt of the parliament to gain knowledge by means of its own experts or from interest groups. The so-called right of parliamentary investigation is one of the means by which parliament seeks such knowledge. Bureaucracy naturally welcomes a poorly informed and hence a powerless parliament – at least insofar as ignorance somehow agrees with the bureaucracy's interests.

The absolute monarch is powerless opposite the superior knowledge of the bureaucratic expert – in a certain sense more powerless than any other political head. All the scornful decrees of Frederick the Great concerning the 'abolition of serfdom' were derailed, as it were, in the course of their realization because the official mechanism simply ignored them as the occasional ideas of a dilettante. When a constitutional king agrees with a socially important part of the governed, he very frequently exerts a greater influence upon the course of administration than does the absolute monarch. The constitutional king can control these experts better because of what is, at least relatively, the public character of criticism, whereas the absolute monarch is dependent for information solely upon the bureaucracy. The Russian czar of the old regime was seldom able to accomplish permanently anything that displeased his bureaucracy and hurt the power interests of the bureaucrats. His ministerial departments, placed directly under him as the autocrat, represented a conglomerate of satrapies, as was correctly noted by Leroy-Beaulieu. These satrapies constantly fought against one another by all the means of personal intrigue, and, especially, they bombarded one another with voluminous 'memorials', in the face of which, the monarch, as a dilettante, was helpless.

With the transition to constitutional government, the concentration of the power of the central bureaucracy in one head became unavoidable. Officialdom was placed under a monocratic head, the prime minister, through whose hands everything had to go before it got to the monarch. This put the latter, to a large extent, under the tutelage of the chief of the bureaucracy. Wilhelm II, in his well-known conflict with Bismarck, fought against this principle, but he had to withdraw his attack very soon. Under the rule of expert knowledge, the actual influence of the monarch can attain steadiness only by a continuous communication with the bureaucratic chiefs; this intercourse must be methodically planned and directed by the head of the bureaucracy.

At the same time, constitutionalism binds the bureaucracy and the ruler into a community of interests against the desires of party chiefs for power in the parliamentary bodies. And if he cannot find support in parliament the constitutional monarch is powerless against the bureaucracy. The desertion of the 'Great of the Reich' – the Prussian ministers and top officials of the Reich – in November 1918, brought a monarch into approximately the same situation as existed in the feudal state in 1056. However, this is an exception, for, on the whole, the power position of a monarch opposite bureaucratic officials is far stronger than it was in any feudal state or in the 'stereotyped' patrimonial state. This is because of the constant presence of aspirant for promotion, with whom the monarch can easily replace inconvenient and independent officials. Other circumstances being equal, only economically independent officials, that is, officials who belong to the propertied strata, can permit themselves to risk the loss of their offices. Today, as always, the recruitment of officials from among propertyless strata increases the power of the rulers. Only officials who belong to a socially influential stratum, whom the monarch believes he must take into account as personal supporters, like the so-called *Kanalrebellen* in Prussia,[5] can permanently and completely paralyse the substance of his will.

Only the expert knowledge of private economic interest groups in the field of 'business' is superior to the expert knowledge of the bureaucracy. This is so because the exact knowledge of facts in their field is vital to the economic existence of businessmen. Errors in official statistics do not have direct economic consequences for the guilty official, but errors in the calculation of a capitalist enterprise are paid for by losses, perhaps by its existence. The 'secret,' as a means of power, is, after all, more safely hidden in the books of an enterpriser than it is in the files of public authorities. For this reason alone authorities are held within narrow barriers when they seek to influence economic life in the capitalist epoch. Very frequently the measures of the state in the field of capitalism take unforeseen and unintended courses, or they are made illusory by the superior expert knowledge of interest groups . . .

THE SOCIOLOGY OF CHARISMATIC AUTHORITY

The General Character of Charisma

Bureaucratic and patriarchal structures are antagonistic in many ways, yet they have in common a most important peculiarity: permanence. In this respect they are both institutions of daily routine. Patriarchal power especially is rooted in the provisioning of recurrent and normal needs of the workaday life. Patriarchal authority thus has its original locus in the economy, that is, in those branches of the economy that can be satisfied by means of normal routine. The patriarch is the 'natural leader' of the daily routine. And in this respect, the bureaucratic structure is only the counter-image of patriarchalism transposed into rationality. As a permanent structure with a system of rational rules, bureaucracy is fashioned to meet calculable and recurrent needs by means of a normal routine.

The provisioning of all demands that go beyond those of everyday routine has had, in principle, an entirely heterogeneous, namely, a charismatic, foundation; the further back we look in history, the more we find this to be the case. This means that the 'natural' leaders — in times of psychic, physical, economic, ethical, religious, political distress — have been neither officeholders nor incumbents of an 'occupation' in the present sense of the word, that is, men who have acquired expert knowledge and who serve for remuneration. The natural leaders in distress have been holders of specific gifts of the body and spirit; and these gifts have been believed to be supernatural, not accessible to everybody. The concept of 'charisma' is here used in a completely 'value-neutral' sense.

The capacity of the Irish culture hero, Cuchulain, or of the Homeric Achilles for heroic frenzy is a manic seizure, just as is that of the Arabian berserk who bites his shield like a mad dog — biting around until he darts off in raving bloodthirstiness. For a long time it has been maintained that the seizure of the berserk is artificially produced through acute poisoning. In Byzantium, a number of 'blond beasts', disposed to such seizures, were kept about, just as war elephants were formerly kept. Shamanist ecstasy is linked to constitutional epilepsy, the possession and the testing of which represents a charismatic qualification. Hence neither is 'edifying' to our minds. They are just as little edifying to us as is the kind of 'revelation', for instance, of the Sacred Book of the Mormons, which, at least from an evaluative standpoint, perhaps would have to be called a 'hoax'. But sociology is not concerned with such questions. In the faith of their followers, the chief of the Mormons has proved himself to be charismatically qualified, as have 'heroes' and 'sorcerers'. All of them have practised their arts and ruled by virtue of this gift (charisma) and, where the idea of God has already been clearly conceived, by virtue of the divine mission lying therein. This holds for doctors and prophets, just as for judges and military leaders, or for leaders of big hunting expeditions.

It is to his credit that Rudolph Sohm brought out the sociological peculiarity of this category of domination-structure for a historically important special case, namely, the historical development of the authority of the early Christian church. Sohm performed this task with logical consistency, and hence, by necessity, he was one-sided from a purely historical point of view. In principle, however, the very same state of affairs recurs universally, although often it is most clearly developed in the field of religion.

In contrast to any kind of bureaucratic organization of offices, the charismatic structure knows nothing of a form or of an ordered procedure of appointment or dismissal. It knows no regulated 'career', 'advancement', 'salary', or regulated and expert training of the holder of charisma or of his aids. It knows no agency of control or appeal, no local bailiwicks or exclusive functional jurisdictions; nor does it embrace permanent institutions like our bureaucratic 'departments', which are independent of persons and of purely personal charisma.

Charisma knows only inner determination and inner restraint. The holder of charisma seizes the task that is adequate for him and demands obedience and a following by virtue of his mission. His success determines whether he finds them. His charismatic claim breaks down if his mission is not recognized by those to whom he feels he has been sent. If they recognize him, he is their master – so long as he knows how to maintain recognition through 'proving' himself. But he does not derive his 'right' from their will, in the manner of an election. Rather, the reverse holds: it is the duty of those to whom he addresses his mission to recognize him as their charismatically qualified leader.

In Chinese theory, the emperor's prerogatives are made dependent upon the recognition of the people. But this does not mean recognition of the sovereignty of the people any more than did the prophet's necessity of getting recognition from the believers in the early Christian community. The Chinese theory, rather, characterizes the charismatic nature of the monarch's position, which adheres to his personal qualification and to his proved worth.

Charisma can be, and of course regularly is, qualitatively particularized. This is an internal rather than an external affair, and results in the qualitative barrier of the charisma holder's mission and power. In meaning and in content the mission may be addressed to a group of men who are delimited locally, ethnically, socially, politically, occupationally, or in some other way. If the mission is thus addressed to a limited group of men, as is the rule, it finds its limits within their circle.

In its economic sub-structure, as in everything else, charismatic domination is the very opposite of bureaucratic domination. If bureaucratic domination depends upon regular income, and hence at least *a posteriori* on a money economy and money taxes, charisma lives in, though not off, this world. This has to be properly understood. Frequently charisma quite deliberately shuns the possession of money and of pecuniary income *per se*, as did Saint Francis and many of his like; but this is of course not the rule. Even a pirate genius may exercise a 'charismatic' domination, in the value-neutral sense intended here. Charismatic political heroes seek booty and, above all, gold. But charisma, and this is decisive, always rejects as undignified any pecuniary gain that is methodical and rational. In general, charisma rejects all rational economic conduct.

The sharp contrast between charisma and any 'patriarchal' structure that rests upon the ordered base of the 'household' lies in this rejection of rational economic conduct. In its 'pure' form, charisma is never a source of private gain for its holders in the sense of economic exploitation by the making of a deal. Nor is it a source of income in the form of pecuniary compensation, and just as little does it involve an orderly taxation for the material requirements of its mission. If the mission is one of peace, individual patrons provide the necessary means for charismatic structures; or those to whom the charisma is addressed provide honorific gifts, donations, or other voluntary contributions. In the case of charismatic warrior heroes, booty represents one of the ends as well as the material means of the mission. 'Pure' charisma is contrary to all patriarchal domination (in the sense of the term used here). It is the opposite of all ordered economy. It is the very force that disregards economy. This also holds, indeed precisely, where the charismatic leader is after the acquisition of goods, as is the case with the charismatic warrior hero. Charisma can do this because by its very nature it is not an 'institutional' and permanent structure, but rather, where its 'pure' type is at work, it is the very opposite of the institutionally permanent.

In order to do justice to their mission, the holders of charisma, the master as well as his disciples and followers, must stand outside the ties of this world, outside of routine occupations, as well as outside the routine obligations of family life. The statutes of the Jesuit order preclude the acceptance of church offices; the members of orders are forbidden to own property or, according to the original rule of St Francis, the order as such is forbidden to do so. The priest and the knight of an order have to live in celibacy, and numerous holders of a prophetic or artistic charisma are actually single. All this is indicative of the unavoidable separation from this world of those who partake ('χλῆϱος') of charisma. In these respects, the economic conditions of participation in charisma may have an (apparently) antagonistic appearance, depending upon the type of charisma – artistic or religious, for instance – and the way of life flowing from its meaning. Modern charismatic movements of artistic origin represent 'independents without gainful employment' (in everyday language, rentiers). Normally such persons are the best qualified to follow a charismatic leader. This is just as logically consistent as was the medieval friar's vow of poverty, which demanded the very opposite.

Foundations and Instability of Charismatic Authority

By its very nature, the existence of charismatic authority is specifically unstable. The holder may forego his charisma; he may feel 'forsaken by his God', as Jesus did on the cross; he may prove to his followers that 'virtue is gone out of him'. It is then that his mission is extinguished, and hope waits and searches for a new holder of charisma. The charismatic holder is deserted by his following, however, (only) because pure charisma does not know any 'legitimacy' other than that flowing from personal strength, that is, one which is constantly being proved. The charismatic hero does not deduce his authority from codes and statutes, as is the case with the jurisdiction of office; nor does he deduce his authority from traditional custom or feudal vows of faith, as is the case with patrimonial power.

The charismatic leader gains and maintains authority solely by proving his strength in life. If he wants to be a prophet, he must perform miracles; if he wants to be a war lord, he must perform heroic deeds. Above all, however, his divine mission must 'prove' itself in that those who faithfully surrender to him must fare well. If they do not fare well, he is obviously not the master sent by the gods.

This very serious meaning of genuine charisma evidently stands in radical contrast to the convenient pretensions of present rulers to a 'divine right of kings', with its reference to the 'inscrutable' will of the Lord, 'to whom alone the monarch is responsible'. The genuinely charismatic ruler is responsible precisely to those whom he rules. He is responsible for but one thing, that he personally and actually be the God-willed master.

During these last decades we have witnessed how the Chinese

monarch impeaches himself before all the people because of his sins and insufficiencies if his administration does not succeed in warding off some distress from the governed, whether it is inundations or unsuccessful wars. Thus does a ruler whose power, even in vestiges and theoretically, is genuinely charismatic deport himself. And if even this penitence does not reconcile the deities, the charismatic emperor faces dispossession and death, which often enough is consummated as a propitiatory sacrifice.

Meng-tse's (Mencius') thesis that the people's voice is 'God's voice' (according to him the only way in which God speaks!) has a very specific meaning: if the people cease to recognize the ruler, it is expressly stated that he simply becomes a private citizen; and if he then wishes to be more, he becomes a usurper deserving of punishment. The state of affairs that corresponds to these phrases, which sound highly revolutionary, recurs under primitive conditions without any such pathos. The charismatic character adheres to almost all primitive authorities with the exception of domestic power in the narrowest sense, and the chieftain is often enough simply deserted if success does not remain faithful to him.

The subjects may extend a more active or passive 'recognition' to the personal mission of the charismatic master. His power rests upon this purely factual recognition and springs from faithful devotion. It is devotion to the extraordinary and unheard-of, to what is strange to all rule and tradition and which therefore is viewed as divine. It is a devotion born of distress and enthusiasm.

Genuine charismatic domination therefore knows of no abstract legal codes and statutes and of no 'formal' way of adjudication. Its 'objective' law emanates concretely from the highly personal experience of heavenly grace and from the god-like strength of the hero. Charismatic domination means a rejection of all ties to any external order in favour of the exclusive glorification of the genuine mentality of the prophet and hero. Hence its attitude is revolutionary and transvalues everything; it makes a sovereign break with all traditional or rational norms: 'It is written, but I say unto you.'

The specifically charismatic form of settling disputes is by way of the prophet's revelation, by way of the oracle, or by way of 'Solomonic' arbitration by a charismatically qualified sage. This arbitration is determined by means of strictly concrete and individual evaluations, which, however, claim absolute validity. Here lies the proper locus of 'Kadi-justice' in the proverbial – not the historical – sense of the phrase. In its actual historical appearance the jurisdiction of the Islamic Kadi is, of course, bound to sacred tradition and is often a highly formalistic interpretation.

Only where these intellectual tools fail does jurisdiction rise to an unfettered individual act valuing the particular case; but then it does indeed. Genuinely charismatic justice always acts in this manner. In its pure form it is the polar opposite of formal and traditional bonds, and it is just as free in the face of the sanctity of tradition as it is in the face of any rationalist deductions from abstract concepts.

This is not the place to discuss how the reference to the *aegum et bonum* in the Roman administration of justice and the original meaning of English 'equity' are related to charismatic justice in general and to the theocratic Kadi-justice of Islamism in particular.[6] Both the *aegum et bonum* and 'equity' are partly the products of a strongly rationalized administration of justice and partly the product of abstract conceptions of natural law. In any case the *ex bona fide* contains a reference to the 'mores' of business life and thus retains just as little of a genuine irrational justice as does, for instance, the German judge's 'free discretion'.

Any kind of ordeal as a means of evidence is, of course, a derivative of charismatic justice. But the ordeal displaces the personal authority of the holder of charisma by a mechanism of rules for formally ascertaining the divine will. This falls in the sphere of the 'routinization' of charisma . . .

THE MEANING OF DISCIPLINE

It is the fate of charisma, whenever it comes into the permanent institutions of a community, to give way to powers of tradition or of rational socialization. This waning of charisma generally indicates the diminishing importance of individual action. And of all those powers that lessen the importance of individual action, the most irresistible is rational discipline.

The force of discipline not only eradicates personal charisma but also stratification by status groups; at least one of its results is the rational transformation of status stratification.

The content of discipline is nothing but the consistently rationalized, methodically trained and exact execution of the received order, in which all personal criticism is unconditionally suspended and the actor is unswervingly and exclusively set for carrying out the command. In addition, this conduct under orders is uniform. Its quality as the communal action of a mass organization conditions the specific effects of such uniformity. Those who obey are not necessarily a simultaneously obedient or an especially large mass, nor are they necessarily united in a specific locality. What is decisive for discipline is that the obedience of a plurality of men is rationally uniform.

Discipline as such is certainly not hostile to charisma or to status group honour. On the contrary, status groups that are attempting to rule over large territories or large organizations – the Venetian aristocratic counsellors, the Spartans, the Jesuits in Paraguay, or a modern officer corps with a prince at its head – can maintain their alertness and their superiority over their subjects only by means of a very strict discipline. This discipline is enforced within their own group, for the blind obedience of subjects can be secured only by training them exclusively for submission under the disciplinary code. The cultivation of stereotyped prestige and style of life of a status group, only for reasons of discipline, will have a strongly conscious and rationally intended character. This factor effects all culture in any way influenced by these status communities; we shall not discuss these effects here. A charismatic hero may make use of discipline in the same way; indeed, he must do so if he wishes to expand his sphere of domination. Thus Napoleon created a strict disciplinary organization for France, which is still effective today.

Discipline in general, like its most rational offspring, bureaucracy, is impersonal. Unfailingly neutral, it places itself at the disposal of every power that claims its service and knows how to promote it. This does not prevent bureaucracy from being intrinsically alien and opposed to charisma, as well as to honour, especially of a feudal sort. The berserk with maniac seizures of frenzy and the feudal knight who measures swords with an equal adversary in order to gain personal honour are equally alien to discipline. The berserk is alien to it because his action is irrational; the knight because his subjective attitude lacks matter-of-factness. In place of individual hero-ecstasy or piety, of spirited enthusiasm or devotion to a leader as a person, of the cult of 'honour', or the exercise of personal ability as an 'art' – discipline substitutes habituation to routinized skill. Insofar as discipline appeals to firm motives of an 'ethical' character, it presupposes a 'sense of duty' and 'conscientiousness' ('Men of Conscience' versus 'Men of Honour', in Cromwell's terms.)

The masses are uniformly conditioned and trained for discipline in order that their optimum of physical and psychic power in attack may be rationally calculated. Enthusiasm and unreserved devotion may, of course, have a place in discipline; every modern conduct of war weighs, frequently above everything else, precisely the 'moral' elements of a troop's endurance. Military leadership uses emotional means of all sorts – just as the most sophisticated techniques of religious discipline, the *exercitia spiritualia* of Ignatius Loyola, do in their way. In combat, military leadership seeks to influence followers through 'inspiration' and, even more, to train them in 'emphatic understanding' of the leader's will. The sociologically decisive points, however, are, first, that everything, and especially these 'imponderable' and irrational emotional factors, are rationally calculated – in principle, at least, in the same manner as one calculates the yields of coal and iron deposits. Secondly, devotion, in its purposefulness and according to its normal content, is of an objective character. It is devotion to a common 'cause', to a rationally intended 'success'; it does not mean devotion to a person as such – however 'personally' tinged it may be in the concrete instance of a fascinating leader.

The case is different only when the prerogatives of a slaveholder create a situation of discipline – on a plantation or in a slave army of the ancient Orient, on galleys manned by slaves or among prisoners in Antiquity and the Middle Ages. Indeed, the individual cannot escape from such a mechanized organization, for routinized training puts him in his place and compels him to 'travel along'. Those who are enlisted in the ranks are forcibly integrated into the whole. This integration is a strong element in the efficacy of all discipline, and especially in every war conducted in a disciplined fashion. It is the only efficacious element and – as *caput mortuum* – it always remains after the 'ethical' qualities of duty and conscientiousness have failed.

The Discipline of Large-Scale Economic Organizations

The discipline of the army gives birth to all discipline. The large-scale economic organization is the second great agency which trains men for discipline. No direct historical and transitional organizations link the Pharaonic workshops and construction work (however little detail about their organization is known) with the Carthaginian Roman plantation, the mines of the late Middle Ages, the slave plantation of colonial economies, and finally the modern factory. However, all of these have in common the one element of discipline.

The slaves of the ancient plantations slept in barracks, living without family and without property. Only the managers – especially the *villicus* – had individual domiciles, somewhat comparable to the lieutenant's domicile or the residence of a manager of a modern, large-scale agricultural enterprise. The *villicus* alone usually had quasi-property (*peculium*, i.e. originally property in cattle) and quasi-marriage (*contubernium*). In the morning the work-slaves lined up in 'squads' (in *decuriae*) and were led to work by overseers (*monitores*); their personal equipment (to use a barrack term) was stored away and handed out according to need. And hospitals and prison cells were not absent. The discipline of the manor of the Middle Ages and the modern era was considerably less strict because it was traditionally stereotyped, and therefore it somewhat limited the lord's power.

No special proof is necessary to show that military discipline is the ideal model for the modern capitalist factory, as it was for the ancient plantation. In contrast to the plantation, organizational discipline in the factory is founded upon a completely rational basis. With the help of appropriate methods of measurement, the optimum profitability of the individual worker is calculated like that of any material means of production. On the basis of this calculation, the American system of 'scientific management' enjoys the greatest triumphs in the rational conditioning and training of work performances. The final consequences are drawn from the mechanization and discipline of the plant, and the psycho-physical apparatus of man is completely adjusted to the demands of the outer world, the tools, the machines – in short, to an individual 'function'. The individual is shorn of his natural rhythm as determined by the structure of his organism; his psycho-physical apparatus is attuned to a new rhythm through a medical specialization of separately functioning muscles, and an optimal economy of forces is established corresponding to the conditions of work. This whole process of rationalization, in the factory as elsewhere, and especially in the bureaucratic state machine, parallels the centralization of the material implements of organization in the discretionary power of the overlord.

The ever-widening grasp of discipline irresistibly proceeds with the rationalization of the supply of economic and political demands. This universal phenomenon increasingly restricts the importance of charisma and of individually differentiated conduct.

Discipline and Charisma

Charisma, as a creative power, recedes in the face of domination, which hardens into lasting institutions, and becomes efficacious only in short-lived mass emotions of incalculable effects, as on elections and similar occasions. Nevertheless charisma remains a highly important element of the social structure, although of course in a greatly changed sense.

We must now return to the economic factors, already mentioned above, which predominantly determine the routinization of charisma: the need of social strata, privileged through existing political, social, and economic orders, to have their social and economic positions 'legitimized'. They wish to see their positions transformed from purely factual power relations into a cosmos of acquired rights, and to know that they are thus sanctified. These interests comprise by far the strongest motive for the conservation of charismatic elements of an objectified nature within the structure of domination. Genuine charisma is absolutely opposed to this objectified form. It does not appeal to an enacted or traditional order, nor does it base its claims upon acquired rights. Genuine charisma rests upon the legitimation of personal heroism or personal revelation. Yet precisely this quality of charisma as an extraordinary, supernatural, divine power transforms it, after its routinization, into a suitable source for the legitimate acquisition of sovereign power by the successors of the charismatic hero. Routinized charisma thus continues to work in favour of all those whose power and possession is guaranteed by that sovereign power, and who thus depend upon the continued existence of such power.

The forms in which a ruler's charismatic legitimation may express itself vary according to the relation of the original charismatic power-holder with the supernatural powers. If the ruler's legitimation cannot be determined, according to unambiguous rules, through hereditary charisma, he is in need of legitimation through some other charismatic power. Normally, this can only be hierocratic power. This holds expressly for the sovereign who represents a divine incarnation, and who thus possesses the highest 'personal charisma'. Unless it is supported and proved by personal deeds, his claim of charisma requires the acknowledgment of professional experts in divinity. Incarnated monarchs are indeed exposed to the peculiar process of interment by close court officials and priests, who are materially and ideally interested in legitimacy. This seclusion may proceed to a permanent palace arrest and even to killing upon maturity, lest the god have occasion to compromise divinity or to free himself from tutelage. Yet generally, according to the genuine view as well as in practice, the weight of responsibility which the charismatic ruler must carry before his subjects works very definitely in the direction of the need for his tutelage.

It is because of their high charismatic qualifications that such rulers as the Oriental Caliph, Sultan, and Shah urgently need, even nowadays (1913), a single personality to assume responsibility for governmental actions, especially for failures and unpopular actions. This is the basis for the traditional and specific position of the 'Grand Vizier' in all those realms. The attempt to abolish and replace the office of the Grand Vizier by bureaucratic departments under ministers with the Shah's personal chairmanship failed in Persia during the last generation. This change would have placed the Shah in the role of a leader of the administration, personally responsible for all its abuses and for all the sufferings of the people. This role not only would have continuously jeopardized him, but would have shaken the belief in his very 'charismatic' legitimacy. The office of Grand Vizier with its responsibilities had to be restored in order to protect the Shah and his charisma.

The Grand Vizier is the Oriental counterpart of the position of the responsible prime minister of the Occident, especially in parliamentary states. The formula, *le roi règne mais il ne gouverne pas*, and the theory that, in the interest of the dignity of his position, the king must not 'figure without ministerial decorations', or, that he must abstain entirely from intervening in the normal administration directed by bureaucratic experts and specialists, or that he must abstain from administration in favour of the political party leaders occupying ministerial positions – all these theories correspond entirely to the enshrinement of the deified, patrimonial sovereign by the experts in tradition and ceremony: priests, court officers, and high dignitaries. In all these cases the sociological nature of charisma plays just as great a part as that of court officials or party leaders and their followings. Despite his lack of parliamentary power, the constitutional monarch is preserved, and above all, his mere existence and his charisma guarantee the legitimacy of the existing social and property order, since decisions are carried out 'in his name'. Besides, all those interested in the social order must fear for the belief in 'legality' lest it be shaken by doubts of its legitimacy.

A president elected according to fixed rules can formally legitimize the governmental actions of the respective victorious party as 'lawful', just as well as a parliamentary monarch. But the monarch, in addition to such legitimation, can perform a function which an elected president cannot fulfil: a parliamentary monarch formally delimits the politicians' quest for power, because the highest position in the state is occupied once and for all. From a political point of view this essentially negative function, associated with the mere existence of a king enthroned according to fixed rules, is of the greatest practical importance. Formulated positively it means, for the archetype of the species, that the king cannot gain an actual share in political power by prerogative (kingdom of prerogative). He can share power only by virtue of outstanding personal ability or social influence (kingdom of influence). Yet he is in position to exert this influence in spite of all parliamentary government, as events and personalities of recent times have shown.

'Parliamentary' kingship in England means a selective admission to actual power for that monarch who qualifies as a statesman. But a mis-step at home or in foreign affairs, or the raising of pretensions that do not correspond with his personal abilities and prestige, may cost him his crown. Thus English parliamentary kingship is formed in a more genuinely charismatic fashion than kingships on the Continent. On the Continent, mere birth-right equally endows the fool and the political genius with the pretensions of a sovereign.

NOTES

1 *Trachtet nach seinem Werk.*
2 *Geist.*
3 Frederick II of Prussia.
4 Cf. *Wirtschaft und Gesellschaft*, pp. 73 ff. and part II. (German Editor.)
5 When, in 1899, the German Reichstag discussed a Bill for the construction of the Mittelland Kanal, the conservative Junker party fought the project. Among the conservative members of the parliamentary party were a number of administrative Junker officials who stood up to the Kaiser who had ordered them to vote for the Bill. The disobedient officials were dubbed *Kanalrebellen* and they were temporarily suspended from office. Cf. Bernard Fürst von Bülow, *Denkwürdigkeiten* (Berlin: 1930), vol. I, pp. 293 ff.
6 Cf. *Wirtschaft und Gesellschaft*, sections 2 and 5 of part II.

3

Max Weber: Legitimation, Method, and the Politics of Theory

SHELDON S. WOLIN

Max Weber is widely regarded as one of the founders of twentieth-century social science and probably its greatest practitioner. Modern and ancient theorists commonly believed that founding – or giving a form or constitution to collective life – was reckoned to be the most notable action of which political man is capable. It is superior to other types of political acts because it aims to shape the lives of citizens by designing the structure or 'dwelling' which they and their posterity will inhabit. In describing this extraordinary action, political theorists often had recourse to architectural metaphors: the founder 'lays foundations'. No such images were invoked to explain the routine acts that occur in the daily life of a polity. Ordinary action is commonly described as 'doing', 'effecting', or 'bringing something about'. If political actors are to bring something about, they presuppose conditions that make possible the action in question and the means for doing it. They also presuppose a context that permits the action to be understood and interpreted. The founder is quintessentially an author of political presuppositions.

By analogy, to found a form of social science entails an act of demarcation that indicates the subject-matter peculiar to the science, the kind of activities that are appropriate (e.g. empirical inquiry), and the norms that are to be invoked in judging the value of the results produced by the activities. These demarcations became presuppositions of subsequent practice. Weber was engaged in founding when he wrote the following:

> The historical and cultural sciences . . . teach us how to
> understand and interpret political, artistic, literary, and social

Source: Sheldon S. Wolin, 'Max Weber: legitimation, method, and the politics of theory', *Political Theory* (August, 1981), pp. 401–24 (copyright, 1981, Sage Publications), reprinted by permission of Sage Publications.

phenomena in terms of their origins. But they give us no answer to the question, whether the existence of these cultural phenomena have been and are worth while ... To take a political stand is one thing, and to analyse political structures and party positions is another.[1]

As this passage indicates, founding attempts to prescribe what shall be considered legitimate activity in a particular field.

But how does the founder acquire his authority to grant or withhold legitimation: who legitimates the legitimator? That question cannot be posed in isolation from the context in which, typically, it arises. The founders of a new science are not in the fortunate position of some of the legendary legislators of antiquity who were able to establish constitutions where none had previously existed. Empty space may be a geographical and even a political reality, but it seems not to be a theoretical possibility. Theories are not like explorations where a flag is planted for the first time. They are, in the revealing language frequently employed, 'attacks' upon another theory. They contest ground that is already held and so they must not only establish their own legitimacy but delegitimate the prevailing theory and its practitioners.

I

Theoretical founding has both a political dimension and a politics. The former is the constitutive activity of laying down basic and general principles which, when legitimated, become the presuppositions of practice, the ethos of practitioners. This definition is modelled upon the Aristotelian conception of 'the political' (*he politike*) as the 'master science' that legislates for the good of the whole that is, for the purpose of shaping the whole to the concept of the good relevant to it. Founding is thus political theorizing.

The politics of founding, or theory destruction, refers to the critical activity of defeating rival theoretical claims. It is Socrates against Thrasymachus. This politics is conducted by means of strategies (e.g. 'the Socratic method', Locke's 'clearing Ground a little, and removing some of the Rubbish') and intellectual weapons (various logics, conceptions of 'facts'). The politics of theory was recognized as early as Plato:

Eleatic   And when combat takes the form of a conflict
of body with body, our natural appropriate
name for it will be *force* ...

Theaetetus	Yes.
Eleatic	But when it is a conflict of argument with argument, can we call it anything but controversy.[2]

We may call this 'profane politics' in order to distinguish it from a 'higher', ontological politics. The latter is illustrated by Aristotle's assertion that the theoretical life is 'more than human . . . We must not follow those who advise us to have human thoughts, since we are (only) men . . . On the contrary, we should try to become immortal.'[3] Ontological politics is preoccupied with gaining access to the highest kind of truth, which is about the nature of ultimate being. The political theorist seeks that truth because he believes that it is the truth about power, the power that holds together the entire structure of things and beings, and holds them together in a perfectly right or just way. The reason why ultimate reality was ultimate was that it contained the solution to the fundamental political riddle, how to combine vast power with perfect right. Holding to this conception of reality, political theorists over many centuries sought to find the way of ordering the life of the collectivity into a right relationship with reality, connecting collective being with ultimate being and thereby assuring that the power and rightness of the one would translate into the safety and well-being of the other. 'For all the laws of men are nourished by one law, the divine law; for it has as much power as it wishes and is sufficient for all and is still left over.'[4] Politics at the ontological level is different from profane politics and more intense. Recall Moses's arguments with Yahweh, Plato's *Phaedrus*, or Augustine's tortuous efforts to find even a small place for the *civitas terrena* in the divine scheme of things. The echoes of ontological politics can still be heard as late as Max Weber's famous essay 'Science as a vocation':

> So long as life remains immanent and is interpreted in its own terms, it knows only of an unceasing struggle of these gods with one another . . . The ultimately possible attitudes toward life are irreconcilable, and hence their struggle can never be brought to a final conclusion. Thus it is necessary to make a decisive choice.[5]

The point of engaging in the politics of theory is to demonstrate the superiority of one set of constitutive principles over another so that in the future these will be recognized as the basis of theoretical inquiry. Thus the founder's action prepares the way for inquiry, that is, for activity which can proceed uninterruptedly because its presuppositions are not in dispute. Inquiry is both a tribute to the triumph of a particular theory and its routinization. Or, to say the same thing differently, inquiry signals that the legitimation struggle is over; it is depoliticized theory. This explains why inquirers are usually quick to deplore as 'political' (or 'ideological') those who challenge the dominant presuppositions and who seek to refound the activity.

As a mode of activity, theorizing has been conceived as a performance whose political significance extends beyond the circle of theorists. It is intended as a model for a new form of politics, not only in the manifest sense of presenting a new political vision, but in the exemplary sense of showing how political action should be conducted extra-murally. To refer to a previous example, Socrates and Thrasymachus not only represented opposing conceptions of theory, one philosophical and the other rhetorical, and contrasting modes of theoretical action (Socratic *elenchus* or cross-examination versus Thrasymachus's set speeches), but also opposing prescriptions of governance. Socrates not only maintains that the true ruler is one who rules for the betterment of the members of the political community, but in the actual course of the dialogue Socrates can be observed at work improving the mental and moral qualities of the participants, including his opponent Thrasymachus. On the other hand, Thrasymachus both maintains that ruling is and should be in the interest of the stronger and he himself seeks to overpower the listeners by the force of his rhetorical style, to diminish them as tyrants diminish their subjects.

It is within this political conception of theory and of theoretical activity that I want to reconsider Max Weber. The appropriate context for analysing the political nature of his activity as a founder is provided by the triumph of modern science. Laying the foundations of social science was a possible action only because of the prestige of the natural sciences. Modern science was a new form of theory that rapidly became paradigmatic for all claims to theoretical knowledge. It achieved that position by defeating rival claimants, such as philosophy, theology and history, and, in the course of more than three centuries of controversy, by delegitimating their respective reality-principles (reason, God, and experience). The spectacular theoretical and practical achievements of science served to obscure the legitimation crisis that was in the making. For centuries science was admired because men thought it provided a true picture of the nature of reality. This had to be so, men reasoned, because of the enormous, god-like power which science was increasingly making accessible to humankind. As long as men continued to believe that science was merely deciphering the laws of nature decreed by a beneficent god, they could preserve sufficient traces of the ancient belief that theoretical knowledge continued to embody the solution to the riddle of power and right. Very few doubted that science had demonstrated its superior ability to generate power. Bacon had compared ancient philosophy to boyish puberty: 'it can talk, but cannot generate.'[6]

This illusion began to dissolve in the nineteenth century. Science appeared to be power without right, an appearance that became all the more unsettling with the realization that science was acknowledging that, by nature, it was incapable of supplying the missing component of rightness, and yet the powers made available by scientific discoveries and technological inventions were increasingly becoming the main influences upon daily life. Equally serious, unlike the discredited forms of theory, such as philosophy, history, and theology, science qua science could not even provide a justification of its own activity. This produced a legitimation crisis within theory, or more precisely, within social science. The triumph of modern science had discredited all of the earlier forms of political theory (philosophy, theology, and history) as well as their reality-principles (reason, revelation, and experience). By dint of this discreditation, social science became the natural successor of political theory.

Max Weber was the ideal type to deal with the developing crisis of the political nature of theory and the politics of theorizing. The title of a book written by his friend Karl Jaspers suggests why: *Max Weber. Politiker. Forscher* (inquirer). *Philosoph.*

Weber was a profoundly political man. At several points in his life he gave serious consideration to abandoning academic life: 'I am born for the pen and the speaker's tribune, not for the academic chair', he once wrote.[7] He was deeply involved in politics before and during the First World War and in the brief period from the armistice to his death in 1920. Max Weber also wrote a great deal about politics, much of it in newspapers, and his formal sociology was laced with political themes. Yet Weber never set down a coherent political theory comparable to the great theories of the tradition of political theory. That inability may well be the meaning of social science.

Although Weber's formal sociology is not much read outside departments of sociology and his studies of the great religions have been largely superseded, the so-called 'methodological essays' continue to attract attention, especially from philosophers interested in the topic of explanation. Virtually all discussions of Weber's methodology assume that his essays on that subject can be strictly separated from his political writings proper, a distinction that was observed by Weber's German editors who collected his *Politische Schriften* in one volume, his *Aufsätze zur Wissenschaftlehre* in another. Following this principle, two of his best-known essays, 'Politics as a vocation' and 'Science as a vocation', were assigned to different volumes on the assumption, no doubt, that each represented a radically different conception of vocation, one political, the other scientific. I shall suggest, in contrast, that they are companion pieces, united by common themes, all of them profoundly political. I shall suggest further that methodology, as conceived by Weber, was a type of political theory transferred to the only plane of action available to the theorist at a time when science, bureaucracy, and capitalism had clamped the world with the tightening grid of rationality. Methodology is mind engaged in the legitimation of its own political activity.

II

In the Prefatory Note to *Wirtschaft und Gesellschaft*, Weber acknowledged what most readers have keenly felt, that the discussion is 'unavoidably abstract and hence gives the impression of remoteness from reality'. He explained that the 'pedantic' air of the work was due to its objective, to supply a 'more exact terminology' for 'what all empirical sociology really means when it deals with the same problems'.[8] When readers first encounter his famous threefold classification of ideal types of legitimation, for example, they are apt to be puzzled because of the absence of any apparent context. Weber simply stipulates that 'there are three pure types of legitimate domination. The validity of the claims may be based on':[9]

(1) rational grounds . . .
(2) traditional grounds . . .
(3) charismatic grounds . . .

The service being rendered 'empirical sociology' was not as innocent as it was made to appear, either in content or form. The bestowing of names is, as any reader of the Book of Genesis will recall, an act of power, an ordering of the world by specifying the place of things. Establishing the basic terms of sociology is a constitutive act that brings order to a distinct realm, especially if that realm has been disturbed by controversy, by a *Methodenstreit*. Weber's definition of the charismatic grounds of authority become relevant at this point: 'resting on devotion to the exceptional sanctity, heroism or exemplary character of an individual person, and of the normative patterns or order revealed or ordained by him.'[10] In keeping with this note of the extraordinary nature of the pattern represented by basic sociological terms, Weber, in a phrase that echoes temple prophets and early philosophers, remarked that 'the most precise formulation cannot always be reconciled with a form which can readily be popularized. In such cases the latter had to be sacrificed.'[11] The context for reading Weber's abstract terms is political, and for the readings of his methodological essays it is political and theoretical. We can begin to construct the context for his terminology by noting the peculiarities of translation surrounding *Herrschaft*. It is often translated as 'authority', but it is not an exact equivalent of *die Autorität*; and the meaning of *Herrschaft* is only obfuscated when translated as 'imperative coordination' by Henderson and Parsons.[12] Although *Herrschaft* may refer specifically to the estate of a noble,[13] a reference which was taken up by Weber in his distinctions between patriarchal and patrimonial dominions, *Herrschaft* typically connotes 'mastery' and 'domination'. Thus Weber would write about the 'domination (*Herrschaft*) of man over man'. This means that while in some contexts it may be perfectly appropriate to translate *Herrschaft* as 'authority' or 'imperative control' and to emphasize the element of 'legitimacy', it is also important to attend to the harsher overtones of *Herrschaft* as domination because these signify its connection to a more universal plane: 'The decisive means for politics is violence . . . who lets himself in for politics, that is, for power and force as means, contracts with diabolical powers'.[14] Conflict and struggle were endemic in society as well as between societies. '"Peace" is nothing more than a change in the form of conflict.'[15] Even when Weber addressed what seemed on its face a purely methodological question, he transformed it into a political engagement, stark, dramatic, and, above all, theological. Thus in the context of 'a non-empirical approach oriented to the interpretation of meaning', he wrote: 'It is really a question not only of alternatives between values but of an irreconcilable death-struggle like that between "God" and the "Devil".'[16]

Even a casual reader of Weber must be struck by the prominence of 'power-words' in his vocabulary; struggle, competition, violence, domination, *Machstaat*, imperialism. The words indicate the presence of a powerful political sensibility seeking a way to thematize its politicalness but finding itself blocked by a paradox of scientific inquiry. Science stipulates that political expression is prohibited in scientific work, but the stipulation is plainly of a normative status and hence its 'validity' (to use Weber's word) cannot be warranted by scientific procedures and is, therefore, lacking in legitimacy. The same would hold true of all prescriptions for correct scientific procedure. As a consequence, instead of a politics of social scientific theory, there was the possibility of anarchy.

At the same time, the modern theoretical mind had come to regard the political and the scientific as mutually exclusive: the political stood for partisanship, the scientific for objectivity. Since science reigned as the paradigmatic form of theory and the political impulse could not be directly expressed in the form of theory, it had to seek its outlet elsewhere, through the circuitous route of ideal-type constructions and more transparently, as we shall see shortly, in the meta-theoretical form of 'methodology'. This meant, however, that social science *qua* science was unable to externalize a political theory and that Weber's political views, which were strongly held and unhesitatingly expressed publicly, could not be legitimated by his science. Accordingly, in 1917 when he published his remarkable essay on the post-war reconstruction of German political institutions, he felt obliged to preface it with the disclaimer that 'it does not claim the authority of any science'.[17]

Although Weber published his political views, his efforts took the form of occasional pieces. He never created a political theory even though the manifest breakdown of German politics and society cried out for one. His political-theoretical impulse was turned inward upon social science where he replicated the problems, dilemmas, and demands which he perceived in the 'real' political world. For that impulse to be released, Weber had to find a way of modifying the scientific prohibition against the injection of politics into scientific inquiry and locate a domain within science where he could theorize both the profane politics of theory and the ontology of theory. The strategy which he followed required that he attack the positivist ideal of a presuppositionless and hence 'value-free' social science but that, at the same time, he defend the scientific character of social science against subjectivist conceptions of social inquiry that emphasized personal intuitions and moral–political concerns. The positivist position called for the elimination of 'values' from scientific work so that 'objectivity' could be preserved; Weber accepted that formulation as the terrain of controversy and proceeded to invest 'values' with political meaning so that, in the end, values functioned as the symbolic equivalent of politics. At the same time, he adopted from the subjectivist argument its starting point of the 'subject', that is, the inquiring self whose passions the positivists had hoped to overcome by the rigours of scientific method. As the price of admitting the morally passionate subject, Weber was willing to concede to the positivists that this would introduce an element of arbitrariness into scientific investigations, but he preferred to gamble that he could revitalize the conception of vocation and make it into a prophylactic that would prevent subjectivity from degenerating into subjectivism.

The initial move that allowed for the political penetration of scientific work was in Weber's definition of social science as one of the 'cultural sciences'. This enabled him to exploit what he saw as the difference between science and culture. The latter was concerned with 'meaning' or 'patterns' rather than with predictions and the closely associated notion of regularities in phenomena.[18] Weberian social science would be devoted to analysing 'the phenomena of life in terms of their cultural significance'. The social scientist, according to Weber, derives his ideas of what is significant and worthy of investigation from the 'value' element accompanying all human actions and historical events. 'The concept of culture is a value-concept.'[19] Significance is grasped as well as expressed by the constructs which Weber designated as 'ideal types'. These are based, he noted, on 'subjective presuppositions' and they are 'formed by the one-sided accentuation of one or more points of view and by the synthesis' of numerous 'concrete individual phenomena'. He likened them to 'a utopia which has been arrived at by the analytical accentuation of certain elements of reality' although they 'cannot be found empirically anywhere in reality'.[20]

The subjective element in these one-sided constructs formed part of Weber's conception of human life: 'every single important activity and ultimately life as a whole . . . is a series of ultimate decisions through which the soul – as in Plato – chooses its own fate.'[21] That conception, first advanced in the context of a methodological discussion, later reappears to colour the whole of Weber's essay on the political 'hero' in *'Politics as a Vocation'*.[22] Choice is the essence of true science as it is of true politics: 'The *objective* validity of all empirical knowledge rests exclusively upon the ordering of the given reality according to categories which are *subjective*.'[23] Scientific activity, Weber argued, represents a series of decisions; it is 'always' from 'particular points of view'.[24]

The effect of these formulations is to politicalize social science, not in the vulgar sense of corrupting it by ideology, but in an allegorical sense. The highest form of available politics is a politics of the soul. In the passage cited earlier, it is revealing that Weber should have referred to Plato's conception of the soul. Classical political theory was remarkable for its profoundly political conception of the soul. Most readers are familiar with Plato's threefold division of the soul (reason, appetite, and passion) and his comparison of it to the 'three orders' that were to 'hold together' his ideal state.[25] For Weber, the politics of the soul appears in the identical virtues which he ascribed to scientific and political man: 'objectivity' or 'distance', 'passion', and 'reponsibility' for the consequences of one's choices.

The complexity that the politics of theory took in Weber's case is all the more interesting when we realize that in the early stages of his career, long before he had become embroiled in methodological controversies, he had championed a radically different view of the relation between social science and politics, a view in which the political nature of theoretical activity was frankly espoused. It was set out in the inaugural lecture which he gave at Freiburg in 1895 under the title 'The Nation State and Political Economy'. The theme of the lecture was political and deliberately provocative. As Weber remarked shortly afterwards, he decided to publish the lecture because of the disagreement it had aroused among his listeners ('*nicht die Zustimmung, sondern Widerspruch*').[26] Midway through the lecture he announced, 'I am a member of the bourgeois class and feel myself to be such, and I have been educated in its outlook and ideals. But it is precisely the vocation of our science to say what will be heard with displeasure'.[27]

A reader who chances upon the Freiburg lecture and who had associated Weber with a strict view of the fact–value distinction, a rigid commitment to 'ethical neutrality' (*Wertfreiheit*) and 'objectivity', and disdain for professors who assumed the role of political prophets, would be startled to find Weber declaring roundly that 'the science of political economy is a *political* science' and that it ought to be 'the servant' of politics; that the nation-state is the ultimate value and political economy should be shaped to its needs.[28] In his prescription for the politicalization of this theoretical science, Weber broke with common belief that political economy should be exploited to promote the material happiness of society; and he rejected the sentiment of liberal free traders that economics should serve the cause of international peace by promoting the ideal of free trade and an international division of labour. 'For the dream of peace and humanity's happiness there stands over the portals of the future of human history: *lasciate ogni speranza* (abandon all hope).'[29] The nature and purpose of political economy, he argued, was dictated by '*Machtkämpfe*', the power struggles in a Darwinian world where nations 'were locked in an endless struggle for existence and domination'.[30] 'The economic policy of a German state', he warned his academic audience, 'like the norm for German economic theoreticians, can only be German'.[31]

The lecture gave not the slightest hint of a possible tension between the conditions needed for scientific inquiry and the requirements of '*die weltliche Machtorganisation der Nation*'.[32] Equally notable in the light of Weber's later pessimism, there was no suggestion that political struggle might be meaningless. Rather there was an air of exaltation at the prospect of participating in 'the eternal struggle for the preservation and improvement of our national type', as though in serving the *Machtstaat* in its quest for 'elbow room'[33] the political economist placed himself in contact with the most elemental force in the political world, the mustering of national power in the fight for survival.

The explicitly political conception of a social science was, however, abandoned over the next decade. Weber suffered a devastating nervous disorder in 1898 and it was not until 1902 that he began to resume his scholarly activity. Beginning in 1903 and continuing over the next several years, he published a series of essays on the methodology of the social sciences. As we have already noted, in the eyes of later commentators and critics, the essays constitute a self-contained series of texts which can be interpreted independently of Weber's sociological and political writings. They are described as the 'philosophy of social science' which Weber worked out in the context of the famous *Methodenstreit*, initiated in 1883 by Schmoller's attack upon Menger over the fundamental nature of the social sciences.[34]

This is, as I have suggested earlier, a far too restrictive context for interpreting the methodological essays and for grasping the meaning of methodology. That context needs to be enlarged to accommodate its author's political concerns. The expression of these concerns was powerfully evident in Weber's substantive, as opposed to his methodological, writings of the same period. Almost simultaneously with the publication (1903–6) of Weber's first methodological essays, those dealing with Roscher and Knies, Weber published what is perhaps his most famous work, *The Protestant Ethic and the Spirit of Capitalism* (1904–5). So much scholarly ink has been expended on the question of whether and in what sense Weber 'explained' the rise of capitalism that the political importance of the work has been almost totally neglected. Yet it contains the most extensive formulation of Weber's ideal conception of the political actor and the most polemical, for it is directed squarely at Marxism. Weber wanted not only to counter the Marxist explanation of the origins of capitalism, but to celebrate the moral and political superiority of the capitalist hero of the past over the proletarian hero of the present and future. In these respects, the *Protestant Ethic* is a complex work concerned with the historical legitimation of capitalism. It is complex because that work also marks the first sustained discussion of a theme that was to preoccupy Weber for the remainder of his life, the meaninglessness of human existence. This intimation of a post-theological theme has been overlooked in most discussions of Weber's methodology, yet it figures prominently in his later essay '"Objectivity" in Social Science'. Meaninglessness was less a concept than a theme. In the *Protestant Ethic* the context for interpreting it was supplied by another crucial theme, 'rationalization'. Rationalization refers to a world shaped by what Weber called 'the special and peculiar rationalism of Western culture'. Rationalization is expressed in the mastery of modern science over nature and of bureaucratic organization over society. It signified the status of human action in a world whose structures encased action in routines and required it to be calculating, instrumentalist, and predictable. Weber attacked that conception of action as its most basic assumption that 'self-interest' is the main motive for action in 'capitalistic culture'.[35] His attack was paradoxical because it was conducted through the figure of a fanatical capitalist who brought an intensity to capital accumulation that would convert it into an epic deed, a spiritual triumph. Puritan zeal would also be brought to bear on human activity and to order it so systematically that it would generate structures of power that would transform the world. The Puritan would be, however, a capitalist without 'purely eudaemonistic self-interest'. He represented, instead, an alternative form of action, the action of a man defined by his 'calling' or vocation, a man who submits to the requirements of a discipline without moderating his passion and who displays 'a certain ascetic tendency' for 'he gets nothing out of his wealth for himself, except the irrational sense of having done his job well.'[36]

The Puritan actor of the *Protestant Ethic* was the prototype for Weber's most famous ideal types, Political Man and Scientific Man, and their respective vocations. His two essays, 'Politics as a vocation' and 'Science as a vocation' appeared in 1919, during which he was at work preparing a revised version of the *Protestant*

Ethic.[37] But the model had not only been developed much earlier, it had exercised a decisive influence upon Weber's conception of scientific activity at the time when he was writing the methodological essays. The exacting, even obsessive, demands which Weber imposed on the social scientist form a counterpart to the Calvinist's adherence to the letter of Scripture and to the rules of piety prescribed by Puritan divines. The Calvinist is, as we have noted, ascetic, but he accumulates material goods with a controlled frenzy. 'The God of Calvinism demanded of his believers not simple good works, but a life of good works combined into a unified system.' The Puritan made no appeal to 'magical sacraments' or confessions; he relied, instead, on 'rational planning' and proceeded 'methodically' to supervise his own conduct and, in the process, to objectify the self.[38] Scientific man is likewise to be a model of rational self-discipline, not only in his scrupulous adherence to scientific protocols, but in controlling his values and biases, and in suppressing the special vice of modern man, his fondness for 'self-expression'. Like the Calvinist, scientific man accumulates, only his activity takes the form of knowledge; yet what he amasses has no more lasting value than other things of the world. Scientific knowledge is always being superseded. Finally, scientific man is also a renunciatory hero. His form of renunciation is dictated by the demands of specialization that require him to abandon the delights of the Renaissance and Goethean ideal of the universal man who seeks to develop as many facets of his personality and as many different fields of knowledge as possible: 'renunciation of the Faustian universality of man . . . is a condition of valuable work in the modern world.'[39]

The extent to which Weber shaped his social scientist in the image of the Calvinist went beyond the attempt to emulate the precision of Calvinism. It extended to Calvinist doctrine, which proved to be an extraordinary move for it meant adopting the demands without being able to presuppose a comparable faith. In Weber's portrait, the most striking feature of the Calvinist's furious dedication to ascetic labour is that, during his unending labours, he can never know whether he has been chosen for election and he can never win it by his own efforts, regardless of how strenuously he tries. The dogma of predestination decrees that the Calvinist will labour amidst unrelieved uncertainty. Scientific man is in a comparable predicament. 'Our highest values' are 'a matter of faith.' Although they are crucial in orienting us toward our scientific work, there is no way that we, as scientists, can be assured that these values are 'true'. Knowledge of values, like the knowledge of secret election by God, is inaccessible.[40] Appropriately, when Weber argued this point in the essay on 'objectivity', he drew upon the oldest theological parallel:

> The fate of an epoch which has eaten of the tree of knowledge is that it must know that we cannot learn the *meaning* of the world from the results of its analysis, be it ever so perfect.[41]

The fundamental premise from which Weber argued for the fact–value distinction, which occupied such an important place in the 'discipline' of Weberian social science, was that values had to be preserved in their unscientific state so that human beings would have to choose.[42] The existence of the fact–value distinction was nothing less than the fundamental article of faith on which rested the entire decisionist framework of Weber's politics of the soul. As long as science could not, in principle, determine choice, men were forced to be free to choose. In that formulation one can see the secular equivalent of the age-old religious controversy over human free will versus divine predestination, only now scientific 'laws' take the place of the providential plan.

Weber laid special emphasis on the transforming effects of Puritan zeal when it was transferred to business activity. It converted money-making into a moral *praxis*, characterized by selflessness and competence. When Weber took the next step of transferring the Calvinist spirit to the domain of social science, he formulated the idea of methodology to serve, not simply as a guide to investigation but as a moral practice and a mode of political action. The Calvinist, Weber wrote,

> strode into the market-place of life, slammed the door of the monastery behind it, and took to penetrate just the daily routine of life, with its methodicalness, to fashion it into a life in the world, but neither of nor for this world.[43]

But as a model for the *bios theoretikos* the Calvinist was worlds removed from the classical idea of theory as contemplative and reflective. 'Scientific work is chained to the course of progress . . . this progress goes on *ad infinitum*.'[44]

As Weber sketched the Calvinist, he injected into his portrait the political themes of struggle which had so sharply defined his own view of politics and especially of international politics as evidenced by the Freiburg lecture. The 'heroism' of the Calvinist was displayed in the 'fight' for 'supremacy against a whole world of hostile forces'. In the end he shattered the powers of church, society, and state, ushering in a new era of 'universal history'.[45] 'Bourgeois classes as such have seldom before and never since displayed heroism'.[46]

The bourgeois actor of Weber's epic is a political hero in the classical sense. He is a founder of a new order, the order of capitalism which has transformed the world. He can stand comparison with another hero, the world-conquering proletariat, a comparison that pits a Protestant hero against a classically inspired one. Marx, particularly in his writings of the early 1840s, likened the proletariat to Prometheus, the rebellious god who saved mankind from destruction by bringing it the techniques of material production. While the proletarian hero signifies material and cultural deprivation and hence implies the promise of gratification, the Protestant is a renunciative hero who disdains the material sensuous pleasures eagerly sought by the materially deprived and sensuously starved man of the *Paris Manuscripts*. A major difference between the two epics is that, unlike Marx, Weber knew that he was composing a portrait of the last hero before the age of rationalization set in and rendered both heroes, Marx's and his own, anachronisms. Henceforth, the possibilities of significant action will be determined and limited by the constraints of rationalization. In the closing pages of the *Protestant Ethic* the fate of action is described in the imagery of the 'iron cage'.

The iron cage is a symbol with many meanings. It symbolizes the transformation of vocation from a religious and moral choice to an economic necessity. It also signifies our helplessness before 'the tremendous cosmos of the modern economic order . . . which today determine[s] the lives of all who are born into this mechanism'. And the iron cage stands for the stage of 'victorious capitalism' when the social order no longer needs the spiritual devotion of the ascetic for 'it rests on mechanical foundations'.[47]

The rationalization of existence foreshadowed by the iron cage became a *leitmotif* in all of Weber's subsequent writings. The cage is iron because the main forces of modern life, science, capitalism, and bureaucratic organization are triumphs of rationality and so the mind has no purchase point to attack them. They are mind incarnated into legal codes and administrative organizations that promise order, predictable decisions, regularity of procedures, and responsible, objective, and qualified officials; into economies that operate according to principles of calculated advantage, efficiency, and means–ends strategies; and into technologies that promote standardization, mechanical behaviour, and uniform tastes. The advantages of rationalization in terms of power and material satisfaction are so overwhelming that the historical process which has brought that system is 'irreversible'. But, finally, the cage is iron because 'the fulfillment of the calling cannot directly be related to the highest spiritual and cultural values'. Instead of being fired by religious, ethical, and political ideals, action has become simply a response to 'economic compulsion' or to 'purely mundane passions'.[48]

Action without the passions that Weber associated with spiritual and moral ideals was 'meaningless', a category that became a major one in Weber's thinking henceforth. Meaninglessness was of special concern in the methodological essays because of the central part which modern science had played in destroying the sources of meaning. Capitalism and bureaucratization may have produced the social and political structures of rationalization but the equation of rationalization with meaninglessness was the special responsibility of modern science. Science had attacked religious, moral, and metaphysical beliefs and had insisted that everything could, in principle, be reduced to rational explanation. Such explanations had no need of gods, spirits, revelations, and metaphysical principles. The result was a bare world, denuded and drained of meaning, which science makes no pretence to replenishing. Science deals with fact, material reality, and rational demonstration. It is so helpless to restore what it has destroyed that, *qua* science, it cannot even justify its own value. Its own activity comes perilously close to being the definition of meaninglessness: 'Chained to the course of progress', its 'fate' is that 'it asks to be "surpassed" and outdated.'[49]

The inherent limitations of science, its inability to make good the deficiencies of the world's meaning, provide the backdrop to the political role of the methodologist. His task is not to undertake scientific investigations or even to instruct his co-workers on how best to conduct research, much less to offer a special field of study. Rather it is to show them that significant action in their chosen realm is possible. It is, therefore, a form of political education in the meaning of vocation. Its politicalness comes from the seriousness, even urgency, of the relationship between vocational action and the world.

In order to bring out the unusual nature of Weberian methodology, a slight excursion is necessary, but it will be one that will re-establish direct contact with our original concern: social science as the post-modern form of political theory. Previously we had noted that Weber frequently asserts that science cannot validate the legitimacy of its own authority. This assertion calls attention to the interesting consideration that Weber never attempted in any systematic fashion to apply his concepts of *legitime Herrschaft* to science, even though the significance of science for the major conceptions of legitimate authority is clear. For example, given Weber's definition of 'traditional authority' as 'resting on an established belief in the sanctity of immemorial traditions and the legitimacy of the status of those exercising authority under them',[50] it is clear that science, which strives to be 'outdated', is hostile to that form of authority. Further, *pace* Kuhn, science as an institutionalized activity appears to be consistent with the 'rational–legal' type of authority which rests on 'a belief in the "legality" of patterns of normative rules and the right of those elevated to authority under such rules to issue commands'.[51] But the most interesting question concerns the possible relations between science and charisma, the form of authority which appears, on its face, to be the least hospitable to science. Charismatic authority, as we have already noted, rests on 'devotion to the specific sanctity, heroism, or exemplary character of an individual person, and of the normative patterns or order revealed or ordained by him'.[52] Now, although Weber never explicitly connected science and charisma, there is a sufficient number of scattered clues to suggest that the connection was in his mind. Science is charisma 'in a godless and prophetless time' and it is displayed by the person 'with an inward calling' who can endure that 'the world is disenchanted'.[53] It is for the chosen few, 'the affair of an intellectual aristocracy'.[54] It is, above all, charisma because science requires 'inspiration' (*Eingebung*). It has nothing to do with any cold calculation.'[55] Weber's discussion of inspiration is compressed but highly suggestive. 'Psychologically' he declared, inspiration was related to 'frenzy' or 'Plato's "mania"' – a reference to the discussion of 'divine madness' in the dialogue *Ion*. 'Whether we have scientific inspiration,' he continued, 'depends upon destinies that are hidden from us, and besides upon "gifts".'[56] 'Gifts' (*Gabe*) clearly refers to a charismatic quality for elsewhere Weber defined charisma as 'the gift of grace', a phrase which he took the pains to associate with 'the vocabulary of early Christianity.'[57] Although the significance of 'grace' (Gr. *caris*) was not explicitly connected by Weber to his discussion of science, a brief account of that term should immediately establish its relevance in the highly decisionistic framework of Weberian social science.

In the New Testament, 'grace' refers to the idea of God's redemptive love which is always actively at work to save sinners and maintain them in the right relationship to Him. Grace is God's free gift, and while it is not the result of man having earned it, there is still an element of choice, though an ambiguous one: 'work out your own salvation,' Paul exhorted his followers, 'with fear and trembling, for God is at work in you' (*Phil.* 2:12–13).

From these considerations we can distill three elements in the idea of charisma: a 'gifted' exceptional person of heroic or risk-taking qualities; a normative pattern that he ordains and that gives him authority; and the element of choice, both for the charismatic figure who commits himself to the revelation entrusted to him and for the others who must decide whether to follow him. Throughout, the decisionist element ('work out your own salvation') rests uneasily with a necessitarian one ('God is at work in you'). All of these elements reappear in Weber's methodological discussions.

But what is the meaning of methodology? What is its connection with the disenchanted world and its meaninglessness? How does it compare as a form of action with political theory?

The word 'methodology' did not come into use until the nineteenth century and it was mostly employed in scientific discussions, at least during the first half of the century. Its etymology is revealing. It is derived from two Greek words, *méthodus* and *logus*. *Méthodus* is itself an interesting compound of *meta* and *hodos*. *Meta*, which is characteristically used as a prefix, had some meanings that bristle with political overtones. They include: sharing, action in common, pursuit or quest. *Hodos*, on the other hand, means 'way.' It is one of the oldest words in the historical lexicon of Greek philosophy. The pre-Socratics, for example, typically described philosophy as a 'way' to the truth or even as a 'way' to ultimate Being. Ancient philosophy, we should recall, deliberately challenged religion, myth, and tradition; its 'way' often provoked opposition, even danger. Thus Parmenides described his 'way' as 'strife-encompassed'.[58]

Logos is probably the richest word in the entire vocabulary of ancient philosophy and theology. It has meant: account, explanation, truth, theory, reason, and, more simply, word. Among several of its usages there is a recurrent element: *logos* as signifying the truth that resides in the deepest layer of Being and that the *logos* has succeeded in embodying. It is represented by a phrase from Parmenides: 'the same thing exists for thinking and for being.'[59]

Methodology might then be rendered as the political action (*meta*) which thought takes on the route (*hodos*) to being (*logos*). Weber referred to it as 'metatheoretical'.[60] The reason for this designation had to do with the political nature of the crisis which gives methodology its *raison d'être*, the kind of crisis experienced by Weber and his contemporaries in the course of the *Methoden-streit* when the nature of the social sciences *qua* science was being contested. Weber took special pains to define the meaning of crisis so that the function of methodology could be made clear. Methodology, he insisted, does not legislate methods; these are 'established and developed' by practising social scientists in the course of dealing with 'substantive problems'. 'Purely epistemological and methodological reflections have never played the crucial role in such developments.'[61] Crises come about because of the dependence of social scientists upon 'evaluative ideas' which give 'significance' to their work. The 'foundation' for empirical inquiry comes not from empirical data but from 'the meta-empirical validity of ultimate final values in which the meaning of our existence is rooted. These foundations, however, tend to shift and even crumble because life itself is 'perpetually in flux . . . The light which emanates from these highest evaluative ideas falls on an ever changing finite segment of the vast chaotic stream of events which flows away through time.'[62] Meanwhile, researchers gradually lose their immediate awareness of the 'ultimate rootedness' in values of their own research. The result is that research falters. 'The significance of the unreflectively utilized viewpoints becomes uncertain' in the mind of the researcher. 'The road is lost in the twilight.' This crisis creates the opportunity for the type of intervention associated with methodology: 'Science . . . prepares to change its standpoint and its analytical apparatus and to view the stream of events from the heights of thought'.[63]

The methodologist seizes the opportunity to show the researcher that science cannot flourish without 'evaluative ideas' for it is these that nourish notions of what is 'significant' and hence worthy of inquiry. 'Significance' becomes the crucial concept in Weber's politics of knowledge. It symbolizes the moment of freedom for the social scientist when he registers his affirmations, when he exchanges the settled routines of inquiry for the risks of action. It is akin to a form of momentary and secular salvation for it creates meaning in an otherwise meaningless world. '"Culture"', Weber declared, 'is a finite segment of the meaningless infinity of the world process, a segment on which human beings confer meaning and significance.' Humans impart significance by taking up 'a deliberate posture (*Stellung*) towards the world'.[64]

The politics of mind in its struggles against meaninglessness finds its most powerful expression in Weber's conception of 'ideal types'. These are the most crucial instruments of social scientific inquiry and hence their nature becomes all important. Ideal types are constructs created by the social scientist to render a particular historical reality intelligible and coherent. They are constructed by abstracting features of a phenomenon (e.g. capitalism or bureaucracy) and reconstructing them to form an internally consistent whole. Ideal types are, Weber emphasized, deliberately constructed to be 'one-sided'; they are meant not only to accentuate the phenomena under study and thereby leave the investigator's mark on a portion of the world, but to accentuate as well the value-orientations of the investigator. Ideal types 'illuminate . . . reality' although they cannot 'exhaust its infinite richness': They are all attempts . . . to bring order into the chaos of these facts which we have drawn into the field circumscribed by our interest.[65]

The investigator does not usually face a situation where no prior constructs exist. Rather he is faced with the challenge of overcoming the constructs of the past. It is not surprising, therefore, to find Weber's description of the use of ideal types reminiscent of descriptions of the *agon* of classical politics. Inherited constructs are 'in constant tension with the new knowledge which we can and desire to rest from reality. The progress of cultural science occurs through this conflict.'[66]

Weber looked upon the ideal type as a means of provoking a 'confrontation with empirical reality'.[67] This somewhat curious formulation reflects the larger problem of political action in a world dominated by huge structures. Where theorists of earlier times were haunted by the fragility of order and by the difficulties of maintaining it, post-modern theory appears to suffer from a surfeit of order. Order is the empirical reality of post-modern theory. And ultimately, of course, the heroic metatheorist will suffer the same fate as the political hero and all charismatics: his *agon* will be routinized. The metatheorist is replaced by the normal social scientist, the metapolitician by the technician.

The fate of the metatheorist is not, perhaps, a great loss. He has turned out to be a theorist *manqué*, his methodology a displaced form of political theory confined within the walls of the academy, but serving a legitimating function once removed. As practised by Weber, methodology provides a rationale for social science, while social science tacitly bestows the peculiar form of legitimacy that is within its power to grant, the legitimacy of fact. Against the *Herrschaft* of facticity, ideal-type constructions afford only a small purchase-point for criticism. Ideal types cannot serve as substitutes for a theoretical counterparadigm, an alternative vision to what is too often the case. Weber's own views about bureaucracy confirm that while an ideal-type construction may highlight how bureaucracy trivializes politics and reduces human beings to classifications, the only rational choice is resignation before its massive facticity: 'The needs of mass administration make [bureaucracy] completely indispensable.'[68]

Weber's torment was that while he prophesied 'a polar night of icy darkness and hardness' and a totally bureaucratized condition wherein mankind would be 'as powerless as the fellahs of ancient Egypt',[69] he could neither turn theory against science – for science *was* theory – nor venture upon the quest for an ontology. His torment was expressed, paradoxically, at the ontological level which science had completely destroyed:

> There are no mysterious incalculable forces . . . One can, in principle, master all things by calculation. This means the world is disenchanted . . . [In antiquity] everybody sacrificed to the gods of his city, so do we still nowadays, only the bearing of man has been disenchanted and denuded of its mystical but inwardly genuine plasticity. Fate, and certainly not 'science' holds sway over these gods and their struggles. One can only understand what the godhead is for the one order or the other, or better, what godhead is in the one or the other order. With this understanding, however, the matter has reached its limits so far as it can be discussed in a lecture-room and by a professor.[70]

Weber's ontological politics, populated with the furious struggles of gods and demons, and seemingly so incongruous in the thought of a founder of the scientific study of society and politics, issues from the frustration of a consciousness that knows that its deepest values are owed to religion but that its vocational commitments are to the enemy. Science has caused the meaning of the universe to 'die out at its very root'. Science is 'specifically [an] irreligious power'.[71] The tension left Weber ambivalent toward science: 'I personally by my very work . . . affirm the value of science . . . and I also do so from precisely the standpoint that hates intellectualism as the worst devil.'[72]

The dramatic rendition of this ontological politics where science destroys the possibility of political renewal is in a figure that reappears frequently in Weber's writings, the prophet. The personal significance of the prophet is obscured because, as was his custom, Weber would frequently throw out sarcastic references about professors playing prophet, or about those who 'cannot bear the fate of the times like a man' and for whom 'the arms of the old church are opened widely and compassionately'.[73] But, of course, it was Weber's prophecies that have made his writings enduring; not so much because they see into the future but because they reveal him deeply engaged with the powers that dominate the soul of modern man: bureaucracy, science, violence, and the 'intellectualism' that has destroyed the spiritual resources on which humankind has fed for three thousand years or more. Prophecy, like religion, was a political symbol for Weber, as evidenced by his treatment of the Old Testament prophets. They were, in his eyes, supremely political figures who 'stood in the midst of their people and were concerned with the fate of the political community'.[74] They practised a 'prophetic politics' while exhorting their people in the midst of 'political disaster'.[75] Prophecy, we might say, is closettheory in the age of science. It achieved pathos in *The Protestant Ethic and the Spirit of Capitalism*, not in the closing pages where Weber pronounced his famous jeremiad about the 'iron cage', but in the introduction which he wrote shortly before his death. They are powerful pages and can only be described as akin to a secular crucifixion. This was because the book, and the prophecy about the future and the myths of the Protestant hero of the past, was considered to be an invasion of special fields or preserves of scholarly experts, 'trespassing' as Weber called it. Acknowledging that he had violated the scientific division of labour, he was prepared to offer himself up for trial. 'The specialist is entitled to a final judgement' and 'one must take the consequences.' To do otherwise would be to 'degrade' the specialist below the 'seer'. 'Whoever wants a sermon,' Weber wrote contemptuously, 'should go to a conventicle.'[76] He then ends on an equivocal note that gives a glimpse of his own agony:

> It is true that the path of human destiny cannot but appall him who surveys a section of it. But he will do well to keep his small personal commentaries to himself, as one does at the sight of the sea or of majestic mountains, unless he knows himself to be called and gifted to give them expression in artistic or prophetic form.[77]

The feebleness of Weber's equivocation corresponded to the powerlessness of the prophet in a 'prophetless and godless' world. Meaninglessness was no longer an aesthetic experience of the few, but a contagion. Having undermined religious, moral, and political beliefs, the forces of rationalization had finally exposed the meaning of meaninglessness to be power without right.

NOTES

1 'Science as a Vocation', *From Max Weber: Essays in Sociology.* (tra.) Hans Gerth and C. Wright Mills (New York, 1946), p. 145. Hereafter this volume will be referred to as *FMW*.
2 *Sophists* 225 A-B (tra.) A. E. Taylor (London, 1971).
3 *Nicomachean Ethics.* 1177b.25 ff., tra. M. Ostwald (Indianapolis, 1962).
4 'Heraclitus', frag. 253, *The Presocratic Philosophers*, (ed.) G. S. Kirk and J. E. Raven (Cambridge, 1957), p. 213.
5 *FMW*, p. 152.
6 'The great instauration', Preface in *Selected Writings of Francis Bacon* (ed.) H. G. Dick (New York: Modern Library, 1955), p. 429.
7 Wolfgang Mommsen, *Max Weber und die deutsche Politik, 1890–1920* (Tübingen, 1959), p. 279. See also the fine study by David Beetham, *Max Weber and the Theory of Modern Politics* (London, 1974); and Anthony Giddens, *Politics and Sociology in the Thought of Max Weber* (London, 1972).
8 *Economy and Society*, (ed.) Guenther Roth and Claus Wittich, 3 vols. (New York, 1968), vol. I, p. 3. Hereafter this will be cited as *E & S*.
9 Ibid, p. 215.
10 Ibid.
11 Ibid, p. 3.
12 Max Weber, *The Theory of Social and Economic Organization* (New York, 1947), p. 152, n. 83.
13 See the comments of the editors, *E & S*, vol. I, p lxxxviii-ix.
14 'Politics as a Vocation', *FMW*, pp. 121, 123.
15 Max Weber, *The Methodology of the Social Sciences* (tra.) E. A. Shils and H. A. Finch (Glencoe, IL, 1949), p. 27. Hereafter referred to as *Methodology*.
16 *Methodology*, p. 17.
17 *E & S*, vol. III, p. 1381.
18 *Methodology*, p. 74ff.
19 Ibid, p. 76.
20 *Methodology*, p. 90.
21 Ibid, p. 18.
22 *FMW*, p. 128.
23 *Methodology*, p. 110 (emphasis in original).
24 Ibid, p. 81.
25 *Republic* 440 B. E. 442 B-D. See also Aristotle, *Nicomachean Ethics* I.2. 1094a27–1094b5.
26 *Gesammelte Politische Schriften.* (2nd edn.) (ed.) J. Winckelmann (Tübingen, 1958), p. 1. Hereafter referred to as *GPS*.
27 Ibid, p. 20.
28 Ibid, p. 14.
29 Ibid, p. 12.

30 Ibid, pp. 12, 14.
31 *GPS*, p. 13.
32 Ibid, p. 14.
33 'Elbow-room in earthly existence will be won only by a hard struggle of man with man', Ibid., p. 12.
34 Examples of this genre are: W. G. Runciman, *A Critique of Max Weber's Philosophy of Social Science* (Cambridge, 1972); R. S. Rudner, *Philosophy of Social Science* (Engelwood Cliffs, NJ, 1966), p. 68ff; Dieter Henrich, *Die Einheit der Wissenschaftslehre* (Tübingen, 1952); and the introductory essays of Guy Okes to his translations of Weber's *Roscher and Knies* (New York, 1975) and *Critique of Stammler* (New York, 1977).
35 *The Protestant Ethic and the Spirit of Capitalism*, (tra.) Talcott Parsons (London, 1930), p. 78. Hereafter referred to as *PE*.
36 *PE*, p. 37.
37 See the translator's note, Ibid, p. ix.
38 Ibid, pp. 117, 153.
39 *PE*, p. 180.
40 *Methodology*, p. 52.
41 *Methodology*, p. 57.
42 Ibid, p. 19.
43 *PE*, p. 154.
44 *FMW*, pp. 137, 138.
45 *PE*, pp. 56, 63, 13.
46 Ibid, p. 37.
47 *PE*, pp. 181–2.
48 *PE*, p. 182.
49 *FMW*, pp. 137, 138.
50 *E & S*, vol. I, p. 215.
51 Ibid. Note the personal remark in 'Science as a vocation' where Weber notes that in promoting young scholars he followed the practice that 'a scholar promoted by me must legitimize and habilitate himself with somebody else at another university.' *FMW*, p. 130.
52 *E & S*, vol. I, p. 215.
53 *FMW*, pp. 148, 153, 155.
54 Ibid, p. 134.
55 Ibid, p. 135.
56 Ibid, p. 136.
57 Ibid. The scriptural passage that seems closest to *Romans* 3:24.
58 fr. 345 in G. S. Kirk and J. E. Raven, *The Presocratic Philosophers* (Cambridge, 1957), p. 271.
59 fr. 344 in Kirk and Raven, p. 269.
60 *Roscher and Knies*, p. 58.
61 *Methodology*, p. 116
62 Ibid, p. 111.
63 Ibid, p. 112.
64 *Methodology*, p. 81

65 *Methodology*, p. 105.
66 Ibid.
67 Ibid, p. 110.
68 *E & S*, vol. I, p. 223.
69 *FMW*, p. 128; *E & S*, vol. III, p. 1402.
70 *FMW*, pp 139, 148.
71 Ibid, p. 142.
72 Ibid, p. 152.
73 *FMW*, p. 155.
74 *Ancient Judaism*, (tra.) H. H. Gerth and Don Martindale (Glencoe, IL, 1952), p. 299. I have slightly revised the translation.
75 Ibid, pp. 301, 319.
76 *The Protestant Ethic*, pp. 28, 29.
77 Ibid, p. 29.

4

Social Conflict, Legitimacy, and Democracy

SEYMOUR MARTIN LIPSET

LEGITIMACY AND EFFECTIVENESS

The stability of any given democracy depends not only on economic development but also upon the effectiveness and the legitimacy of its political system. Effectiveness means actual performance, the extent to which the system satisfies the basic functions of government as most of the population and such powerful groups within it as big business or the armed forces see them. Legitimacy involves the capacity of the system to engender and maintain the belief that the existing political institutions are the most appropriate ones for the society. The extent to which contemporary democratic political systems are legitimate depends in large measure upon the ways in which the key issues which have historically divided the society have been resolved.

While effectiveness is primarily instrumental, legitimacy is evaluative. Groups regard a political system as legitimate or illegitimate according to the way in which its values fit with theirs. Important segments of the German Army, civil service, and aristocratic classes rejected the Weimar Republic, not because it was ineffective, but because its symbolism and basic values negated their own. Legitimacy, in and of itself, may be associated with many forms of political organization, including oppressive ones. Feudal societies, before the advent of industrialism, undoubtedly enjoyed the basic loyalty of most of their members. Crises of legitimacy are primarily a recent historical phenomenon, following the rise of sharp cleavages among groups which are able, because of mass communication, to organize around different values than those previously considered to be the only acceptable ones.

Source: Seymour Martin Lipset, *Political Man: The Social Bases of Politics* (Baltimore: Johns Hopkins University Press, expanded edition, 1981), reprinted by permission of Seymour Martin Lipset.

A crisis of legitimacy is a crisis of change. Therefore, its roots must be sought in the character of change in modern society. Crises of legitimacy occur during a transition to a new social structure, if (1) the *status* of major conservative institutions is threatened during the period of structural change; (2) all the major groups in the society do not have access to the political system in the transitional period, or at least as soon as they develop political demands. After a new social structure is established, if the new system is unable to sustain the expectations of major groups (on the grounds of 'effectiveness') for a long enough period to develop legitimacy upon the new basis, a new crisis may develop.

Tocqueville gives a graphic description of the first general type of loss of legitimacy, referring mainly to countries which moved from aristocratic monarchies to democratic republics: '. . . epochs sometimes occur in the life of a nation when the old customs of a people are changed, public morality is destroyed, religious belief shaken, and the spell of tradition broken . . .' The citizens then have neither the instinctive patriotism of a monarchy nor the reflecting patriotism of a republic; . . . they have stopped between the two in the midst of confusion and distress.'[1]

If, however, the status of major conservative groups and symbols is not threatened during this transitional period, even though they lose most of their power, democracy seems to be much more secure. And thus we have the absurd fact that ten out of the twelve stable European and English-speaking democracies are monarchies.[2] Great Britain, Sweden, Norway, Denmark, the Netherlands, Belgium, Luxembourg, Australia, Canada, and New Zealand are kingdoms, or dominions of a monarch, while the only republics which meet the conditions of stable democratic procedures are the United States and Switzerland, plus Uruguay in Latin America.

The preservation of the monarchy has apparently retained for these nations the loyalty of the aristocratic, traditionalist, and clerical sectors of the population which resented increased democratization and equalitarianism. And by accepting the lower strata and not resisting to the point where revolution might be necessary, the conservative orders won or retained the loyalty of the new 'citizens'. In countries where monarchy was overthrown by revolution, and orderly succession was broken, forces aligned with the throne have sometimes continued to refuse legitimacy to republican successors down to the fifth generation or more.

The one constitutional monarchy which became a Fascist dictatorship, Italy, was, like the French Republic, considered illegitimate by major groups in the society. The House of Savoy alienated the Catholics by destroying the temporal power of the Popes, and was also not a legitimate successor in the old Kingdom of the Two Sicilies. Catholics were, in fact, forbidden by the church to participate in Italian politics until almost World War I, and the church finally rescinded its position only because of its fear of the Socialists. French Catholics took a similar attitude to the Third Republic during the same period. Both the Italian and French democracies have had to operate for much of their histories without loyal support from important groups in their societies, on both the left and the right. Thus one main source of legitimacy lies in the continuity of important traditional integrative institutions during a transitional period in which new institutions are emerging.

The second general type of loss of legitimacy is related to the ways in which different societies handle the 'entry into politics' crisis – the decision as to when new social groups shall obtain access to the political process. In the nineteenth century these new groups were primarily industrial workers; in the twentieth, colonial elites and peasant peoples. Whenever new groups become politically active (e.g. when the workers first seek access to economic and political power through economic organization and the suffrage, when the bourgeoisie demand access to and participation in government, when colonial elites insist on control over their own system), easy access to the legitimate political institutions tends to win the loyalty of the new groups to the system, and they in turn can permit the old dominating strata to maintain their own status. In nations like Germany where access was denied for prolonged periods, first to the bourgeoisie and later to the workers, and where force was used to restrict access, the lower strata were alienated from the system and adopted extremist ideologies which, in turn, kept the more established groups from accepting the workers' political movement as a legitimate alternative.

Political systems which deny new strata access to power except by revolution also inhibit the growth of legitimacy by introducing millennial hopes into the political arena. Groups which have to push their way into the body politic by force are apt to over-exaggerate the possibilities which political participation affords. Consequently, democratic regimes born under such stress not only face the difficulty of being regarded as illegitimate by groups loyal to the *ancien régime* but may also be rejected by those whose millennial hopes are not fulfilled by the change. France, where right-wing clericalists have viewed the Republic as illegitimate and sections of the lower strata have found their expectations far from satisfied, is an example. And today many of the newly independent nations of Asia and Africa face the thorny problem of winning the loyalties of the masses to democratic states which can do little to meet the utopian objectives set by nationalist movements during the period of colonialism and the transitional struggle to independence.

In general, even when the political system is reasonably effective, if at any time the status of major conservative groups is threatened, or if access to politics is denied to emerging groups at crucial periods, the system's legitimacy will remain in question. On the other hand, a breakdown of effectiveness, repeatedly or for a long period, will endanger even a legitimate system's stability.

A major test of legitimacy is the extent to which given nations have developed a common 'secular political culture', mainly national rituals and holidays.[3] The United States has developed a common homogeneous culture in the veneration accorded the Founding Fathers, Abraham Lincoln, Theodore Roosevelt, and their principles. These common elements, to which all American politicians appeal, are not present in all democratic societies. In some European countries, the left and the right have a different set of symbols and different historical heroes. France offers the clearest example of such a nation. Here battles involving the use of different symbols which started in 1789 are, as Herbert Luethy points out, 'still in progress, and the issue is still open; every one of these dates [of major political controversy] still divides left and right, clerical and anti-clerical, progressive, and reactionary, in all their historically determined constellations'.[4]

Knowledge concerning the relative degree of legitimacy of a nation's political institutions is of key importance in any attempt to analyse the stability of these institutions when faced with a crisis of effectiveness. The relationship between different degrees of legitimacy and effectiveness in specific political systems may be presented in the form of a fourfold table, with examples of countries characterized by the various possible combinations:

		Effectiveness	
		+	−
Legitimacy	+	A	B
	−	C	D

Societies which fall in box A, which are, that is, high on the scales of both legitimacy and effectiveness, have stable political systems, like the United States, Sweden, and Britain.[5] Ineffective and illegitimate regimes, which fall in box D, are by definition unstable and break down, unless they are dictatorships maintaining themselves by force, like the governments of Hungary and Eastern Germany today.

The political experiences of different countries in the early 1930s illustrate the effect of other combinations. In the late 1920s, neither the German nor the Austrian republic was held legitimate by large and powerful segments of its population. Nevertheless, both remained reasonably effective.[6] In terms of the table, they fell in box C. When the effectiveness of various governments broke down in the 1930s, those societies which were high on the scale of legitimacy remained democratic, while such countries as Germany, Austria, and Spain lost their freedom, and France narrowly escaped a similar fate. Or, to put the changes in terms of the table, countries which shifted from A to B remained democratic, while those which shifted from C to D broke down. The military defeat of 1940 underlined French democracy's low position on the scale of legitimacy. It was the sole defeated democracy which furnished large-scale support for a Quisling regime.[7]

Situations like these demonstrate the usefulness of this type of analysis. From a short-range point of view, a highly effective but illegitimate system, such as a well governed colony, is more unstable than regimes which are relatively low in effectiveness and high in legitimacy. The social stability of a nation like Thailand, despite its periodic *coups d'état*, stands out in sharp contrast to the situation in neighbouring former colonial nations. On the other hand, prolonged effectiveness over a number of generations may give legitimacy to a political system. In the modern world, such effectiveness means primarily constant economic development. Those nations which have adapted most successfully to the requirements of an industrial system have the fewest internal political strains, and have either preserved their traditional legitimacy or developed strong new symbols.

The social and economic structure which Latin America inherited from the Iberian peninsula prevented it from following the lead of the former English colonies, and its republics never developed the symbols and aura of legitimacy. In large measure, the survival of the new political democracies of Asia and Africa will depend on their ability to meet the needs of their populations over a prolonged period, which will probably mean their ability to cope with industrialization.

LEGITIMACY AND CONFLICT

Inherent in all democratic systems is the constant threat that the group conflicts which are democracy's lifeblood may solidify to the point where they threaten to distintegrate the society. Hence conditions which serve to moderate the intensity of partisan battle are among the key requisites of democratic government.

Since the existence of a moderate state of conflict is in fact another way of defining a legitimate democracy, it is not surprising that the principal factors determining such an optimum state are closely related to those which produce legitimacy viewed in terms of continuities of symbols and statuses. The character and content of the major cleavages affecting the political stability of a society are largely determined by historical factors which have affected the way in which major issues dividing society have been solved or left unresolved over time.

In modern times, three major issues have emerged in Western nations: first, the place of the church and/or various religions within the nation; second, the admission of the lower strata, particularly the workers, to full political and economic 'citizenship' through universal suffrage and the right to bargain collectively; and third, the continuing struggle over the distribution of the national income.

The significant question here is, Were these issues dealt with one by one, with each more or less solved before the next arose; or did the problems accumulate, so that traditional sources of cleavage mixed with newer ones? Resolving tensions one at a time contributes to a stable political system; carrying over issues from one historical period to another makes for a political atmosphere characterized by bitterness and frustration rather than tolerance and compromise. Men and parties come to differ with each other, not simply on ways of settling current problems, but on fundamental and opposed outlooks. This means that they see the political victory of their opponents as a major moral threat, and the whole system, as a result, lacks effective value-integration.

The place of the church in society was fought through and solved in most of the Protestant nations in the eighteenth and nineteenth centuries. In some, the United States, for example, the church was disestablished and accepted the fact. In others, like Britain, Scandinavia, and Switzerland, religion is still state-supported, but the state churches, like constitutional monarchs, have ceased to be major sources of controversy. It remains for the Catholic countries of Europe to provide us with examples of situations in which the historic controversy between clerical and anti-clerical forces has continued to divide men politically down to the present day. In such countries as France, Italy, Spain, and Austria, being Catholic has meant being allied with rightist or conservative groups in politics, while being anticlerical, or a member of a minority religion, has most often meant alliance with the left. In a number of these countries, newer issues have been superimposed on the religious question. For conservative Catholics the fight against socialism has been not simply an economic struggle, or a controversy over social institutions, but a deep-rooted conflict between God and Satan.[8] For many secular intellectuals in contemporary Italy, opposition to the church legitimizes alliance with the Communists. And as long as religious ties reinforce secular political alignments, the chances for compromise and democratic give-and-take are weak.

The 'citizenship' issue has also been resolved in various ways. The United States and Britain gave the workers suffrage in the nineteenth century. In countries like Sweden, which resisted until the first part of the twentieth century, the struggle for citizenship became combined with socialism as a political movement, thereby producing a revolutionary socialism. Or, to put it in other terms, where the workers were denied both economic and political rights their struggle for redistribution of income and status was superimposed on a revolutionary ideology. Where the economic and status struggle developed outside of this context, the ideology with which it was linked tended to be that of gradualist reform. The workers in Prussia, for example, were denied free and equal suffrage until the revolution of 1918, and thereby clung to revolutionary Marxism. In southern Germany, where full citizenship rights were granted in the late nineteenth century, reformist, democratic, and non-revolutionary socialism was dominant. However, the national Social Democratic party continued to embrace revolutionary dogmas. These served to give ultra-leftists a voice in party leadership, enabled the Communists to win strength after the military defeat, and, perhaps even more important historically, frightened large sections of the German middle class who feared that a socialist victory would end all their privileges and status.

In France, the workers won the suffrage but were refused basic economic rights until after World War II. Large numbers of French employers refused to recognize French trade unions and sought to weaken or destroy them after every union victory. The instability of the French unions, and their constant need to preserve militancy in order to survive, made the workers susceptible to the appeals of extremist political groups. Communist domination of the French labour movement can in large part be traced to the tactics of the French business classes.

These examples do not explain why different countries varied in the way they handled basic national cleavages. They should suffice, however, to illustrate the way in which the conditions for stable democratic government are related to the bases of diversity. Where a number of historic cleavages intermix and create the basis for ideological politics, democracy will be unstable and weak, for by definition such politics does not include the concept of tolerance.

Parties with such total ideologies attempt to create what the German-American political scientist Sigmund Neumann has called an 'integrated' environment, in which the lives of the members are encased within ideologically linked activities. These actions are based on the party's assumption that it is important to isolate its followers from the 'falsehoods' expressed by non believers. Neumann has suggested the need for a basic analytic distinction between parties of representation, which strengthen democracy, and parties of integration, which weaken it.[9] The former are typified by most parties in the English-speaking democracies and Scandinavia, plus most centrist and conservative parties other than religious ones. These parties view their function as primarily one of securing votes around election time. The parties of integration, on the other hand, are concerned with making the world conform to their basic philosophy. They do not see themselves as contestants in a give-and-take game of pressure politics, but as partisans in a mighty struggle between divine or historic truth on one side and fundamental error on the other. Given this conception of the world, it becomes necessary to prevent their followers from being exposed to the cross-pressures flowing from contact with outsiders which will reduce their faith.

The two major non-totalitarian groups which have followed such procedures have been the Catholics and the Socialists. In much of Europe before 1939 the Catholics and Socialists attempted to increase intra-religious or intra-class communications by creating a network of social and economic organizations within which their followers could live their entire lives. Austria offers perhaps the best example of a situation in which two groups, the Social Catholics and the Social Democrats, dividing over all three historic issues and carrying on most of their social activities in party or church-linked organizations, managed to split the country into two hostile camps.[10] Totalitarian organizations, Fascist and Communist alike, expand the integrationist character of political life to the furthest limit possible by defining the world completely in terms of struggle.

Efforts, even by democratic parties, to isolate their social base from cross-pressures clearly undermine stable democracy, which requires shifts from one election to another and the resolving of issues between parties over long periods of time. Isolation may intensify loyalty to a party or church, but it will also prevent the party from reaching new groups. The Austrian situation illustrates the way in which the electoral process is frustrated when most of the electorate is confined within parties of integration. The necessary rules of democratic politics assume that conversion both ways, into and out of a party, is possible and proper, and parties which hope to gain a majority by democratic methods must ultimately give up their integrationist emphasis. As the working class has gained complete citizenship in the political and economic spheres in different countries, the Socialist parties of Europe have dropped their integrationist emphasis. The only non-totalitarian parties which now maintain such policies are religious parties like the Catholic parties or the Calvinist Anti-Revolutionary party of Holland. Clearly the Catholic and Dutch Calvinist churches are not 'democratic' in the sphere of religion. They insist there is but one truth, as the Communists and Fascists do in politics. Catholics may accept the assumptions of political democracy, but never those of religious tolerance. And where the political conflict between religion and irreligion is viewed as salient by Catholics or other believers in one true church, then a real dilemma exists for the democratic process. Many political issues which might easily be compromised are reinforced by the religious issue and cannot be settled.

Wherever the social structure operates so as to isolate *naturally* individuals or groups with the same political outlook from contact with those who hold different views, the isolated individuals or groups tend to back political extremists. It has been repeatedly noted, for example, that workers in so-called 'isolated' industries – miners, sailors, fishermen, lumbermen, sheepshearers, and longshoremen – who live in communities predominately inhabited by others in the same occupation usually give overwhelming support to the more left-wing platforms.[11] Such districts tend to vote Communist or Socialist by large majorities, sometimes to the point of having what is essentially a 'one-party' system. The political intolerance of farm-based groups in times of crisis may be another illustration of this same pattern, since farmers, like workers in isolated industries, have a more homogeneous political environment than do those employed in most urban occupations.[12]

These conclusions are confirmed by studies of individual voting behaviour which indicate that individuals under cross-pressures – those who belong to groups predisposing them in different directions, or who have friends supporting different parties, or who are regularly exposed to the propaganda of different groups – are less likely to be strongly committed politically.[13]

Multiple and politically inconsistent affiliations, loyalties, and stimuli reduce the emotion and aggressiveness involved in political choice. For example, in contemporary Germany, a working-class Catholic, pulled in two directions, will most probably vote Christian-Democratic, but is much more tolerant of the Social Democrats than the average middle-class Catholic.[14] Where a man belongs to a variety of groups that all predispose him toward the same political choice, he is in the situation of the isolated worker and is much less likely to be tolerant of other opinions.

The available evidence suggests that the chances for stable democracy are enhanced to the extent that groups and individuals have a number of cross-cutting, politically relevant affiliations. To the degree that a significant proportion of the population is pulled among conflicting forces, its members have an interest in reducing the intensity of political conflict.[15] As Robert Dahl and Talcott Parsons have pointed out, such groups and individuals also have an interest in protecting the rights of political minorities.[16]

A stable democracy requires relatively moderate tension among its contending political forces. And political moderation is facilitated by the system's capacity to resolve key dividing issues before new ones arise. If the issues of religion, citizenship, and 'collective bargaining' are allowed to accumulate, they reinforce each other, and the more reinforced and correlated the sources of cleavage, the less likelihood for political tolerance. Similarly, the greater the isolation from heterogeneous political stimuli, the more the background factors 'pile up' in one direction, the greater the chances that the group or individual will have an extremist perspective. These two relationships, one on the level of partisan issues, the other on the level of party support, are joined by the fact that parties reflecting accumulated unresolved issues will further seek to isolate their followers from conflicting stimuli. The best conditions for political cosmopolitanism are again those of economic development – the growth of urbanization, education, communications media, and increased wealth. Most of the obviously isolated occupations – mining, lumbering, agriculture – are precisely those whose relative share of the labour force declines sharply with industrialization.[17]

Thus the factors involved in modernization or economic development are linked to those which establish legitimacy and tolerance. But it should always be remembered that correlations are only statements about relative degrees of congruence, and that another condition for political action is that the correlation never be so clear-cut that men feel they cannot change the direction of affairs by their actions. And this lack of high correlation also means that for analytic purposes the variables should be kept distinct even if they intercorrelate. For example, the analysis of cleavage presented here suggests specific ways in which different electoral and constitutional arrangements may affect the chances for democracy. These are discussed in the following section.

SYSTEMS OF GOVERNMENT

If cross-cutting bases of cleavage make a more vital democracy, it follows that, all other factors being constant, two-party systems are better than multi-party systems, that the election of officials on a territorial basis is preferable to proportional representation, and federalism is superior to a unitary state. Of course there have been and are stable democracies with multi-party systems, proportional representation, and a unitary state. In fact, I would argue that such variations in systems of government are much less important than those derived from the basic differences in social structure discussed in the previous sections. Nevertheless, they may contribute to overall stability or instability.

The argument for the two-party system rests on the assumption that in a complex society parties must necessarily be broad coalitions which do not serve the interests of one major group, and that they must not be parties of integration but must seek to win support among groups which are preponderantly allied to the opposition party. The British Conservative or American Republic parties, for instance, must not basically antagonize the manual workers, since a large part of their votes must come from them. The Democratic and Labour parties are faced with a similar problem *vis-à-vis* the middle classes. Parties which are never oriented toward gaining a majority seek to win the greatest possible electoral support from a limited base − a 'workers' party will accentuate working-class interests, and a party appealing primarily to small businessmen will do the same for its group. For these splinter parties, elections, instead of being occasions for seeking the broadest possible base of support by convincing divergent groups of their common interests, become events in which they stress the cleavages separating their supporters from other segments of the society.

The proposition that proportional representation weakens rather than strengthens democracy rests on an analysis of the differences between multi-party and majority party situations. If it is true, as suggested above, that the existence of many parties accentuates differences and reduces consensus, then any electoral system which increases the chance for more rather than fewer parties serves democracy badly.

Besides, as the German sociologist Georg Simmel has pointed out, the system of electing members of parliament to represent territorial constituencies rather than groups (as proportional representation encourages), forces the various groups to secure their ends within an electoral framework that involves concern with many interests and the need for compromise.[18]

Federalism increases the opportunity for multiple sources of cleavage by adding regional interests and values to the others which cross-cut the social structure. A major exception to this generalization occurs when federalism divides a country across the lines of basic cleavage, e.g. between different ethnic, religious, or linguistic areas, as it does in India and Canada. Democracy needs cleavage within linguistic or religious groups, not between them. But where such divisions do not exist, federalism seems to serve democracy well. Besides creating a further source of cross-cutting cleavage, it provides the various functions which Tocqueville noted it shared with strong voluntary associations – resistance to centralization of power, the training of new political leaders, and a means of giving the out party a stake in the system as a whole, since both national parties usually continue to control some units of the system.

I might emphasize again that I do not consider these aspects of the political structure essential for democratic systems. If the underlying social conditions facilitate democracy, as they seem to in, say, Sweden, then the combination of many parties, proportional representation, and a unitary state does not seriously weaken it. At most it permits irresponsible minorities to gain a foothold in parliament. On the other hand, in countries like Weimar Germany and France, where a low level of effectiveness and legitimacy weakens the foundations of democracy, constitutional factors encouraging the growth of many parties further reduce the chances that the system will survive . . .

NOTES

1 Alexis de Tocqueville, *Democracy in America*, Vol. I (New York: Alfred A. Knopf, Vintage edn, 1945), pp. 251–2.
2 Walter Lippman in referring to the seemingly greater capacity of the constitutional monarchies than the republics of Europe to 'preserve order with freedom' suggests that this may be because 'in a republic the governing power, being wholly secularized, loses much of its prestige; it is stripped, if one prefers, of all the illusions of intrinsic majesty.' See his *The Public Philosophy* (New York: Mentor Books, 1956), p. 50.
3 See Gabriel Almond, 'Comparative political systems', *Journal of Politics*, 18 (1956), pp. 391–409.
4 Herbert Luethy, *The State of France* (London: Secker and Warburg, 1955), p. 29.
5 The race problem in the American South does constitute one basic challenge to the legitimacy of the system, and at one time did cause a breakdown of the national order. This conflict has reduced the commitment of many White southerners to the democratic game down to the present. Great Britain had a comparable problem as long as Catholic Ireland remained part of the United Kingdom. Effective government could not satisfy Ireland. Political practices by both sides in Northern Ireland, Ulster, also illustrate the problem of a regime which is not legitimate to a major segment of its population.
6 For an excellent analysis of the permanent crisis of the Austrian republic which flowed from the fact that it was viewed as an illegitimate regime by the Catholics and conservatives, see Charles Gulick, *Austria from Hapsburg to Hitler* (Berkeley: University of California Press, 1948).
7 The French legitimacy problem is well described by Katherine Munro. 'The Right wing parties never quite forgot the possibility of a counter revolution while the Left wing parties revived the Revolution militant in their Marxism or Communism; each side suspected the other of using the Republic to achieve its own ends and of being legal only so far as it suited it. This suspicion threatened time and time again to make the Republic unworkable, since it led to obstruction in both the political and the economic sphere, and difficulties of government in turn undermined confidence in the regime and its rulers.' Quoted in Charles Micaud, 'French political parties: ideological myths and social realities', in Sigmund Neumann (ed.), *Modern Political Parties* (Chicago: University of Chicago Press, 1956), p. 108.
8 The linkage between democratic instability and Catholicism may also be accounted for by elements inherent in Catholicism as a religious system. Democracy requires a universalistic political belief system in the sense that it accepts various different ideologies as legitimate. And it might be assumed that religious value systems which are more universalistic, in the sense of placing less stress on being the only true

church, will be more compatible with democracy than those which assume that they are the only truth. The latter belief, which is held much more strongly by the Catholic than by most other Christian churches, makes it difficult for the religious value system to help legitimate a political system which requires as part of its basic value system the belief that 'good' is served best through conflict among opposing beliefs.

Kingsley Davis has argued that a Catholic state church tends to be irreconcilable with democracy since 'Catholicism attempts to control so many aspects of life, to encourage so much fixity of status and submission to authority, and to remain so independent of secular authority that it invariably clashes with the liberalism, individualism, freedom, mobility and sovereignty of the democratic nation.' See 'Political ambivalence in Latin America', *Journal of Legal and Political Sociology*, 1 (1943), reprinted in A. N. Christensen, *The Evolution of Latin American Government* (New York: Henry Holt, 1951), p. 240.

9 See Sigmund Neumann, *Die Deutschen Parteien: Wesen und Wandel nach dem Kriege* (Berlin: Junker und Dünnhaupt Verlag, 1932) for exposition of the distinction between parties of integration and parties of representation. Neumann has further distinguished between parties of 'democratic integration' (the Catholic and Social Democratic parties) and those of 'total integration' (Fascist and Communist parties) in his more recent chapter, 'Toward a comparative study of political parties', in the volume which he edited: *Modern Political Parties*, pp. 403–5.

10 See Charles Gulick, *Austria from Hapsburg to Hitler*.

11 See Seymour Martin Lipset, *Political Man: The Social Bases of Politics*, pp. 233–5, 249.

12 This tendency obviously varies with relation to urban communities, type of rural stratification, and so forth. For a discussion of the role of vocational homogeneity and political communication among farmers, see S. M. Lipset, *Agrarian Socialism* (Berkeley: University of California Press, 1950), Chap 10, 'Social structure and political activity'. For evidence on the undemocratic propensities of rural populations see Samuel A. Stouffer, *Communism, Conformity, and Civil Liberties* (New York: Doubleday & Co., Inc., 1955), pp. 138–9. National Public Opinion Institute of Japan, Report No. 26, *A Survey Concerning the Protection of Civil Liberties* (Tokyo, 1951) reports that the farmers were the occupational group by far the least concerned with civil liberties. Carl Friedrich, in accounting for the strength of natonalism and Nazism among German farmers, suggests similar factors to the ones discussed here; that 'the rural population is more homogeneous, that it contains a smaller number of outsiders and foreigners, that it has much less contact with foreign countries and peoples, and finally that its mobility is much more limited'. Carl J. Friedrich, 'The agricultural basis of emotional nationalism', *Public Opinion Quarterly*, 1 (1937), pp. 50–1.

13 Perhaps the first general statement of the consequences of 'cross-pressures' on individual and group behaviour may be found in a work written over 50 years ago by Georg Simmel, *Conflict and the Web of Group Affiliations* (Glencoe: The Free Press, 1956), pp. 126–95. It is an interesting example of discontinuity in social research that the concept of cross-pressures was used by Simmel, but had to be independently rediscovered in voting research. For a detailed application of the effect of multiple-group affiliations on the political process in general, see David Truman, *The Governmental Process* (New York: Alfred A. Knopf, 1951).

14 See Juan Linz, The Social Bases of German Politics (unpublished PhD thesis, Department of Sociology, Columbia University, 1958).

15 See Bernard Berelson, Paul F. Lazarsfeld, and William McPhee, *Voting* (Chicago: University of Chicago Press, 1954), for an exposition of the usefulness of cross-pressure as an explanatory concept. Also, see Lipset, *Political Man*, Ch. VI for an attempt to specify the consequences of different group memberships for voting behaviour, and a review of the literature.

16 As Dahl puts it, 'If most individuals in the society identify with more than one group, then there is some positive probability that any majority contains individuals who identify for certain purposes with the threatened minority. Members of the threatened minority who strongly prefer their alternative will make their feelings known to those members of the tentative majority who also, at some psychological level, identify with the minority. Some of these sympathizers will shift their support away from the majority alternative and the majority will crumble.' See Robert A. Dahl, *A Preface to Democratic Theory* (Chicago: University of Chicago Press, 1956), pp. 104–5. Parsons suggests that 'pushing the implications of political difference too far activates the solidarities between adherents of the two parties which exist on other, nonpolitical bases so that members of the political majority come to defend those who share other of their interests who differ from them politically.' See Parsons' essay 'Voting and the equilibrium of the American political system', in E. Burdick and A. Brodbeck (eds), *American Voting Behavior* (Glencoe: The Free Press, 1959), p. 93. A recent discussion of this problem in a Norwegian context points up 'the integrative functions of cross-cutting conflict . . . [when] the conflict lines between the voter groups cut across the divisions between readers of newspapers of different political tendencies and this places a considerable proportion of the electorate in a situation of cross-pressure . . . In the Norwegian situation there is an interesting two way process of mutual restraints: on the one hand a majority of the Socialist voters are regularly exposed to newspaper messages from the opposition parties, on the other hand the non-Socialist papers, just because they in so many cases dominate their community and address themselves to a variety of politically heterogeneous groups, are found to exercise a great deal of restraint in the

expression of conflicting opinions.' Stein Rokkan and Per Torsvik, 'The voter, the reader and the party press' (Mimeo, Oslo: 1959).
17 Colin Clark, *The Conditions of Economic Progress* (New York: Macmillan, 1940).
18 Georg Simmel, *Conflict and the Web of Group Affiliations* (Glencoe: The Free Press, 1956), pp. 191–4. Talcott Parsons has recently made a similar point that one of the mechanisms for preventing a 'progressively deepening rift in the electorate' is the 'involvement of voting with the ramified solidarity structure of the society in such a way, that, though there is a correlation, there is no exact correspondence between political polarization and other bases of differentiation'. Talcott Parsons, *The Social System* (Glencoe: The Free Press, 1951), pp. 92–3.

5
Legitimacy in the Modern State

JOHN H. SCHAAR

I

Authority is a word on everyone's lips today. The young attack it and the old demand respect for it. Parents have lost it and policemen enforce it. Experts claim it and artists spurn it, while scholars seek it and lawyers cite it. Philosophers reconcile it with liberty and theologians demonstrate its compatibility with conscience. Bureaucrats pretend they have it and politicians wish they did. Everybody agrees that there is less of it than there used to be. It seems that the matter stands now as a certain Mr. Wildman thought it stood in 1648: 'Authority hath been broken into pieces.'[1]

About the only people left who seem little affected by the situation are the political scientists. Authority used to be a central term in learned political discourse, perhaps the governing term in philosophical treatments of politics. Except for a few renegade Catholic philosophers, that is obviously no longer the case. You can read a dozen authoritative texts on the American political system, for example, and not find the concept seriously treated. Its use is restricted to discussions of such ritual matters as 'the authority of the people' or to descriptions of the 'authority' of this or that institution or office. Even the recent spate of writing on the theory of democracy contains no substantial treatment of the topic.[2]

Max Weber pretty thoroughly did our work for us here. His exposition of the three types of authority, or the three grounds upon which claims to legitimate authority can be based, has the same status in social science that an older trinity has in Christian theology. Since Weber, we have been busy putting the phenomena into one or another of his three boxes and charting the progress by which charismatic authority becomes routinized into traditional

Source: John Schaar, 'Legitimacy in the modern state', in *Power and Community: Dissenting Essays in Political Science*, Philip Green and Sanford Levinson (eds.) (New York: Random House, 1969), pp. 278–80, 282–8, 294–313, 317–27, reprinted by permission of Random House.

authority, which, under the impact of science and secularism, gives way in turn to rational-legal authority. It all looks pretty good to the political scientists, as more and more traditional societies enter the transitional stage and gather their resources for the hopeful journey toward the modern stage, where rational-legal authority holds sway, along with prosperity, moderation, and a 'participant' and empathetic citizenry. It is admitted, to be sure, that there are many obstacles on the path, that some traditional folk still hold out, and that there are even one or two troublesome cases of regression. But on the whole, history is the story of the rational-legal state.[3]

But while the discipline cumulates, things outside jump. We hear of riots and rebellions, demonstrations and assassinations. Heads of state in many modern countries cannot safely go among the citizenry. Dignified ceremonies are raucously interrupted by riotous crowds chanting obscenities at the officials. Policemen have been transformed from protectors into pigs. A log of young people are trying drugs, and a lot of older people are buying guns. In 1969 a man entered the employment security building in Olympia, Washington, and tried to murder a computer. He failed, however, because 1401's brains were protected by a bulletproof steel plate. Some developers recently announced plans for a 'maximum security subdivision' in Maryland at a minimum cost of $200,000 per house. The subdivision will be ringed by a steel fence and patrolled by armed guards, the shrubbery will hide electronic detectors, and visitors will be checked through a blockhouse. In 1968, American governmental units hired 26,000 additional policemen, an increase of 7 per cent over 1967; 1968 was the second year in a row during which police employment rose more steeply than any other kind of public employment.[4]

We can feel the chill of some sentences Henry Adams wrote over 60 years ago:

> The assumption of unity which was the mark of human thought in the middle-ages has yielded very slowly to the proofs of complexity . . . Yet it is quite sure . . . that, at the accelerated rate of progression shown since 1600, it will not need another century or half century to tip thought upside down. Law, in that case, would disappear as theory or *a priori* principle, and give place to force. Morality would become police. Explosives would reach cosmic violence. Disintegration would overcome integration.[5]

It is the thesis of this essay that legitimate authority is declining in the modern states; that, in a real sense, 'law and order' *is* the basic political question of our day. The seamless web of socialization described by such leading students of the subject as Easton, Greenstein, Hess, and Hyman shows rips and frays. Many of the sons are no longer sure they want the legacy of the fathers. Among young people, the peer group increasingly takes priority as the agency of socialization, and the values it sponsors are new and hostile to those of the adult world. Many people are seeking ways to live in the system without belonging to it: their hearts are elsewhere. Others, convinced that the organized system will not in the long run permit the escape into private liberty, or feeling that such an escape is ignoble, are acting politically to transform the system. In the eyes of large and growing numbers of men, the social and political landscape of America, the most advanced of the advanced states, is no green and gentle place, where men may long abide. That landscape is, rather, a scene of wracked shapes and desert spaces. What we mainly see are the eroded forms of once authoritative institutions and ideas. What we mainly hear are the hollow winds of once compelling ideologies, and the unnerving gusts of new moods and slogans. What we mainly feel in our hearts is the granite consolidation of the technological and bureaucratic order, which may bring physical comfort and great collective power, or sterility, but not political liberty and moral autonomy. All the modern states, with the United States in the vanguard, are well advanced along a path toward a crisis of legitimacy.[6]

The essay has two subsidiary theses. First, that the crisis of legitimacy is a function of some of the basic, defining orientations of modernity itself; specifically, rationality, the cult of efficiency and power, ethical relativism, and equalitarianism. In effect, it will be argued that the modern mind, having now reached nearly full development, is turning back upon itself and undermining the very principles that once sustained order and obedience in the modern state. Secondly, it will be argued (mainly indirectly) that contemporary social science has failed to appreciate the precariousness of legitimate authority in the modern states because it is largely a product of the same phenomena it seeks to describe and therefore suffers the blindness of the eye examining itself.

What the thesis essentially asserts, then, is that the philosophical and experiential foundations of legitimacy in the modern states are gravely weakened, leaving obedience a matter of lingering habit, or expediency, or necessity, but not a matter of reason and principle, and of deepest sentiment and conviction. We are nearing the end of an era, and it is becoming clear that the decline of legitimate authority is the product of the ideal and material forces that have been the defining attributes of modern authority itself. This movement has been visible for a long time in most of the non-political sectors of life – family, economy, education, religion – and it is now spreading rapidly into the political realm. The gigantic and seemingly impregnable control structures that surround and dominate men in the modern states are increasingly found to have at their centres, not a vital principle of authority, but something approaching a hollow space, a moral vacuum.

A preliminary word on the scope and perspective of the essay, and on its political and methodological orientations.

The major thesis and its subsidiaries can be expanded and elucidated in a number of ways. Its critical terms can be defined with precision, and its relevance to the contemporary political scene in the United States can be shown. Empirical evidence can be brought to bear on the propositions. But these propositions cannot be made operational, tested, and verified or falsified beyond reasonable doubt by the criteria of a rigorous behaviouralism. This essay will report no opinion survey, present no input–output charts, attempt no stimulus-response or cognitive–dissonance analysis of legitimacy. It will, instead, utilize a variety of materials that help illuminate the problem, including some materials of dubious scientific quality. Perhaps it really is possible to say something about the truth without first polling a sample of one's contemporaries in order to get the facts . . .

II

Start by comparing the traditional and common meanings of legitimacy with the usage of leading modern social scientists. The *Oxford English Dictionary* says the following:

Legitimacy: (a) of a government or the title of a sovereign: the condition of being in accordance with law or principle . . . (b) conformity to a rule or principle; lawfulness. In logic, conformity to sound reasoning.

Legitimate: (a) etymologically, the word expresses a status, which has been conferred or ratified by some authority; (b) conformable to law or rule. Sanctioned or authorized by law or right, lawful, proper; (c) normal, regular; conformable to a recognized standard type; (d) sanctioned by the laws of reasoning; logically admissible or inferable.

The most relevant entries from Webster's *Unabridged* are:

Legitimate: (1) lawfully begotten . . . (2) real, genuine; not false, counterfeit, or spurious; (3) accordant with law or with established legal forms and requirements; lawful; (4) conforming to recognized principles, or accepted rules or standards.

Now, three current professional definitions:

(1) Legitimacy involves the capacity of the system to engender and maintain the belief that the existing political institutions are the most appropriate ones for the society.[7]
(2) In the tradition of Weber, legitimacy has been defined as 'the degree to which institutions are valued for themselves and considered right and proper'.[8]
(3) We may define political legitimacy as the quality of 'ought-ness' that is perceived by the public to inhere in a political regime. That government is legitimate which is viewed as morally proper for a society.[9]

The contrast between the two sets of definitions, the traditional and lexical on the one side and the current scientific usage on the other, is basic and obvious. The older definitions all revolve around the element of law or right, and rest the force of a claim (whether it be a claim to political power or to the validity of a conclusion in an argument) upon foundations external to and independent of the mere assertion or opinion of the claimant (e.g. the laws of inheritance, the laws of logic). Thus, a claim to political power is legitimate only when the claimant can invoke some source of authority beyond or above himself. History shows a variety of such sources: immemorial custom, divine law, the law of nature, a constitution. As Arendt has pointed out, 'In all these cases, legitimacy derives from something outside the range of human deeds; it it either not man-made at all . . . or has at least not been made by those who happen to be in power.'[10]

The new definitions all dissolve legitimacy into belief or opinion. If a people holds the belief that existing institutions are 'appropriate' or 'morally proper', then those institutions are legitimate. That's all there is to it. By a surgical procedure, the older concept has been trimmed of its cumbersome 'normative' and 'philosophical' parts, leaving the term leaner, no doubt, but now fit for scientific duty. It might turn out that Occam's Razor has cut off a part or two that will be missed later on.

A few implications of these new formulations should be articulated.

First of all, when legitimacy is defined as consisting in belief alone, then the investigator can examine nothing outside popular opinion in order to decide whether a given regime or institution or command is legitimate or illegitimate. To borrow the language of the law, there can be no independent inquiry into the title. In effect, this analysis dissolves legitimacy into acceptance or acquiescence, thereby rendering opaque whole classes of basic and recurrent political phenomena, e.g. a group or individual refuses consent and obedience to the orders of a regime or institution on the ground that the regime or institution is illegitimate; a regime or institution is acknowledged to be legitimate as such, but consent is withheld from a particular order on the ground that the regime had no legitimate right to make that order; one consents or acquiesces out of interest or necessity, although he regards a regime or an order as illegitimate. In short, legitimacy and acquiescence, and legitimacy and consensus, are not the same, and the relations between them are heterogeneous. The older formulations made these empirical situations comprehensible, while the newer usages obfuscate them. The phenomenon of legitimacy, far from being identical with consensus, is rather, as Friedrich says, 'a very particular form of consensus, which revolves around the question of the right or title to rule'.[11] Legitimacy is that aspect of authority which refers to entitlement.

Another important feature of these new formulations, which emerges clearly when the definitions are examined within the context of the larger works in which they appear, is that they see legitimacy as a function of a system's ability to persuade members of its own appropriateness. The flow is from leaders to followers. Leaders lay down rules, promulgate policies, and disseminate symbols which tell followers how and what they should do and feel. Thus, Merelman explains legitimacy within the framework of stimulus-response psychology, which he rather narrowly equates with learning theory. The regime or the leaders provide the stimuli, first in the form of policies improving citizen welfare and later in the form of symbolic materials which function as secondary reinforcements, and the followers provide the responses, in the form of favourable attitudes toward the stimulators – which, to reiterate, is what Merelman means by legitimacy. The symbols become, in the minds of the followers, condensations of the practices and intentions of the rulers. Over time, if the rulers manipulate symbols skilfully, symbolic rewards alone may suffice to maintain supportive attitudes.[12] The symbols may actually conceal rather than reveal the real nature of the regime's policies and practices, as the symbols of democracy becloud the actual processes of rule in the modern states.

We should be clear about the understanding of the relationship between 'community' and control that informs such a conception of legitimacy. Merelman and others in this tradition see a polity not as a people with a culture seeking together the forms of order and action that will preserve and enhance that culture, but as a mass or collective that is made into a unit of control by propaganda.[13] That is no doubt a fairly accurate conception of most modern systems of rule, but it is worth remembering that a politics of propaganda and ideology is not the only possible politics.[14]

Legitimacy, then, is almost entirely a matter of sentiment. Followers believe in a regime, or have faith in it, and that is what legitimacy is. The faith may be the product of conditioning, or it may be the fruit of symbolic bedazzlement, but in neither case is it in any significant degree the work of reason, judgement, or active participation in the processes of rule. In this analysis, people do not attribute legitimacy to authority because they recognize its claim to a foundation in some principle or source outside itself. This emerges clearly in Lipset's treatment of the specific institutional arrangements and procedures which are conducive to legitimacy: cross-pressures; widespread and multiple membership in voluntary associations; the two-party system; federalism, territorial rather than proportional representation.[15] In a most confusing way, an analysis of something called legitimacy first equates legitimacy with opinion, then goes to a restatement of the standard liberal-pluralist description of the structure of power in the United States, turns next to a discussion of stability, and finally resolves stability into passivity or acquiescence caused by cognitive confusion, conflict of interest, and inability to translate one's desires into political decisions due to certain institutional arrangements. Obviously, we are no longer talking about faith or belief at all, let alone legitimacy, but about confusion and indifference, stability and efficiency. There is where the contemporary social treatment of legitimate power rests. A fuller view is needed.

No matter where we go in space, nor how far back in time, we find power. Power is ancient and ubiquitous, a universal feature of social life. But if it is a fact, it is nonetheless a complex fact:

Power exists . . . only through the concurrence of all [its] properties . . . it draws its inner strength and the material succour which it receives, both from the continuously helping hand of habit and also from the imagination; it must possess both a reasonable authority and a magical influence; it must operate like nature herself, both by visible means and by hidden influence.[16]

Force can bring political power into being but cannot maintain it. For that, something else is required: 'Will, not force,' said T. H. Green, 'is the basis of the state'. Once power is established and set on course, as it were, then obedience is largely a matter of habit. But there are two critical points in the life of power when habit does not suffice. The first is at its birth, when habits of obedience have not formed. The other comes when the customary ways and limits of power are altered, when subjects are presented with new and disturbing uses of power and are asked to assume new burdens and accept new claims. At those two points – and most of the states of our day, old and new, are at one or the other of the two – theory must be called in to buttress and justify obedience. There is no denying a certain pragmatic or expediential element in all theories of legitimacy. Such theories are never offered idly, they never appear accidentally. Rather, they appear when the uses of power are matters of controversy, and they are weapons in the struggles of men to enjoy the benefits and escape the burdens of power. This is not to say that all theories of legitimacy are only or merely 'rationalizations'; rather, it is to say that they have an element of rationalization in them.

Theory, then, by making power legitimate, turns it into authority. All theories of legitimacy take the form of establishing a principle which, while it resides outside power and is independent of it, locates or embeds power in a realm of things beyond the wills of the holders of power: the legitimacy of power stems from its *origin*. In addition, most theories of legitimacy simultaneously attempt to justify power by reference to its *ends*. As was suggested by the earlier quotation from Arendt, the originating principles have been many and diverse. So too have the ends. But in our time this great complexity has been reduced, in virtually all states, to a gratifying simplicity: for power to become authority, it must originate in 'democratic consent' and aim at the 'common good' or 'public interest' . . .

III

A serious account of the contemporary problem of 'law and order' would be an account of the hollowing out of the theoretical and empirical foundations upon which authority (*de jure* and *de facto*) has rested in the states of the West. Weber thought that the day of charismatic and traditional structures of legitimacy was over and that both were being displaced by rational-legal authority. But he did not see far enough into the matter, for rational-legal authority has also been undermined, leaving the great institutions it brought into being gravely weakened from within. I cannot supply anything like a full map of the routes leading to this end. What follows is a sketch of the main routes on this journey into emptiness.

The Epistemological Route

This route consists in charting the connections between the status of the concept of truth on the one side, and the growing feeling of disengagement or alienation from authoritative structures of order on the other. Until recently, the concept of truth rested upon certain assumptions about the relations between the knower and the known. Two of these assumptions are of greatest importance: (1) the notion that man's cognitive apparatus did not itself basically condition the quality and nature of what was known; and (2) the notion that there existed a kingdom of order outside man and independent of him (e.g. the laws of nature, God, the laws of history). Given the first assumption, truth always meant discovery. Given the second, truth meant discovery of a *pre-established* order. Discoveries made by the methods of science, philosophy, and theology were not fabrications of the human mind, but faithful reflections or representations of an order independent of the discoverer. For man to increase his own harmony with the pre-established harmony outside himself, he had only to increase his knowledge of the world.[17] Given the right methods and concepts, increasing knowledge brought increasing harmony between man and the world. Anthropological and mythological researches have shown that in the ages before philosophy and science, myth served this same function of bringing men into contact with the sources of order outside themselves.

Given this concept of truth, social and political life too could be seen as a harmonious association of self and society with an objective order external to man and constituted by some force independent of him. Political societies were not works of human art and will, but were embedded in and even constituted by a larger order of being. Human authority rested on bases more 'solid' than individual choice and will.

That older view of knowledge and truth has now just about

disappeared, and with its disappearance men have lost most of their older principles of legitimation. In the older view, a structure of order could base its claim to legitimacy on some foundation other than the choices and opinions of the members. In the newer view, order becomes dependent upon will, with no source of rewards and punishments external to the system and its members. With that, the social and political world becomes 'unfrozen' as it were, movable by skill and power, for it is seen that there is no necessity in any given arrangement of things. All things could be other than they are. It is the world of Sorel, rather than the world of Plato. It is not even a world in which change or becoming follows a necessary pattern. It is the world of Sartre, rather than the world of Hegel.[18]

Furthermore, the death of the older views also spelled death for the authoritative classes of priests and nobles who claimed a right to rule on the grounds that they possessed knowledge of the true order of things and of the methods needed for gaining further knowledge of that order. The oldest and most basic justification for hierarchy has dissolved. The only class that could conceivably make that claim today is the class of scientists. But in order to occupy this role, the scientific estate would have to transform itself into something very like a priesthood, along lines which Comte understood perfectly. The foundations for that are already present. For the masses, science is largely a matter of miracle, mystery, and authority. Translated into educational terms, the slogan that through science man has gained increasing knowledge of nature really means that a few men now know a great deal about how nature 'works', while the rest of us are about as ignorant as we have always been. Translated into political terms, the slogan that through knowledge man has gained power really means that a few men have gained the means of unprecedented power over a great many other men. On the other hand, there are good reasons for thinking that the scientists and experts may not be able to perform the priestly role with enduring success. I shall indicate some of these reasons later.

When the secret that nature is no guide is finally known to all – the secret exposed by the Sophists and in our age by Nietzsche – the whole question of legitimacy will have to be reopened. Order will be seen as artificial, the result of will and choice alone, as vulnerable to change and challenge as will itself is. Structures of authority will not be able to invoke the ancient and once ubiquitous idea that each thing under the sun has its own right nature and place in the constitution of the whole. For centuries, this sense of the fitness and rightness of things set boundaries to men's pretensions to control and shaped their moral attitudes concerning the permissible limits within which they might legitimately impose their desires on the world around them. A basic piety toward the world and toward the processes that sustain it will disappear, and all things, including polities and men themselves, will come to appear artificial and malleable.[19] Whole new sets of arguments and images imposing limits on man's urge to satisfy his desires will have to be found. And until they are found, the idea and the very experience of legitimate authority cannot have anything like the bedrock importance they have heretofore had in political life.

The Moral Route

The knowledge that civilization begins when men understand that any shared custom at all is better than none is as old as Homer and as new as the researches of Lévi-Strauss. All morality is in the beginning group morality. Each tribe believes that there is no morality outside the tribe and that the tribe without its morality is no longer a tribe. Morality is, then, both a means and the basic means for preserving a community – holding it together, marking pathways through the landscape of social relations, defending it against threats from strangers and the gods. Men everywhere are taught to fear those who violate morality and to revere its authors and upholders.

Furthermore, as Nietzsche understood, and as scientific research increasingly confirms, nations and communities are 'born'.[20] And birth requires a father or author, the one who, whether mythologically or actually, brought the original laws and customs, thereby making a people a people.[21] The founder of a people is usually either a god or a messenger and mediator between gods and men: the creative moment in the birth of a nation is the birth of a religion.[22] Even the Enlightened American Founding Fathers saw the Constitution as a partial embodiment of that higher order called the Laws of Nature and of Nature's God. Prophets and messengers appear not only at the original birth, but also at times after the founding when the boundaries have been altered or obscured and need to be rectified. In addition, through actions based on myth and ritual, the people themselves also re-enact and reaffirm the harmony between the ontological order and their own human realm. In sum, founders and prophets create and correct, and myth and ritual recreate and restore, a community identity set within a cosmology. Identity and legitimacy are thus inseparable.[23]

No one needs to be told that these ancient patterns of thought no longer prevail. The old moralities of custom and religion are husks and shells. With the growth of the special modern form of individual self-consiousness as consciousness of separation, men lose sight of the dependence of the group upon morality and of the dependence of morality upon the group. These paths run parallel to the one, discussed earlier, by which men have journeyed toward epistemological emptiness. Individual withdrawal from the group consciousness and individual rejection of received knowledge proceed concurrently. There is an intimate connection between the decline of custom and 'nature' as the setter of boundaries in the social realm, and the Cartesian and Hobbesian rejection of received opinion as the starting point of the individual knower's search for knowledge. Each man becomes his own author and oracle, his own boundary setter and truth maker. The ego recognizes no source of truth and morality external to itself.

Bacon, Descartes, and Hobbes first decisively stated this modern perspective, and Rousseau formulated the basic political problem stemming from it. He was the first to understand fully, I think, that ours is the task of developing the theory and institutions of a community in which men can be *both* conscious and individual *and* share the moral bonds and limits of the group. Rousseau thought – and much modern experience suggests he was right – that until such a polity was built, modern men would often be, and would even more often feel like, slaves, and that no modern state would be truly legitimate.

Hobbes and just about all later writers in the liberal line – T. H. Green nearly escaped – left this problem on shaky foundations. Hobbes never conceived the possibility of a selfhood which transcended the purely individual. Hence, for him, there is no trouble so long as one self does not impinge upon another. When that happens, Leviathan puts curbs on all. In this perspective, order is a question of power, and legitimacy is reduced to prudent calculations of self-interest. That line of thought remains dominant in Sartre, though the vocabulary has shifted to 'seriality', and in much contemporary behavioural science, though the Hobbesian vocabulary of 'prudence' has shifted to 'satisficing' and 'maximizing utility'.

All this might be made a little more concrete by bringing it closer to home. The United States can be seen as a great experiment in the working out of these ideas. As Lipset has pointed out, the United States is in a very real sense the 'first new nation'. Our founding took place at an advanced stage of the progress toward epistemological and moral individualism which was sketched above. At the time of the founding, the doctrine and sentiment were already widespread that each individual comes into this world morally complete and self-sufficient, clothed with natural rights which are his by birth, and not in need of fellowship for moral growth and fulfilment. The human material of this new republic consisted of a gathering of men, each of whom sought self-sufficiency and the satisfaction of his own desires. Wave after wave of immigrants replenished those urges, for to the immigrant, America largely meant freedom from inherited authorities and freedom to get rich. Community and society meant little more than the ground upon which each challenged or used others for his own gain. Others were accepted insofar as they were useful to him in his search for self-sufficiency. But once that goal was reached, the less one had to put up with the others the better. Millions upon millions of Americans strive for that goal, and what is more important, base their political views upon it. The state is a convenience in a private search; and when that search seems to succeed, it is no wonder that men tend to deny the desirability of political bonds, of acting together with others for the life that is just for all. We have no political or moral teaching that tells men they must remain bound to each other even one step beyond the point where those bonds are a drag and a burden on one's personal desires. Americans have always been dedicated to 'getting ahead'; and getting ahead has always meant leaving others behind. Surely a large part of the zealous repression of radical protest in America yesterday and today has its roots in the fact that millions of men who are apparently 'insiders' know how vulnerable the system is because they know how ambiguous their own attachments to it are. The slightest moral challenge exposes the fragile foundations of legitimacy in the modern state.

I am aware that my argument and conclusions here stand in opposition to the standard liberal-pluralist view of American politics. In that view, Americans are enthusiastic joiners. They seek goals through associational means more readily than do citizens in other lands.[24] In addition, Americans have been found to be less cynical about politics than the citizens of some other states. And early on, Americans learn attitudes of trust and respect for their regime and its authority figures.

But this literature is largely beside the point; and to the degree that it has been expressed doctrinally – as evidence for the democratic and participatory character of political decision making in the United States – it is misleading.[25] What matter here are questions of quality, not quantity. The professional literature glorifies the sheer, gross quantity of associational life – though it has never quite known what to say about the majority of adults who are members of no association except a religious one. Little is said about the quality and meaning of associational life, the narrowness of the constituencies, or the intentions that bring men together.[26] The associational life praised in the literature originates in and is pervaded by the kinds of liberal intentions and feelings described above. The individual takes little part in 'group life', apart from lending his quantum of power to the whole. Membership is instrumental: the association is an efficient means for the achievement of individual goals, not an expression of a way of life valued in and for itself.

Affective life centres almost exclusively on the family, and other associations are more or less useful in the pursuit of private goals. Once the goal of self-sufficiency is reached, the individual retreats from group life. Or individuals are held in formal association by the subtle arts of managerial psychology, the not-so-subtle arts of bureaucratic control, the revision upwards of personal desires and demands, and the redefinition of material goals in symbolic terms. It is, then, a question not of how many associations there are, but of what being together means.[27]

This point, however, is a minor one, even though discussion of it occupies a large place in the professional literature. The main point remains: modern man has determined to live without collective ideals and disciplines, and thus without obedience to and reliance upon the authorities that embody, defend, and replenish those ideals. The work of dissolution is almost complete, and modern man now appears ready to attempt a life built upon no other ideal than happiness, comfort and self-expression. But if this is nihilism, it is nihilism with a change of accent that makes all the difference. Gone is the terror, and gone too the dedication to self-overcoming of the greatest nihilist. All ideals are suspect, all renunciations and disciplines seen as snares and stupidities, all corporate commitments nothing but self-imprisonments. Modern prophets rise to pronounce sublimation and self-mutilation the same. We, especially the young among us, presume that an individual can live fully and freely, with no counsel or authority other than his desires, engaged completely in the development of all his capacities save two – the capacity for memory and the capacity for faith.

No one can say where this will lead, for the attempt is without illuminating precedent. But it is clear that for our time, as Rieff has written, 'the question is no longer as Dostoevski put it: "Can civilized men believe?" Rather: Can unbelieving men be civilized?'[28] Perhaps new prophets will appear; perhaps tribalism will reappear; perhaps the old faiths will be reborn; perhaps Weber's 'specialists without spirit, sensualists without heart' will stalk the land; or perhaps we really shall see the new technological Garden tilled by children – simple, kind, sincere innocents, barbarians with good hearts. But however it comes out, we must be clear that already the development of the post-moral mentality places the question of authority and legitimacy on a wholly new footing.[29]

Rationality and Bureaucratic Coordination

At least one portion of the liberal impulse has reached near completion in the modern state: the urge to replace the visible with the unseen hand.[30] Personal and visible power and leadership decline, supplanted by impersonal, anonymous, and automatic mechanisms of control and coordination. Overall, we are confronted not with a situation of 'power without authority', as Berle, Drucker, and others have described it, though that is part of it, but with a situation of the 'autonomy of process', as Ellul and Arendt have described it. The results, as they bear on the meaning of authority and legitimacy, are mainly two: a reduction in the scope for human freedom and responsibility; and the dehumanization – in concrete ways – of leadership. We are beginning to gather the bitter harvest of these triumphs of rationality in the seemingly irrational, nihilistic, and self-indulgent violent outburts of our day.

It was mentioned before that modern civilizations seem committed to no ideal beyond their own reproduction and growth. A man from another era might say that collectively we have sunk into mere life; the men of our era prefer to call it a celebration of life. Setting that matter of judgement aside, the point which must be understood is that this condition, combined with some of the basic characteristics of modern social systems and some of the basic components of the modern climate of opinion, decisively alters most of our inherited conceptions of authority and leadership.

Our familiar ways of thinking prepare us to imagine that a society must have 'someone' in charge, that there must be somewhere a centre of power and authority. Things just would not work unless someone, somewhere, knew how they worked and was responsible for their working right. That image and experience of authority has almost no meaning today – as the people in power are the first to say. Modern societies have become increasingly like self-regulating machines, whose human tenders are needed only to make the minor adjustments demanded by the machine itself. As the whole system grows more and more complex, each individual is able to understand and control less and less of it. In area after area of both public and private life, no single identifiable office or individual commands either the knowledge or the authority to make decisions. A search for the responsible party leads through an endless maze of committees, bureaus, offices, and anonymous bodies.[31]

The functions of planning and control, and ultimately of decision making, are increasingly taken away from men and given over to machines and routine processes. Human participation in planning and control tends to be limited to supplying the machines with inputs of data and materials. And still the complexity grows. Modern man is haunted by the vision of a system grown so complex and so huge that it baffles human control. Perhaps the final solution to the problem of human governance will be to make a machine king. That is surely the immanent end toward which the efforts of all the linear programmers and systems analysts are headed.[32]

This is what I mean to suggest by the autonomy of process. The system works, not because recognizable human authority is in charge, but because its basic ends and its procedural assumptions are taken for granted and programmed into men and machines. Given the basic assumptions of growth as the main goal, and efficiency as the criterion of performance, human intervention is largely limited to making incremental adjustments, fundamentally of an equilibrating kind. The system is glacially resistant to genuine innovation, for it proceeds by its own momentum, imposes its own demands, and systematically screens out information of all kinds but one. The basic law of the whole is: Because we already have machines and processes and things of certain kinds, we shall get more machines and processes and things of closely related kinds, and this by the most efficient means. Ortega was profoundly right when a generation ago he described this situation as one of drift, though at that time men still thought they were in command. That delusion is no longer so widespread.[33]

The organization of the human resources needed to serve this process is done in the bureaucratic mode. It would be superfluous here to describe the essential characteristics of bureaucracy: that has been done capably by a number of writers. What I want to do instead is describe briefly what can best be called the bureaucratic epistemology, the operative definition of knowledge or information which is characteristic of all highly developed modern bureaucracies, for this is the screen through which information must pass before it becomes useful knowledge. This screen is one of the basic agencies by which the autonomy of process is assured.[34]

We are taught that the three great planning and control processes of modern society – bureaucracy, technology, and science – are all value-free means or instruments, just tools, which men must decide how to use by standards drawn from some other source than the realms of science, technology, and bureaucracy. This fairy tale is widely believed among the sophisticated and the naïve alike. Many things could be said about it, but here one thing is most important.[35] It is misleading to say that bureaucracy, for example – to focus on the force that matters most in a discussion of legitimacy – is a neutral means that can be used to achieve any end. Here, as in all human affairs, the means profoundly shape the ends. Bureaucracy may have no ultimate values, but it has a host of instrumental values, and among these is a conception of what counts as knowledge or useful information. This bureaucratic epistemology decisively shapes the outcomes – so decisively, in fact, that if you assign a certain task to a bureaucratic agency, you can largely say beforehand how the bureaucratic epistemology will constitute and alter the task itself. To put what follows in a phrase, if you were to assign the task of devising a religion to a bureaucracy, you could say beforehand that the product would be all law and no prophecy, all rule and no revelation.

More and more of men's energies are channelled through bureaucratic forms. Bureaucracy had advanced, as Weber pointed out, by virtue of its superiorities over other modes of directing human energy toward the ends of mastery over nature and other men. It is superior in speed, precision, economy, and clarity over alternative modes of controlling men and coordinating their energies. Hence, one can say, again with Weber, that modern bureaucracy is one of the supreme achievements of modern Western man. It is simultaneously an expression of the drive for rationality and predictability and one of the chief agencies in making the world ever more rational and predictable, for the bureaucratic mode of knowing becomes constitutive of the things known. In a way Hegel might barely recognize, the rational does become the real, and the real the rational.

Bureaucracy is rational in certain specific ways. First, it is in principle objective and impersonal, treating all cases without regard to their personal idiosyncrasies: all must stand in line. The objects of bureaucratic management are depersonalized (though, typically, each bureaucracy has a favoured clientele group – all others must stand in line.) Secondly, bureaucracy is objective in the sense that the official is expected to detach his feelings from the conduct of his office. Subjectivity is for the private life. Thirdly, since bureaucracy proceeds by fixed rules and techniques, the incumbent of an office is in principle replaceable by any other individual who knows the rules and procedures governing that office and commands the skills appropriate to it.

This form of organizing human effort has a conception of knowledge which is also rational in specifiable senses. In the bureaucratic epistemology, the only legitimate instrument of knowledge is objective, technically trained intellect, and the only acceptable mode of discourse is the cognitive mode. The quest for knowledge must follow specified rules and procedures. Thus, many other paths to knowledge are blocked. Specifically, everything thought of as 'subjective' and tainted by 'feeling' must be suppressed. Any bureaucrat who based his decisions upon conscience, trained prudence, intuition, dreams, empathy, or even common sense and personal experience would be *ipso facto* guilty of malfeasance. The bureaucratic must define whatever is to be done as a problem, which implies that there is a solution and that finding the right solution is a matter of finding the right technique. In order to solve a problem, it must be broken down into its component parts. Wholes can appear as nothing more than clusters of parts, as a whole car or watch is an ensemble of parts. In order for wholes to be broken into parts, things that are in appearance dissimilar must be made similar. This is done by extracting one or a few aspects which all the objects dealt with have in common and then treating those aspects as though they were the whole. Thus, there is in this conception of knowledge an urge toward abstraction and toward comparison and grouping by common attributes. Abstraction and comparison in turn require measuring tools that will yield comparable units: among the favoured ones are units of money, time, weight, distance, and power. All such measurements and comparisons subordinate qualitative dimensions, contextual meanings, and unique and variable properties to the common, external, and quantifiable.[36]

This conception of knowledge also entails a whole conception of reality. Reality is that which is tangible, discrete, external, quantifiable, and capable of being precisely conveyed to others. Everything that is left over – and some might think that this is half of life – becomes curiously unreal or epiphenomenal. If it persists in its intrusions on the 'real' world, then it must be treated as trouble; and those who act from motives embedded in the unreal world are treated as deviant cases, in need of repair or reproof. Bureaucrats still cannot quite believe that the human objects of 'urban renewal' see themselves as victims.

All that remains to be added is the obvious point that he who would gain this kind of knowledge of this kind of reality must himself be a certain kind of man. The model is the knowledge seeker who is perfectly 'objective' and dispassionate, detached from the objects of knowledge and manipulation, and blind to those aspects of the world that lie outside his immediate problem.

Now, when men treat themselves and their world this way, they and it increasingly become this way.[37] And somehow, this way includes consequences that an older vocabulary would have called horrible or evil. But if this is evil, it is evil of a special quality, the quality that Arendt calls banality. Bureaucracies staffed by 'perfectly normal men' somehow perform horrors, but not out of ideology or love of evil. In 1576 the Duke of Alba marched into the Low Countries at the head of a uniform and thoroughly disciplined army of soldiers wholly devoted to the True Faith. When those soldiers, contrary to their disciplined and predictable appearance, began furiously burning and pillaging, the people called them 'machines with devils inside'. Today when we see bureaucracies perform their work of classifying, herding, expediting, and exterminating when necessary, we know they are machines without devils inside. What is inside is merely a certain conception of knowledge and the self, which has been long growing and which is widely distributed. It is a conception which means by thought only a process of rational and efficient calculation of the most efficient way to handle materials, a conception which trains men how to behave efficiently, but not how to act responsibly. When thought is so defined, the roles once filled by human leaders wither and computers can perform them better than men. Computer 1401 is worth much more to the State of Washington than the man who tried to kill it. In some remarkable way, Eichmann was no more responsible than a computer. Bureaucratic behaviour is the most nearly perfect example (along with certain areas of scientific and technical experimentation) of that mode of conduct which denies responsibility for the consequences of action on the grounds that it lacks full knowledge of the reasons for action. All bureaucrats are innocent.

IV

Weber's account of charismatic authority leaves one with a divided impression. On the one hand, he understood the strong bonds and powerful currents of feeling that are possible between leaders and followers, and sensed that in some way these relations were distinctively human. On the other, Weber's tone suggests that charismatic authority is for the childhood of the race and that the spread of rational–legal authority, even though it too comes at a price, is somehow progressive, more fitted to mature and independent adulthood. He frequently argues that we cannot return to that earlier condition of ignorance and innocence, for 'disenchantment' has gone too far, and he recommends the Church with its music and incense for those who are too 'weak' to bear the burdens of the present. 'Science as a vocation' concludes on a note of warning to those 'who today tarry for new prophets and saviors' and urges all to 'set to work and meet the demands of the day'. Modern life is disenchanted and hollowed of meaning, but we must manfully live it anyway and not yearn for the gifts of faith and charisma. Each of us must, like Weber himself, see how much he can bear.

But Weber's formulation puts this whole question on the wrong footing. First of all, Weber 'romanticized' charismatic authority, making it seem much more mysterious than it really is. He also dealt mainly with very 'strong' figures, thereby skewing perception away from charismalike phenomena on a smaller scale and even in everyday life. He emphasized its dark aspects and saw it nearly always as the ravishing of the weak and gullible by the strong and hypnotic, almost as Mann described it in 'Mario and the Magician'. But more importantly, the basic opposition is not between charismatic and rational authority, but between what can only be called personal and human authority on the one side and bureaucratic–rational manipulation and coordination on the other. It is obviously not charismatic leadership that has been driven out by rational–legal authority, for our age abounds in charismatic figures and putative prophets: Rome of the second century of the Christian Era was no richer. Such men have set the destinies of states, and they may be met on every street corner and in every rock band. The proliferation of these figures is plainly the dialectical fruit of technological and bureaucratic coordination.

Rather, what is missing is humanly meaningful authority and leadership. For this, the age shows a total incapacity. Establishment officials and hippies alike share the conviction that the only alternatives to the present system of coordination are repression or the riot of passion and anarchy. Both groups, the high and the low, are unable to escape the crushing opposites that the world presents to us and that Weber taught us to believe are the only possible choices. Both groups conceive of authority almost exclusively in terms of repression and denial and can hardly imagine obedience based on mutual respect and affection. Confronted with the structures of bureaucratic and technological coordination, the young fear all authority and flee into the unreason of drugs, music, astrology, and the *Book of Changes*, justifying the flight by the doctrine of 'do your own thing' – something that has never appeared on a large scale among any populace outside Bedlam and the nursery, where it can be indulged because there is a keeper who holds ultimate power over the inmates. No doctrine was ever better designed to provide its holders with the illusion of autonomy while delivering real power to the custodians. When those in high positions are confronted with challenges, their first response is to isolate themselves from the challengers by tightening the old rules and imposing tougher new rules. When the managers do attempt reforms in a 'humanistic' direction, the result is nearly always a deformity: to humanize leadership, institute coffee hours, fabricate human-interest stories to show that the powerful one is human after all, and bring in the make-up artists when he has to go on television; to humanize bureaucracy, appoint T-groups and ombudsmen; to humanize the law, introduce the indeterminate sentence, special procedures and officials for juvenile offenders, and psychiatrists who will put a technical name on any state of mind for a fee. It is always an alliance between 'democratic' ideology and expert manipulation, in a hopeless attempt to reconstruct something now almost forgotten – the idea and the experience of genuine authority.

To escape this trap, we must reject Weber's false opposites, and with it his test of manliness. It is not a question of either retreating to charisma or advancing bravely to the rational–legal destiny, but of developing something different from both. It is perfectly possible that the march toward the rationally integrated world is not progressive at all, but a wrong turning, a mistake, whose baneful consequences need not be supinely accepted as inevitable or slavishly rationalized as developmental.[38]

It is certainly necessary to understand that natural human authority has been overwhelmed by the combined impact of the very forces, structures, and intellectual and moral orientations that we identify with modernity. A mere partial listing must suffice. Huge populations have made men strangers to each other and have made it necessary to develop efficient means of mass measurement and control. Centrally controlled communications systems can reach into all corners of the society, encroaching upon small human units of unique experience and outlook. Furthermore, the communications revolution makes possible the elaborate feedback circuitry necessary to the processes of automatic control. Intricate division of labour reduces common experience, producing both pluralistic ignorance and fragmentation of the process of work. The data explosion has produced microspecialization of the mind and the narrowing of perspectives on human problems. The relativization, materialization, and secularization of values makes it impossible for men to relate to one another on the basis of shared commitments to transcendent and demanding purposes and values. The sheer quantity and variety of artefacts and material needs and desires requires a vast system of administrative regulation and control, and thoroughly blurs the distinction between public and private, with the result that authorities cannot pretend to speak for public and objective goods but must accept the popular equation of private desire with public right.[39] The decline of tradition removes another rich source of shared meanings and limits, while rapid technological change proceeds by its own imperatives and enslaves its human attendants. All these add up to a scope and complexity so vast that humanly meaningful authority and leadership are baffled. Control must be accomplished either by bureaucratic coordination and self-regulating devices that govern the technical system by standards generated by the system itself, or by deliberately fabricated ideologies and images.

All these structures and processes will have to be confronted — and radically revised, in ways that no man can clearly foresee — before humanly meaningful authority and leadership can reappear.[40] But before that confrontation can begin — or begin in ways that offer some prospect of a worthy and merciful outcome — there must be an even more basic shift in our understanding of the kind of knowledge that can properly be accepted as constituting a claim to authority in the human realm. I presented the administrative and scientific conception of knowledge as a specimen of what such knowledge must not be. It remains to sketch what it must be.

All leaders perform the same functions. They interpret events, explore possible responses to problematic situations, recommend courses of action, and vouch for the rightness and success of actions taken. They advise, recommend, warn, reprove, and command.[41] All this is so manifest in common experience that the large social science literature which attempted to 'explain' leadership by distinguishing between 'functional' and 'trait' theories should have been seen from the outset as superficial and unimportant, doomed to trivial answers because it asked trivial questions. The fact that it has been taken seriously supports the suggestion made earlier that certain experiences of leadership and authority really have become rare among men in the modern states. The question is not whether leaders hold their positions by performing certain functions or possessing certain traits. The question is, rather, precisely how those functions are construed and what kind of knowledge is understood to be appropriate to their performance.

Each man is born, lives among others, and dies. Hence, each man's life has three great underpinnings, which no matter how far he travels must always be returned to and can never be escaped for long. The three underpinnings present themselves to each man as problems and as mysteries: the problem and mystery of becoming a unique self: but still a self living among and sharing much with others in family and society: and finally a unique self among some significant others, but still sharing with all humanity the condition of being human and mortal. Who am I as an individual? Who am I as a member of this society? Who am I as a man, a member of humanity? Each of the three questions contains within itself a host of questions, and the way a man formulates and responds to them composes the centre and the structure of his life.

Given this, it can be said quite simply that humanly significant authorities are those who help men answer these questions in terms that men themselves implicitly understand. The leader offers interpretations and recommendations which set off resonances in the minds and spirits of other men. When leaders and followers interact on levels of mutual, subjective comprehension and sharing of meaning, then we can say that there exists humanly significant leadership. The relationship is one of mutuality, identification, and co-performance. The leader finds himself in the followers, and they find themselves in the leader. I am aware that to the rational and objective men of our day, this is mysticism. But it is those same rational men who cannot understand why the rational, objective, and expert administrators are losing authority, if not yet power, in all the modern states. The answer is mysteriously simple: to the degree that the rational, expert administrative leader achieves the objectivity and expertise which are the badges of his competence, he loses the ability to enter a relationship of mutual understanding with those who rely on him for counsel and encouragement . . .

Events, institutions, and moral and epistemological ideas which, taken together, constitute modernity have virtually driven humanly meaningful authority and leadership from the field, replacing it with bureaucratic coordination and automatic control processes, supplemented when necessary by ideology and phony charisma. Furthermore, our methods of study have blocked us from seeing that such mechanisms of control are inherently vulnerable and in the long run unworkable, incapable of responding to men's needs for understanding and counsel on the basic, inescapable questions of human existence. So long as men remain what we have hitherto called human, they will require of power which strives to become authority that it respond to those questions in ways that have meaning for men. The current epidemic of revolts and uprisings, the current challenging of established institutions and processes, the thickening atmosphere of resentment and hostility, the drop-out cultures of the young – these are something other than the romantic, reactionary, or nihilistic spasms which they are seen as in some quarters of the academy and the state. They are the cries of people who feel that the processes and powers which control their lives are inhuman and destructive. They are the desperate questionings of people who fear that their institutions and officials have no answers. They are overt signs of the underlying crisis of legitimacy in the modern state.

NOTES

1 From 'The Whitehall Debates', in A.S.P. Wodehouse (ed.) *Puritanism and Liberty* (London: J. M. Dent, 1938), p. 127.
2 The only important exception is Yves R. Simon, *Philosophy of Democratic Government* (Chicago: University of Chicago Press, 1951), pp. 1–72. Simon's book lies within the Aristotelian–Thomist tradition.
3 For a recent specimen, see the sections by Lerner in Daniel Lerner and Wilbur Schramm (eds) *Communication and Change in the Developing Countries* (Honolulu: East-West Center Press, 1967).
4 *San Francisco Chronicle*, 5 June, 1969, p. 42.
5 Letter to Henry Osborne Taylor, January 17, 1905. In Harold Dean Cater (ed.) *Henry Adams and His Friends*. Quoted here from William H. Jordy, *Henry Adams: Scientific Historian* (New Haven: Yale University Press, 1963), p. xi.
6 When I refer to a crisis of legitimacy, I mean more than an intensification of controversy about various public issues and policies – the kind of thing Dahl discusses in his analysis of the periodicity of opposition in the United States; or the kind of thing treated by the Michigan group under the category of critical or realigning elections. For a study of American voting patterns and electoral behaviour that is important to an understanding of legitimacy in the United States, see Walter Dean Burnham, 'The changing shape of the American political universe', *American Political Science Review*, LIX, No. 1 (March 1965), pp. 7–28. What I mean by legitimacy will become clear as the essay proceeds.

7 Seymour Martin Lipset, *Political Man* (Garden City, NY: Doubleday, 1960), p. 77.

8 Robert Bierstedt, 'Legitimacy', in *Dictionary of the Social Sciences* (New York: The Free Press, 1964), p. 386. Bierstedt is here paraphrasing Lipset, *Political Man*.

9 Richard M. Merelman, 'Learning and legitimacy', *American Political Science Review*, LX, No. 3 (September 1966), p. 548.

10 Hannah Arendt, 'What was authority?' in Carl J. Friedrich (ed.) Authority (Cambridge, Mass.: Harvard University Press, 1958), p. 83.

11 Carl Joachim Friedrich, *Man and His Government: An Empirical Theory of Politics* (New York: McGraw-Hill, 1963), p. 233.

12 There is evidence that in the United States symbolic rewards alone do largely suffice. See Herbert McClosky, 'Consensus and ideology in American politics', *American Political Science Review*, LVIII, No. 2 (June 1964), pp. 361–82. A study of the tables on cynicism and futility shows that on item after item members of the general electorate express a strong sense of their own political powerlessness. Yet, 90 per cent of the respondents say that they 'usually have confidence that the government will do what is right'.

13 David Easton's treatment, in *A Systems Analysis of Political Life* (New York: John Wiley, 1965), especially Ch. 18, also remains within this perspective, although his reification of 'the system' and his employment of the term as a noun of agency becloud what actually goes on. But consider: 'Under the usual conception of legitimacy as a belief in the right of authorities to rule and members to obey . . . the major stimulus for the input of diffuse support would arise from efforts to reinforce such ideological convictions among the membership' (p. 288).

14 Lipset also sees legitimacy largely in terms of symbol manipulation. Thus, he says that 'a major test of legitimacy is the extent to which given nations have developed a common "secular political culture", mainly national rituals and holidays'. The United States has passed the test, for it possesses 'a common homogeneous culture in the veneration accorded the Founding Fathers, Abraham Lincoln, Theodore Roosevelt, and their principles'. (Lipset, *Political Man*, p. 80.) I refrain from comment on this pantheon.

15 Ibid., pp. 88–92.

16 In Necker, *Du Pouvoir executif dans les Grands États* (1972) p. 22. Quoted here from Bertrand de Jouvenel, *Power*, tr. J. F. Huntingdon (London: Barchworth Press, 1948), p. 30.

17 Even Hume's thought reflects these patterns. Hume is, of course, famous for shattering the 2000-year-old concept of natural law – the idea that man could, by rational processes alone, discover universal norms of moral and political conduct. But while Hume, through his sceptical analysis of the character and functions of reason, undermined the ancient rationalist and transcendental conception of natural law, he replaced it by still another, more empirical, conception of natural law whose norms were as certain as those they replaced. He tried to show

that the empirical existence of universal norms could be established by observation and that these norms were necessary products of social life. His logic was similar to that of the ancient theorists of the *jus gentium* and remarkably like that of modern linguistic philosophers, who argue that certain broad and necessary truths can be derived from the prerequisite conditions essential for the existence of a language. See Hume, *Treatise of Human Nature*, Book III, Part II, Sections I–VI; Part III, Section VI. See also his essay 'That Politics May Be Reduced to a Science'.

18 The scientific, objective, manipulative epistemology presupposes that the knower stands outside nature and studies it by assault. Thus: 'A long time ago, we developed modern science as veritable outsiders of nature. In order to become scientific observers, we had to denature ourselves. We have succeeded. When we say, now, that we are reasonable we mean that we are engaged in calculations. When we hold something to be irrational we are merely indignant that our predictions have not been borne out, or perhaps, we are amused, for we make rash distinctions between the irrational and the stupid. When we say "naturally", we are hardly ever right.' Hans Speier, 'Shakespeare's "The Tempest",' reprinted in Speier, *Social Order and the Risks of War* (Cambridge, Mass.: MIT Press, 1969), p. 132.

19 For the impact of this upon the scope and nature of violence in the modern world, see Sheldon S. Wolin, 'Violence and the Western political tradition', *American Journal of Orthopsychiatry*, XXXIII, No. 1 (January 1963), pp. 15–29.

20 The words *nature* and *nation* come from the same root, the word for birth. Etymologically, a nation is a birth, hence a group of persons made kindred by common origin. Nations are also continually reborn, through the death of old customs and institutions and the generation of new ones. A nation has a unique birth and is also a continuous rebirth.

21 Law means limit or boundary. In Greek, the words for law, boundary line, and shepherd had the same root.

22 Vico expressed the point perfectly in his assertion that there were as many Joves, with as many names, as there are nations. *The New Science of Giambattista Vico*, tr. Thomas Goddard Bergin and Max Harold Fisch (Garden City, NY: Doubleday Anchor Books, 1961), pp. xxix, 31.

23 Machiavelli, obviously not under the spell of mythological thought, gave great attention to this problem of how to keep alive and intact the guiding spirit of a polity and in the end saw it as almost synonymous with popular remembrance of the founding premises: order and action perpetually recreated and renewed through remembrance of origins.

24 Tocqueville is frequently cited at this point in the standard exposition. But Tocqueville has been abused. He hoped and thought that, through voluntary associations, Americans could break out of the cell of individualism and learn the art of politics. But for this to happen, the associations themselves would have to be democratic and political in

their internal character. That is rarely the case; but in its absence, Tocqueville's argument simply does not support the uses to which it has been put by contemporary pluralists.

25 Hopefully, Grant McConnell's work *Private Power and American Democracy* (New York: Alfred A. Knopf, 1966) will put an end to the idealization of the interest-group system as a process of partisan mutual adjustment which assures rationality and secures the public interest, thereby meeting the criteria of democracy. McConnell shows that 'to a very considerable degree (the system of private power) makes a mockery of the vision by which one interest opposes another and ambition checks ambition. The large element of autonomy accorded to various fragments of government has gone far to isolate important matters of public policy from supposedly countervailing influences' (ibid., p. 164).

26 I am, of course, speaking here of American writers, not of the European pluralist tradition of Von Gierke, Maitland, Duguit, Figgis, *et al.* Mary Parker Follett's *The New State: Group Organization the Solution of Popular Government* escapes these strictures.

27 At the least, it is a question of authorities here. Against the professional view of the seamless web of political socialization stand Malcom X's *Autobiography* and, say, the two major studies by Kenneth Keniston. Against the voluminous professional accounts of the American as joiner stands the literature of the great American novels, which, from Melville to Faulkner, is an exploration of metaphysical and social isolation, a literature which sees the American as the wanderer, the one who does not belong.

28 Philip Rieff, *The Triumph of the Therapeutic: Uses of Faith After Freud* (New York: Harper and Row, Publishers, 1966), p. 4. Rieff's book is an important attempt to come to an understanding of the meanings of 'postcommunal culture'.

29 The spread of this new, postmoral mentality is bound to have corrosive consequences for the liberal doctrine of contract – the doctrine which bases government on consent of the governed and postulates an original contract by which the people who voluntarily set themselves under authority reserve the right to resist government when it abuses the agreement. The doctrine has always been a quicksand for logicians, a despair for sociologists and historians, and an invitation to resistance for men of conscience and just plain egoists. Historically, obedience has rarely been founded on contract; and as Hume said, 'in the few cases where consent may seem to have taken place, it was commonly so irregular, so confined, or so much intermixed either with fraud or violence, that it cannot have any great authority'. ('Of the original contract', in Frederick Watkins (ed.) *Hume: Theory of Politics* (Edinburgh: Nelson, 1951), p. 201). Few men really consent to government, whether openly or tacitly. And as Jefferson understood, the logic of contract is incapable of binding men to the promises made by their predecessors. These logical shortcomings all become otiose in

the face of the simple sociological fact that 'obedience or subjugation becomes so familiar that most men never make any enquiry about its origin or cause, more than about the principle of gravity' (ibid., p. 197). But all such habits are weakening in the modern states. As they weaken, the doctrine of consent becomes explosive. Every society rests upon a fiction, which usually encompasses both the society's origins and its ends, thereby helping make life and the world intelligible and endurable. Most of these fictions have failed. The fiction of contract and consent was never one of the best (strongest). To take it seriously now would mean the dissolution of the modern state.

30 Ironic evidence is provided by the 'Who governs?' literature. After prodigious professional labours we still have no authoritative answer. Apparently, everybody governs. Or nobody.

31 Admittedly, there are more sanguine vocabularies for describing the situation: 'The fundamental axiom in the theory and practice of American pluralism is, I believe, this: Instead of a single center of sovereign power there must be multiple centers of power, none of which is or can be wholly sovereign . . . Why this axiom? The theory and practice of American pluralism tends to assume, as I see it, that the existence of multiple centers of power, none of which is wholly sovereign, will help (may indeed be necessary) to tame power, to secure the consent of all, and to settle conflicts peacefully.' Robert Dahl, *Pluralist Democracy in the United States* (Chicago: Rand McNally 1967), p. 24.

   This description, I believe, misses three central features of the situation: (1) it fails to point out that with all this dispersion there is still a powerful central tendency of policy, a pattern of movement; (2) it fails to point out that some persons and groups in the right positions and possessed of the right resources benefit much more from the system than do others – 'noncumulative inequalities' is a dangerous euphemism; and (3) it fails to point out both the real nature of what is lost by the losers – identity, self-respect, and faith in others, as well as wealth and power – and the reparations those losers might some day demand. Thus: The chief of an Indian tribe, seeking redress for a grievance felt by his people, was advised to present his case to the government. He went from this office to that, was sent from one official to another and back again and again. He met no one who looked like himself, though everybody seemed to listen politely enough in the special way that bureaucrats listen. But much time passed, and nothing happened. The chief sadly concluded that the fault was his, because, despite his many interviews and diligent searchings, he had apparently failed to find the 'government'. Here indeed power was tamed, consent obtained, and conflict settled, but that Indian may not always conclude that the fault was his.

32 See Robert Boguslaw, *The New Utopians* (Englewood Cliffs, NJ: Prentice-Hall, 1965).

33 The description is not limited to control processes in the non-

governmental sector. In fact, any distinction between public and private, in both process and substance (except for the military power) would be very hard to draw in the United States. In 1908, Henry Adams wrote: 'The assimilation of our forms of government to the form of an industrial corporation . . . seems to me steady though slow.' (W. C. Ford (ed.) *Letters of Henry Adams* (Boston: Houghton Mifflin, 1930), Vol II, p. 482.) Public, governmental bureaucracy grows apace: In 1947, there were about 5.8 million people in government civilian employment, and in 1963 there were 9.7 million; government expenditures, exclusive of 'defence', space, veteran, and debt outlays, grew eightfold between 1938 and 1963. The main impulse of large organizations, as most students of the subject agree, is toward the maintenance and growth of the organization itself, which requires increasing control over all aspects of the organizational environment.

34 The following draws heavily on Weber's classic analysis and on the equally incisive work of Kenneth Keniston, *The Uncommitted: Alienated Youth in American Society* (New York: Dell Publishing, 1967), especially pp. 253–72.

35 Though I cannot resist adding a brief appeal to those who still believe that science – especially social science – acquires 'objective' knowledge and that any such knowledge that can be acquired is worthy of being acquired. Nietzsche exposed the fallacies here. The number of things one might want to know is, in principle, infinite. Therefore, every act of knowing requires a prior act of choosing and desiring. The knowledge sought and gained necessarily reflects, in many ways, the impulses (values, intentions, urges) which launched the search. Since it is a manifestation of desire and choice, knowledge is subject to moral judgement; and its 'worth' is partly a function of the motives that led to its acquisition. Our age, for example, has chosen to know how to command *power* over nature and other men. Since Nietzsche, we must recognize both the psychology and the morality of knowledge.

36 As a measure of the bureaucratization of American higher education, consider Clark Kerr's incisive definition of the multiversity as 'a mechanism held together by administrative rules and powered by money'. *The Uses of the University* (Cambridge, Mass.: Harvard University Press, 1963), p. 20. He is talking about what used to be called the community of scholars.

37 Reread W. H. Auden's 'The unknown citizen,' dedicated to JS/07/M/378, in *Another Time* (New York: Random House, 1940). Or C. Virgil Gheorghiu, *The Twenty-Fifth Hour* (New York: Alfred A. Knopf, 1950).

38 I wish to make it explicit here that while I have often treated Weber critically, the 'real' Weber was a far more powerful man than the Weber canonized by social science. Social scientists have borrowed Weber's discussion of the ideal-typical characteristics of bureaucracy, but without his passionate concern to defend politics against bureaucracy. They have enthroned his fact-value distinction but have

not begun to come to terms with his profound criticism of the social science model of cumulative knowledge. They cite his dedication to science and rationality, but they ignore his acceptance of Nietzsche's view of contemporary conceptions of science and rationality as potentially dehumanizing forces. What was not 'operational' in Weber has been largely ignored.

39 Perhaps this is excessive. Perhaps it is not yet a 'popular equation'. Most adult Americans do limit private desire by public right. But among the young the equation is surely growing: either private desire is equated with public right, or the existence of anything like public right is simply denied, leaving only private desire.

40 In the earlier ages of man, leaders were made by art to appear as more than human: as divine or semi-divine personages. Today the ones who stand at the command posts and switching points are made by art to appear as more than mechanical: as human beings.

41 This formulation cuts across Jouvenel's distinction between *dux* and *rex*, though that distinction is very useful for locating the performance of leadership roles within a social setting. Jouvenel, *Sovereignty*, especially pp. 40–70.

6

What does a Legitimation crisis mean today? Legitimation Problems in late Capitalism

JÜRGEN HABERMAS

The expression 'late capitalism' implicitly asserts that, even in state-regulated capitalism, social developments are still passing through 'contradictions' or crises. I would therefore like to begin by elucidating the concept of *crisis*.

Prior to its use in economics, we are familiar with the concept of crisis in medicine. It refers to that phase of a disease in which it is decided whether the self-healing powers of the organism are sufficient for recovery. The critical process, the disease, seems to be something objective. A contagious disease, for instance, affects the organism from outside. The deviations of the organism from what it should be – i.e. the patient's normal condition – can be observed and, if necessary, measured with the help of indicators. The patient's consciousness plays no part in this. How the patient feels and how he experiences his illness is at most a symptom of events that he himself can barely influence. Nevertheless, we would not speak of a crisis in a medical situation of life or death if the patient were not trapped in this process with all his subjectivity. A crisis cannot be separated from the victim's inner view. He experiences his impotence toward the objectivity of his illness only because he is a subject doomed to passivity and temporarily unable to be a subject in full possession of his strength.

Crisis suggests the notion of an objective power depriving a subject of part of his normal sovereignty. If we interpret a process as a crisis, we are tacitly giving it a normative meaning. When the crisis is resolved, the trapped subject is liberated.

This becomes clearer when we pass from the medical to the

Source: Jürgen Habermas, 'What does a legitimation crisis mean today? Legitimation problems in late capitalism', *Social Research* (Winter, 1973), reprinted with permission of *Social Research*.

dramaturgical notion of crisis. In classical aesthetics from Aristotle to Hegel, crisis signifies the turning point of a fateful process which, although fully objective, does not simply break in from the outside. There is a contradiction expressed in the catastrophic culmination of a conflict of action, and that contradiction is inherent in the very structure of the system of action and in the personality systems of the characters. Fate is revealed in conflicting norms that destroy the identities of the characters unless they in turn manage to regain their freedom by smashing the mythical power of fate.

The notion of crisis developed by classical tragedy has its counterpart in the notion of crisis to be found in the doctrine of salvation. Recurring throughout the philosophy of history in the eighteenth century, this figure of thought enters the evolutionary social theories of the nineteenth century. Marx is the first to develop a sociological concept of system crisis. It is against that background that we now speak of social or economic crises. In any discussion of, say, the great economic crisis in the early thirties, the Marxist overtones are unmistakable.

Since capitalist societies have the capacity of steadily developing technological productive forces, Marx conceives an economic crisis as a crisis-ridden process of economic growth. Accumulation of capital is tied to the acquisition of surplus. This means for Marx that economic growth is regulated by a mechanism that both establishes and conceals a power relationship. Thus the model of rising complexity is contradictory in the sense that the economic system keeps creating new and more problems as it solves others. The total accumulation of capital passes through periodic devaluations of capital components: this forms the cycle of crises, which Marx in his time was able to observe. He tried to explain the classical type of crisis by applying the theory of value with the help of the law of the tendential fall of the rate of profit. But that is outside my purpose at the moment. My question is really, 'Is late capitalism following the same or similar self-destructive pattern of development as classical – i.e. competitive – capitalism? Or has the organizing principle of late capitalism changed so greatly that the accumulation process no longer generates any problems jeopardizing its existence?

My starting point will be a rough descriptive model of the most important structural features of late-capitalist societies. I will then mention three crisis tendencies which today, though not specific to the system, are major topics of discussion. And finally, I will deal with various explanations of the crisis tendencies in late capitalism.

STRUCTURAL FEATURES OF LATE-CAPITALIST SOCIETIES

The expression 'organized or state-regulated capitalism' refers to two classes of phenomena both of which can be traced back to the advanced stage of the accumulation process. One such class is the process of economic concentration (the creation of national and by now even multinational corporations) and the organization of markets for goods, capital, and labour. On the other hand, the interventionist state keeps filling the increasing functional gaps in the market. The spread of oligopolistic market structures certainly spells the end of competitive capitalism. But no matter how far companies may see into the future or extend their control over the environment, the steering mechanism of the market will continue to function as long as investments are determined by company profits. At the same time, by complementing and partially replacing the market mechanism, government intervention means the end of liberal capitalism. But no matter how much the state may restrict the owner of goods in his private autonomous activity, there will be no political planning to allocate scarce resources as long as the overall societal priorities develop naturally – i.e. as indirect results of the strategies of private enterprise. In advanced capitalist societies, the economic, the administrative, and the legitimation systems can be characterized as follows.

The Economic System

During the 1960s, various authors, using the example of the United States, developed a three-sector model based on the distinction between the private and public areas. Private production is market-oriented, one sector still regulated by competition, another by the market strategies of the oligopolies that tolerate a competitive fringe. However, the public area, especially in the wake of armament and space-travel production, has witnessed the rise of great industries which, in their investment decisions, can operate independently of the market. These are either enterprises directly controlled by the government or private firms living on government contracts. The monopolistic and the public sectors are dominated by capital-intensive industries; the competitive sector is dominated by labour-intensive industries. In the monopolistic and the public sectors, the industries are faced with powerful unions. But in the competitive sector, labour is not as well organized, and the salary levels are correspondingly different. In the monopolistic sector, we can observe relatively rapid progress in production. However, in the public sector, the companies do not need to be, and in the competitive sector they cannot be, that efficient.

The Administrative System

The state apparatus regulates the overall economic cycle by means of global planning. On the other hand, it also improves the conditions for utilizing capital.

Global planning is limited by private autonomous use of the means of production (the investment freedom of private enterprises cannot be restricted). It is limited on the other hand by the general purpose of crisis management. There are fiscal and financial measures to regulate cycles, as well as individual measures to regulate investments and overall demand (credits, price guarantees, subsidies, loans, secondary redistribution of income, government contracts based on business-cycle policies, indirect labour-market policies, etc.). All these measures have the reactive character of avoidance strategies within the context of a well-known preference system. This system is determined by a didactically demanded compromise between competing imperatives: steady growth, stability of money value, full employment, and balance of trade.

Global planning manipulates the marginal conditions of decisions made by private enterprise. It does so in order to correct the market mechanism by neutralizing dysfunctional side effects. The state, however, supplants the market mechanism wherever the government creates and improves conditions for utilizing excess accumulated capital. It does so:

(1) by 'strengthening the competitive capacity of the nation', by organizing supranational economic blocks, by an imperialistic safeguarding of international stratification, etc.;

(2) by unproductive government consumption (armament and space-travel industry);

(3) by politically structured guidance of capital in sectors neglected by an autonomous market;

(4) by improving the material infrastructure (transportation, education and health, vocation centres, urban and regional planning, housing, etc.);

(5) by improving the immaterial infrastructure (promotion of scientific research, capital expenditure in research and development, intermediary of patents, etc.);

(6) by increasing the productivity of human labour (universal education, vocational schooling, programmes of training and re-education, etc.);

(7) by paying for the social costs and real consequences of private production (unemployment, welfare, ecological damage).

The Legitimation System

With the functional weaknesses of the market and the dysfunctional side effects of the market mechanism, the basic bourgeois ideology of fair exchange also collapsed. Yet there is a need for even greater legitimation. The government apparatus no longer merely safeguards the prerequisites for the production process. It also, on its own initiative, intervenes in that process. It must therefore be legitimated in the growing realms of state intervention, even though there is now no possibility of reverting to the traditions that have been undermined and worn out in competitive capitalism. The universalistic value systems of bourgeois ideology have made civil rights, including suffrage, universal. Independent of general elections, legitimation can thus be gotten only in extraordinary circumstances and temporarily. The resulting problem is resolved through formal democracy.

A wide participation by the citizens in the process of shaping political will – i.e. genuine democracy – would have to expose the contradiction between administratively socialized production and a still private form of acquiring the produced values. In order to keep the contradiction from being thematized, one thing is necessary. The administrative system has to be sufficiently independent of the shaping of legitimating will. This occurs in a legitimation process that elicits mass loyalty but avoids participation. In the midst of an objectively politicized society, the members enjoy the status of passive citizens with the right to withhold their acclaim. The private autonomous decision about investments is complemented by the civil privatism of the population.

Class Structure

The structures of late capitalism can be regarded as a kind of reaction formation. To stave off the system crisis, late-capitalist societies focus all socially integrative strength on the conflict that is structurally most probable. They do so in order all the more effectively to keep that conflict latent.

In this connection, an important part is played by the quasi-political wage structure, which depends on negotiations between companies and unions. Price fixing, which has replaced price competition in the oligopolistic markets, has its counterpart in the labour market. The great industries almost administratively control the prices in their marketing territories. Likewise, through wage negotiations, they achieve quasi-political compromises with their union adversaries. In those industrial branches of the monopolistic and public sectors that are crucial to economic development, the commodity known as labour has a 'political' price. The 'wage-scale partners' find a broad zone of compromise, since increased labour costs can be passed on into the prices, and the middle-range demands made by both sides against the government tend to converge. The main consequences of immunizing the original conflict zone are as follows: (1) disparate wage developments; (2) a permanent inflation with the corresponding short-lived redistribution of incomes to the disadvantages of unorganized wage earners and other marginal groups; (3) a permanent crisis in government finances, coupled with public poverty – i.e. pauperization of public transportation, education, housing, and health; (4) an insufficient balance of disproportionate economic developments, both sectoral (e.g. agricultural) and regional (marginal areas).

Since World War II, the most advanced capitalist countries have kept the class conflict latent in its essential areas. They have extended the business cycle, transforming the periodic pressures of capital devaluation into a permanent inflationary crisis with milder cyclical fluctuations. And they have filtered down the dysfunctional side effects of the intercepted economic crisis and scattered them over quasi-groups (such as consumers, school children and their parents, transportation users, the sick, the elderly) or divided groups difficult to organize. This process breaks down the social identity of the classes and fragments class consciousness. In the class compromise now part of the structure of late capitalism, nearly everyone both participates and is affected as an individual – although, with the clear and sometimes growing unequal distribution of monetary values and power, one can well distinguish between those belonging more to the one or to the other category.

THREE DEVELOPING CRISES

The rapid growth processes of late-capitalist societies have confronted the system of world society with new problems. These problems cannot be regarded as crisis phenomena specific to the system, even though the possibilities of coping with the crises are specific to the system and therefore limited. I am thinking of the disturbance of the ecological balance, the violation of the personality system (alienation), and the explosive strain on international relations.

The Ecological Balance

If physically economic growth can be traced back to the technologically sophisticated use of more energy to increase the productivity of human labour, then the societal formation of capitalism is remarkable for impressively solving the problem of economic growth. To be sure, capital accumulation originally pushes economic growth ahead, so there is no option for the conscious steering of this process. The growth imperatives originally followed by capitalism have meanwhile achieved a global validity by way of system competition and worldwide diffusion (despite the stagnation or even retrogressive trends in some Third World countries).

The mechanisms of growth are forcing an increase of both population and production on a worldwide scale. The economic needs of a growing population and the productive exploitation of nature are faced with material restrictions: on the one hand, finite resources (cultivable and inhabitable land, fresh water, metals, minerals, etc.); on the other hand, irreplaceable ecological systems that absorb pollutants such as fallout, carbon dioxide, and waste heat. Forrester and others have estimated the limits of the exponential growth of population, industrial production, exploitation of natural resources, and environmental pollution. To be sure, their estimates have rather weak empirical foundations. The mechanisms of population growth are as little known as the maximum limits of the earth's potential for absorbing even the major pollutants. Moreover, we cannot forecast technological development accurately enough to know which raw materials will be replaced or renovated by future technology.

However, despite any optimistic assurances, we are able to indicate (if not precisely determine) *one* absolute limitation on growth: the thermal strain on the environment due to consumption of energy. If economic growth is necessarily coupled with increasing consumption of energy, and if all natural energy that is transformed into economically useful energy is ultimately released as heat, it will eventually raise the temperature of the atmosphere. Again, determining the deadline is not easy. Nevertheless, these reflections show that an exponential growth of population and production – i.e. an expanded control over external nature – will some day run up against the limits of the biological capacity of the environment.

This is not limited to complex societal systems. Specific to these systems are the possibilities of warding off dangers to the ecology. Late-capitalist societies would have a very hard time limiting their growth without abandoning their principle of organization, because an overall shift from spontaneous capitalist growth to qualitative growth would require production planning in terms of use-values.

The Anthropological Balance

While the disturbance of the ecological balance points out the negative aspect of the exploitation of natural resources, there are no sure signals for the capacity limits of personality systems. I doubt whether it is possible to identify such things as psychological constants of human nature that inwardly limit the socialization process. I do, however, see a limitation in the kind of socializing that societal systems have been using to create motives for action. Our behaviour is oriented by norms requiring justification and by interpretative systems guaranteeing identity. Such a communicative organization of behaviour can become an obstacle in complex societies for a simple reason. The adaptive capacity in organizations increases proportionately as the administrative authorities become independent of the particular motivations of the members. The choice and achievement of organization goals in systems of high intrinsic complexity have to be independent of the influx of narrowly delimited motives. This requires a generalized willingness to comply (in political systems, such willingness has the form of legitimation). As long as socialization brings inner nature into a communicative behavioural organization, no legitimation for norms of action could conceivably secure an unmotivated acceptance of decisions. In regard to decisions whose contents are still undetermined, people will comply if convinced that those decisions are based on a legitimate norm of action. If the motives for acting were no longer to pass through norms requiring justification, and if the personality structures no longer had to find their unity under interpretative systems guaranteeing identity, then (and only then) the unmotivated acceptance of decisions would become an irreproachable routine, and the readiness to comply could thus be produced to any desirable degree.

The International Balance

The dangers of destroying the world system with thermonuclear weapons are on a different level. The accumulated potential for annihiliation is a result of the advanced stage of productive forces. Its basis is technologically neutral, and so the productive forces can also take the form of destructive forces (which has happened because international communication is still undeveloped). Today, mortal damage to the natural substratum of global society is quite possible. International communication is therefore governed by a historically new imperative of self-limitation. Once again, this is not limited to all highly militarized societal systems, but the possibilities of tackling this problem have limits specific to the systems. An actual disarmament may be unlikely because of the forces behind capitalist and post-capitalist class societies. Yet regulating the arms race is not basically incompatible with the structure of late-capitalist societies if it is possible to increase technologically the use-value of capital to the degree that the capacity effect of the government's demand for unproductive consumer goods can be balanced.

DISTURBANCES SPECIFIC TO THE SYSTEM

I would now like to leave these three global consequences of late-capitalist growth and investigate disturbances specific to the system. I will start with a thesis, widespread among Marxists, that the basic capitalist structures continue unaltered and create econo-mic crises in altered manifestations. In late capitalism, the state pursues the politics of capital with other means. This thesis occurs in two versions.

Orthodox state-theory maintains that the activities of the inter-ventionist state, no less than the exchange processes in liberal capitalism, obey economic laws. The altered manifestations (the crisis of state finances and permanent inflation, growing disparities between public poverty and private wealth, etc.) are due to the fact that the self-regulation of the realization process is governed by power rather than by exchange. However, the crisis tendency is determined, as much as ever, by the law of value, the structurally forced asymmetry in the exchange of wage labour for capital. As a result, state activity cannot permanently compensate for the tendency of falling rates of profit. It can at best mediate that trend –

i.e. consummate it with political means. The replacement of market functions by state functions does not alter the unconscious nature of the overall economic process. This is shown by the narrow limits of the state's possibilities for manipulation. The state cannot substantially intervene in the property structure without causing an investment strike. Neither can it manage permanently to avoid cyclical stagnation tendencies of the accumulation process – i.e. stagnation tendencies that are created endogenously.

A revisionist version of the Marxist theory of the state is current among leading economists in the German Democratic Republic. According to this version, the state apparatus, instead of naturally obeying the logic of the law of value, is consciously supporting the interests of united monopoly capitalists. This agency theory, adapted to late capitalism, regards the state not as a blind organ of the realization process but as a potent supreme capitalist who makes the accumulation of capital the substance of his political planning. The high degree of the socialization of production brings together the individual interests of the large corporations and the interest in maintaining the system. And all the more so because its existence is threatened internally by forces transcending the system. This leads to an overall capitalist interest, which the united monopolies sustain with the aid of the state apparatus.

I consider both versions of the theory of economic crises inadequate. One version underestimates the state, the other overestimates it.

In regard to the orthodox thesis, I wonder if the state-controlled organization of scientific and technological progress and the system of collective bargaining (a system producing a class compromise, especially in the capital- and growth-intensive economic sectors) have not altered the mode of production. The state, having been drawn into the process of production, has modified the determinants of the process of utilizing capital. On the basis of a partial class compromise, the administrative system has gained a limited planning capacity. This can be used within the framework of the democratic acquisition of legitimation for purposes of reactive avoidance of crises. The cycle of crises is deactivated and rendered less harmful in its social consequences. It is replaced by inflation and a permanent crisis of public finances. The question as to whether these surrogates indicate a successful halting of the economic crisis or merely its temporary shift into the political system is an empirical one. Ultimately, this depends on whether the indirectly productive capital invested in research, development, and education can continue the process of accumulation. It can manage to do so by making labour more productive, raising the rate of surplus value, and cheapening the fixed components of capital.

The revisionist theory has elicited the following reservations. For one thing, we cannot empirically support the assumption that the state apparatus, no matter in whose interest, can actively plan, as well as draft and carry through, a central economic strategy. The theory of state-monopoly capitalism (akin to Western theories of technocracy) fails to recognize the limits of administrative planning in late capitalism. Bureaucracies for planning always reactively avoid crises. The various bureaucracies are not fully coordinated, and because of their limited capacity for perceiving and steering, they tend to depend largely on the influence of their clients. It is because of this very inefficiency that organized partial interests have a chance to penetrate the administrative apparatus. Nor can we empirically support the other assumption that the state is active as the agent of the united monopolists. The theory of state-monopoly capitalism (akin to Western elite theories) overrates the significance of personal contacts and direct influence. Studies on the recruiting, make-up, and interaction of the various power elites fail to explain cogently the functional connections between the economic and administrative systems.

In my opinion, the late-capitalist state can be properly understood neither as the unconscious executive organ of economic laws nor as a systematic agent of the united monopoly capitalists. Instead, I would join Claus Offe in advocating the theory that late-capitalist societies are faced with two difficulties caused by the state's having to intervene in the growing functional gaps of the market. We can regard the state as a system that uses legitimate power. Its output consists in sovereignly executing administrative decisions. To this end, it needs an input of mass loyalty that is as unspecific as possible. Both directions can lead to crisis-like disturbances. Output crises have the form of the efficiency crisis. The administrative system fails to fulfil the steering imperative that it has taken over from the economic system. This results in the disorganization of different areas of life. Input crises have the form of the legitimation crisis. The legitimation system fails to maintain the necessary level of mass loyalty. We can clarify this with the example of the acute difficulties in public finances, with which all late-capitalist societies are now struggling.

The government budget, as I have said, is burdened with the public expenses of an increasingly socialized production. It bears the costs of international competition and of the demand for unproductive consumer goods (armament and space-travel). It bears the costs for the infrastructural output (transportation and communication, scientific and technological progress, vocational training). It bears the costs of the social consumption indirectly concerned with production (housing, transportation, health, leisure, general education, social security). It bears the costs of providing for the unemployed. And finally, it bears the externalized costs of environmental damage caused by private production. Ultimately, these expenses have to be met by taxes. The state apparatus thus has two simultaneous tasks. It has to levy the necessary taxes from profits and income and employ them so efficiently as to prevent any crises from disturbing growth. In addition the selective raising of taxes, the recognizable priority model of their utilization, and the administrative performance have to function in such a way as to satisfy the resulting need for legitimation. If the state fails in the former task, the result is a deficit in administrative efficiency. If it fails in the latter task, the result is a deficit in legitimation.

THEOREMS OF THE LEGITIMATION CRISIS

I would like to restrict myself to the legitimation problem. There is nothing mysterious about its genesis. Legitimate power has to be available for administrative planning. The functions accruing to the state apparatus in late capitalism and the expansion of social areas treated by administration increase the need for legitimation. Liberal capitalism constituted itself in the forms of bourgeois democracy, which is easy to explain in terms of the bourgeois revolution. As a result, the growing need for legitimation now has to work with the means of political democracy (on the basis of universal suffrage). The formal democratic means, however, are expensive. After all, the state apparatus does not just see itself in the role of the supreme capitalist facing the conflicting interests of the various capital factions. It also has to consider the generalizable interests of the population as far as necessary to retain mass loyalty and prevent a conflict-ridden withdrawal of legitimation. The state has to gauge these three interest areas (individual capitalism, state capitalism, and generalizable interests), in order to find a compromise for competing demands. A theorem of crisis has to explain not only why the state apparatus encounters difficulties but also why certain problems remain unsolved in the long run.

First, an obvious objection. The state can avoid legitimation problems to the extent that it can manage to make the administrative system independent of the formation of legitimating will. To that end, it can, say, separate expressive symbols (which create a universal willingness to follow) from the instrumental functions of administration. Well-known strategies of this sort are: the personalizing of objective issues, the symbolic use of inquiries, expert opinions, legal incantations, etc. Advertising techniques, borrowed from oligopolistic competition, both confirm and exploit current structures of prejudice. By resorting to emotional appeals, they arouse unconscious motives, occupy certain contents positively, and devalue others. The public, which is engineered for purposes of legitimation, primarily has the function of structuring attention by means of areas of themes and thereby of pushing uncomfortable themes, problems, and arguments below the threshold of attention. As Niklas Luhmann put it, the political system takes over tasks of ideology planning.

The scope for manipulation, however, is narrowly delimited, for the cultural system remains peculiarly resistant to administrative control. There is no administrative creation of meaning, there is at best an ideological erosion of cultural values. The acquisition of legitimation is self-destructive as soon as the mode of acquisition is exposed. Thus there is a systematic limit for attempts at making up for legitimation deficits by means of well-aimed manipulation. This limit is the structural dissimilarity between areas of administrative action and cultural tradition.

A crisis argument, to be sure, can be constructed out of these considerations only with the viewpoint that the expansion of state activity has the side-effect of disproportionately increasing the need for legitimation. I regard such an overproportionate increase as likely because things that are taken for granted culturally, and have so far been external conditions of the political systems, are now being drawn into the planning area of administration. This process thematizes traditions which previously were not part of public programming, much less of practical discourse. An example of such direct administrative processing of cultural tradition is educational planning, especially the planning of the curriculum. Hitherto, the school administration merely had to codify a given naturally evolved canon. But now the planning of the curriculum is based on the premise that the tradition models can also be different. Administrative planning creates a universal compulsion for justification toward a sphere that was actually distinguished by the power of self-legitimation.

In regard to the direct disturbance of things that were culturally taken for granted, there are further examples in regional and urban planning (private ownership of land), health planning ('classless hospital'), and family planning and marriage-law planning (which are shaking sexual taboos and facilitating emancipation).

An awareness of contingency is created not just for contents of tradition but also for the techniques of tradition – i.e. socialization. Among pre-school children, formal schooling is already competing with family upbringing. The new problems afflicting the educational routine, and the widespread awareness of these problems, are reflected by, among other indications, a new type of pedagogical and psychological writing addressed to the general public.

On all these levels, administrative planning has unintentional effects of disquieting and publicizing. These effects weaken the justification potential of traditions that have been forced out of their natural condition. Once they are no longer indisputable, their demands for validity can be stabilized only by way of discourse. Thus, the forcible shift of things that have been culturally taken for granted further politicizes areas of life that previously could be assigned to the private domain. However, this spells danger for bourgeois privatism, which is informally assured by the structures of the public. I see signs of this danger in strivings for participation and in models for alternatives, such as have developed particularly in secondary and primary schools, in the press, the church, theatres, publishing, etc.

These arguments support the contention that late-capitalist societies are afflicted with serious problems of legitimation. But do these arguments suffice to explain why these problems cannot be solved? Do they explain the prediction of a crisis in legitimation? Let us assume the state apparatus could succeed in making labour more productive and in distributing the gains in productivity in such a way as to assure an economic growth free of crises (if not disturbances). Such growth would nevertheless proceed in terms of priorities independent of the generalizable interests of the population. The priority models that Galbraith has analysed from the viewpoint of 'private wealth versus public poverty' result from a class structure which, as always, is still being kept latent. This structure is ultimately the cause of the legitimation deficit.

We have seen that the state cannot simply take over the cultural system and that, in fact, the expansion of areas for state planning creates problems for things that are culturally taken for granted. 'Meaning' is an increasingly scarce resource, which is why those expectations that are governed by concrete and identifiable needs – i.e. that can be checked by their success – keep mounting in the civil population. The rising level of aspirations is proportionate to the growing need for legitimation. The resource of 'value', siphoned off by the tax office, has to make up for the scanty resource of 'meaning'. Missing legitimations have to be replaced by social rewards such as money, time, and security. A crisis of legitimation arises as soon as the demands for these rewards mount more rapidly than the available mass of values, or if expectations come about that are different and cannot be satisfied by those categories of rewards conforming with the present system.

Why then, should not the level of demands keep within operable limits? As long as the welfare state's programming in connection with a widespread technocratic consciousness (which makes uninfluenceable system-restraints responsible for bottlenecks) maintains a sufficient amount of civil privatism, then the legitimation emergencies do not have to turn into crises. To be sure, the democratic form of legitimation could cause expenses that cannot be covered if that form drives the competing parties to outdo one another in their platforms and thereby raise the expectations of the population higher and higher. Granted, this argument could be amply demonstrated empirically. But we would still have to explain why late-capitalist societies even bother to retain formal democracy. Merely in terms of the administrative system, formal democracy could just as easily be replaced by a variant – a conservative, authoritarian welfare state that reduces the political participation of the citizens to a harmless level; or a Fascist authoritarian state that keeps the population toeing the mark on a relatively high level of permanent mobilization. Evidently, both variants are in the long run less compatible with developed capitalism than a party state based on mass democracy. The socio-cultural system creates demands that cannot be satisfied in authoritarian systems.

This reflection leads me to the following thesis: only a rigid socio-cultural system, incapable of being randomly functionalized for the needs of the administrative system, could explain how legitimation difficulties result in a legitimation crisis. This development must therefore be based on a motivation crisis – i.e. a discrepancy between the need for motives that the state and the occupational system announce and the supply of motivation offered by the socio-cultural system.

THEOREMS OF THE MOTIVATION CRISIS

The most important motivation contributed by the socio-cultural system in late-capitalist societies consists in syndromes of civil and family/vocational privatism. Civil privatism means strong interests in the administrative system's output and minor participation in the process of will-formation (high-output orientation versus low-input orientation). Civil privatism thus corresponds to the structures of a depoliticized public. Family and vocational privatism complements civil privatism. It consists of a family orientation with consumer and leisure interests, and of a career orientation consistent with status competition. This privatism thus corresponds to the structures of educational and occupational systems regulated by competitive performance.

The motivational syndromes mentioned are vital to the political and economic system. However, bourgeois ideologies have components directly relevant to privatistic orientations, and social changes deprive those components of their basis. A brief outline may clarify this.

Performance Ideology

According to bourgeois notions which have remained constant from the beginnings of modern natural law to contemporary election speeches, social rewards should be distributed on the basis of individual achievement. The distribution of gratifications should correlate to every individual's performance. A basic condition is equal opportunity to participate in a competition which is regulated in such a way that external influences can be neutralized. One such allocation mechanism was the market. But ever since the general public realized that social violence is practised in the forms of exchange, the market has been losing its credibility as a mechanism for distributing rewards based on performance. Thus, in the more recent versions of performance ideology, market success is being replaced by the professional success mediated by formal schooling. However, this version can claim credibility only when the following conditions have been fulfilled:

(1) equal opportunity of access to higher schools;
(2) non-discriminatory evaluation standards for school performance;
(3) synchronic developments of the educational and occupational systems;
(4) work processes whose objective structure permits evaluation according to performances that can be ascribed to individuals.

'School justice' in terms of opportunity of access and standards of evaluation has increased in all advanced capitalist societies at least to some degree. But a counter-trend can be observed in the two other dimensions. The expansion of the educational system is becoming more and more independent of changes in the occupational system, so that ultimately the connection between formal schooling and professional success will most likely loosen. At the same time, there are more and more areas in which production structures and work dynamics make it increasingly difficult to evaluate individual performance. Instead, the extrafunctional elements of occupational roles are becoming more and more important for conferring occupational status.

Moreover, fragmented and monotonous work processes are increasingly entering sectors in which previously a personal identity could be developed through the vocational role. An intrinsic motivation for performance is getting less and less support from the structure of the work process in market-dependent work areas. An instrumentalist attitude toward work is spreading even in the traditionally bourgeois professions (white-collar workers, professionals). A performance motivation coming from outside can, however, be sufficiently stimulated by wage income only if:

(1) the reserve army on the labour market exercises an effective competitive pressure;
(2) a sufficient income differential exists between the lower wage groups and the inactive work population.

Both conditions are not necessarily met today. Even in capitalist countries with chronic unemployment (such as the United States), the division of the labour market (into organized and competitive sectors) interferes with the natural mechanism of competition. With a mounting poverty line (recognized by the welfare state), the living standards of the lower income groups and the groups temporarily released from the labour process are mutually assimilating on the other side in the sub-proletarian strata.

Possessive Individualism

Bourgeois society sees itself as an instrumental group that accumulates social wealth only by way of private wealth – i.e. guarantees economic growth and general welfare through competition between strategically acting private persons. Collective goals, under such circumstances, can be achieved only by way of individual utility orientations. This preference system, of course, presupposes:

(1) that the private economic subjects can with subjective unambiguity recognize and calculate needs that remain constant over given time periods;

(2) that this need can be satisfied by individually demandable goods (normally, by way of monetary decisions that conform to the system).

Both presuppositions are no longer fulfilled as a matter of course in the developed capitalist societies. These societies have reached a level of societal wealth far beyond warding off a few fundamental hazards to life and the satisfying of basic needs. This is why the individualistic system of preference is becoming vague. The steady interpreting and reinterpreting of needs is becoming a matter of the collective formation of the will, a fact which opens the alternatives of either free and quasi-political communication among consumers as citizens or massive manipulation – i.e. strong indirect steering. The greater the degree of freedom for the preference system of the demanders, the more urgent the problem of sales policies for the suppliers – at least if they are to maintain the illusion that the consumers can make private and autonomous decisions. Opportunistic adjustment of the consumers to market strategies is the ironical form of every consumer autonomy, which is to be maintained as the facade of possessive individualism. In addition, with increasing socialization of production, the quota of collective commodities among the consumer goods keeps growing. The urban living conditions in complex societies are more and more dependent on an infrastructure (transportation, leisure, health, education, etc.) that is withdrawing further and further from the forms of differential demand and private appropriation.

Exchange-value Orientation

Here I have to mention the tendencies that weaken the socialization effects of the market, especially the increase of those parts of the population that do not reproduce their lives through income from work (students, welfare recipients, social security recipients, invalids, criminals, soldiers, etc.) as well as the expansion of areas of activity in which, as in civil service or in teaching, abstract work is replaced by concrete work. In addition, the relevance that leisure acquires with fewer working hours (and higher real income), compared with the relevance of issues within the occupational sphere of life, does not in the long run privilege those needs that can be satisfied monetarily.

The erosion of bourgeois tradition brings out normative structures that are no longer appropriate to reproducing civil and family
and professional privatism. The now dominant components of
cultural heritage crystallize around a faith in science, a 'postauratic'
art, and universalistic values. Irreversible developments have occurred in each of these areas. As a result, functional inequalities of the
economic and the political systems are blocked by cultural barriers,
and they can be broken down only at the psychological cost of
regressions – i.e. with extraordinary motivational damage. German
fascism was an example of the wasteful attempt at a collectively
organized regression of consciousness below the thresholds of
fundamental scientistic convictions, modern art, and universalistic
law and morals.

Scientism

The political consequences of the authority enjoyed by the scientific
system in developed societies are ambivalent. The rise of modern
science established a demand for discursive justification, and
traditionalistic attitudes cannot hold out against that demand. On
the other hand, short-lived popular syntheses of scientific data
(which have replaced global interpretations) guarantee the authority of science in the abstract. The authority known as 'science' can
thus cover both things: the broadly effective criticism of any
prejudice, as well as the new esoterics of specialized knowledge and
expertise. A self-affirmation of the sciences can further a positivistic
common sense on the part of the depoliticized public. Yet scientism
establishes standards by which it can also be criticized itself and
found guilty of residual dogmatism. Theories of technocracy and of
democratic elitism, asserting the necessity of an institutionalized
civic privatism, come forth with the presumption of theories. But
this does not make them immune to criticism.

Postauratic Art

The consequences of modern art are somewhat less ambivalent.
The modern age has radicalized the autonomy of bourgeois art in
regard to the external purposes for which art could be used. For the
first time, bourgeois society itself produced a counter-culture
against the bourgeois life style of possessive individualism,
performance, and practicality. The *Bohème*, first established in
Paris, the capital of the nineteenth century, embodies a critical
demand that had arisen, unpolemically still, in the aura of the

bourgeois artwork. The alter ego of the businessman, the 'human being', whom the bourgeois used to encounter in the lonesome contemplation of the artwork, soon split away from him. In the shape of the artistic avant garde, it confronted him as a hostile, at best seductive, force. In artistic beauty, the bourgeoisie had been able to experience its own ideals and the (as always) fictitious redemption of the promise of happiness which was merely suspended in everyday life. In radicalized art, however, the bourgeois soon had to recognize the negation of social practice as its complement.

Modern art is the outer covering in which the transformation of bourgeois art into a counter-culture was prepared. Surrealism marks the historical moment when modern art programmatically destroyed the outer covering of no-longer beautiful illusion in order to enter life desublimated. The levelling of the different reality degrees of art and life was accelerated (although not, as Walter Benjamin assumed, introduced) by the new techniques of mass reproduction and mass reception. Modern art had already sloughed off the aura of classical bourgeois art in that the art work made the production process visible and presented itself as a made product. But art enters the ensemble of utility values only when abandoning its autonomous status. The process is certainly ambivalent. It can signify the degeneration of art into a propagandistic mass art or commercialized mass culture, or else its transformation into a subversive counter-culture.

Universalist Morality

The blockage which bourgeois ideologies, stripped of their functional components, create for developing the political and economic system, is even clearer in the moral system than in the authority of science and the self-disintegration of modern art. The moment traditional societies enter a process of modernization, the growing complexity results in steering problems that necessitate an accelerated change of social norms. The tempo inherent in natural cultural tradition has to be heightened. This leads to bourgeois formal law which permits releasing the norm contents from the dogmatic structure of mere tradition and defining them in terms of intention. The legal norms are uncoupled from the corps of privatized moral norms. In addition, they need to be created (and justified) according to principles. Abstract law counts only for that area pacified by state power. But the morality of bourgeois private persons, a morality likewise raised to the level of universal principles, encounters no barrier in the continuing natural condition between the states. Since principled morality is sanctioned only by the purely inward authority of the conscience, its claim to universality conflicts with public morality, which is still bound to a concrete state-subject. This is the conflict between the cosmopolitanism of the human being and the loyalties of the citizen.

If we follow the developmental logic of overall societal systems of norms (leaving the area of historical examples), we can settle that conflict. But its resolution is conceivable only under certain conditions. The dichotomy between inner and outer morality has to disappear. The contrast between morally and legally regulated areas has to be relativized. And the validity of *all* norms has to be tied to the discursive formation of the will of the people potentially affected.

Competitive capitalism for the first time gave a binding force to strictly universalistic value systems. This occurred because the system of exchange had to be regulated universalistically and because the exchange of equivalents offered a basic ideology effective in the bourgeois class. In organized capitalism, the bottom drops out of this legitimation model. At the same time, new and increased demands for legitimation arise. However, the system of science cannot intentionally fall behind an attained stage of cumulative knowledge. Similarly, the moral system, once practical discourse has been admitted, cannot simply make us forget a collectively attained stage of moral consciousness.

I would like to conclude with a final reflection. If no sufficient concordance exists between the normative structures that still have some power today and the politico-economic system, then we can still avoid motivation crises by uncoupling the cultural system. Culture would then become a non-obligatory leisure occupation or the object of professional knowledge. This solution would be blocked if the basic convictions of a communicative ethics and the experience complexes of counter-cultures (in which postauratic art is embodied) acquired a motive-forming power determining typical socialization processes. Such a conjecture is supported by several behaviour syndromes spreading more and more among young people – either retreat as a reaction to an exorbitant claim on the personality resources; or protest as a result of an autonomous ego organization that cannot be stabilized without conflicts under given conditions. On the activist side we find the student movements, revolts by high-school students and apprentices, pacifists, women's lib. The retreatist side is represented by hippies, Jesus people, the drug subculture, phenomena of undermotivation in schools, etc. These are the primary areas for checking our hypothesis that late-capitalist societies are endangered by a collapse of legitimation.

7

Legitimation Problems in Advanced Capitalism

THOMAS McCARTHY

Habermas's reflections on the 'contradictions' and 'crisis tenden-cies' endemic to 'advanced' or 'organized' capitalism are based on concepts and principles developed in chapters 1 to 4. Briefly he argues that the basic contradiction of the capitalist order remains the private appropriation of public wealth – in terms of the discourse model of practical reason: the suppression of generaliz-able interests through treating them as particular. As a conse-quence, political decisions that reflect the existing organizational principle of society *ipso facto* do not admit of rational consensus. They could not be justified in a general and unrestricted discussion of what, in the light of present and possible circumstances, is in the best interests of all affected by them. Hence the stability of the capitalist social formation depends on the continued effectiveness of legitimations that could not withstand discursive examination. The problem, in short, is how to distribute socially produced wealth inequitably and yet legitimately.

Stated in this way, Habermas's critique appears to be essentially moral; social reality is measured against an abstract standard of reason and found wanting. However if we recall his views on the nature of critical social theory – from the 'empirical philosophy of history with a practical intent' to the 'reconstruction of historical materialism' – we might expect that he would not leave off with a moral condemnation. And in fact the burden of his argument in *Legitimation Crisis* is to the effect that the basic contradiction of contemporary capitalism issues in crisis tendencies that can be empirically ascertained. The critique as a whole, then, assumes a Marxist form: what is morally required is being empirically prepared: the seeds of the new society are being formed in the

Source: Thomas McCarthy, *The Critical Theory of Jürgen Habermas* (New York: MIT Press, 1978), pp. 358–77, 385–6, reprinted with permission of MIT Press and the Hutchinson Publishing Group.

womb of the old. But it is a Marxist critique with important differences. In the first place, the crisis tendencies pregnant with the future are no longer located immediately in the economic sphere but in the socio-cultural sphere, they do not directly concern the reproduction of the material conditions of life but the reproduction of reliable structures of intersubjectivity. Habermas thus attempts to make a case for the likelihood of a legitimation crisis, not an economic crisis. (And this, of course, is what we might expect. As we saw earlier, the core of his disagreement with orthodox Marxism was precisely its overemphasis on economic factors to the exclusion of 'superstructural' considerations. This was the point of his distinction between labour and interaction and the dominant motif in his reconstruction of historical materialism.)

Other important differences concern the structure and status of the crisis argument itself. Habermas distinguishes four types of 'possible crisis tendencies' in advanced capitalism, tendencies rooted in the functioning of the economy and the administration, and in the needs for legitimation and motivation.[1] Any one of these tendencies, or more probably some combination of them, could, he holds, erupt into an actual crisis.[2] But to say that a crisis could occur is not to say that it will occur. and it is the latter claim that is characteristic of Marxist critique. Accordingly the question to which Habermas addresses himself is, Can a crisis of advanced capitalism be systematically predicted today? His response is neither a clear 'yes' nor a clear 'no' but a qualified conditional thesis.

In the first place, he does not think it possible at the moment to decide cogently the 'question about the chances for a self-transformation (*Selbstaufhebung*) of advanced capitalism', that is, for an evolutionary self-transcendence of the capitalist principle of organization.[3]

Assuming that this does not happen, it is possible, he maintains, to construct a systematic argument for a crisis, but not an economic crisis: 'I do not exclude the possibility that economic crisis can be permanently averted, although only in such a way that the contradictory steering imperatives that assert themselves in the pressure for capital realization would produce a series of other crisis tendencies. The continuing tendency toward disturbance of capitalist growth can be administratively processed and transferred by stages through the political and into the socio-cultural system'.[4] 'Administrative processing' of cyclical economic crises gives rise to 'a bundle of crisis tendencies that, from a genetic point of view, represent a hierarchy of crisis phenomena shifted upwards from below.'[5] The end result of this displacement process is, Habermas argues, a tendency toward a legitimation crisis.

But even the force of this argument is held to be conditional on the continued existence of a truth-dependent mode of socialization, one still 'bound to reason'. Habermas is thinking here of the chances for a 'brave new world' in which the pressure for legitimation would be removed by 'uncoupling' the socialization process from norms that require justification. In part 3 of *Legitimation Crisis* he critically reviews the thesis of 'the end of the individual' in general and Luhmann's systems-theoretic version of it in particular. His conclusion is that this too is an open question.[6] Thus the argument for a legitimation crisis is twice conditioned: neither the possibility of a self-transformation of capitalism nor that of an 'uncoupling' of motive formation from reason can be empirically excluded at present.

Even with this double conditional, the legitimation crisis argument claims no more than a 'certain plausibility'.[7] From the start Habermas warns against confusing 'the clarification of very general strutures of hypotheses' with 'empirical results'.[8] And he ends by acknowledging that his 'argumentation sketch' falls short of providing theoretical certainty.[9] In short one has to distinguish between the predictive form of the argument and its hypothetical status.

These qualifications notwithstanding, *Legitimation Crisis* offers an insightful analysis of contemporary society, of its endemic problems and prospective fate. In these few pages I shall examine the 'argumentation sketch' advanced there.

The basic elements of the concept of crisis were already worked out in the aesthetics of the classical tragedy.

> In classical aesthetics, from Aristotle to Hegel, crisis signifies the turning point in a fateful process that, despite all objectivity, does not simply impose itself from outside and does not remain external to the identity of the persons caught up in it. The contradiction expressed in the catastrophic culmination of conflict, is inherent in the structure of the action system and in the personality systems of the principal characters. Fate is fulfilled in the revelation of the conflicting norms against which the identities of the participants shatter, unless they are able to summon up the strength to win back their freedom by shattering the mythical power of fate through the formation of new identities.[10]

Through the traditions of *Heilsgeschichte*, eighteenth-century philosophy of history and nineteenth-century evolutionary social theory, this constellation of objectivity and identity, conflict and catastrophe, entered into the formative process of modern social theory. In his 'historical materialism' and 'critique of political economy', Marx claimed to have finally placed it on a scientific footing.

These same elements figure in Habermas's concept of crisis, but they are interpreted in the light of his theory of social evolution. On his understanding, the 'objectivity of the fateful process' is to be construed in terms of systems theory – as 'structurally inherent system-imperatives that are incompatible and cannot be hierarchically integrated.'[11] This occurs when the 'organizational principle' of a society does not permit the resolution of problems that are critical for its continued existence. But problems of 'system integration' lead to crises only when they pose a threat to 'social integration', that is, when they undermine the consensual foundations of social interaction. In such cases unresolved system problems lead to the disintegration of social institutions: the 'identity of the persons caught up in the fateful process' is at stake: 'Crisis occurrences owe their objectivity to the fact that they issue from unresolved steering problems. Although the subjects are not generally conscious of them, these steering problems create secondary problems that do affect consciousness in a specific way – precisely in such a way as to endanger social integration. The question is, when do such steering problems arise.'[12]

Marx's answer to this question *a propos* liberal capitalism is well known.[13] The organizational principle in question is the relationship of wage labour to capital anchored in the system of bourgeois law. The institutional nucleus of this system is not the state – which merely secures the structural prerequisites of the capitalist process of reproduction (civil law and its enforcement, labour legislation, education, transportation, communication, tax, banking, and business law and so on) – but the market mechanism: economic exchange is the dominant steering medium. That is, system integration (in Parsons's terms, adaptation and goal attainment) is left to the semi-autonomous workings of labour, commodity, and capital markets. On Marx's analysis, this mode of organization regularly leads to structurally insoluble problems in the form, above all, of tendencies to a falling rate of profit (crises of capital accumulation) and to reduced powers of consumption and incentives to invest (crises of capital realization). Consequently the cycle of prosperity, crisis, and depression is typical of liberal capitalism. The underlying systems problems reside directly in the economic sphere; they assume crisis proportions because this same sphere has also taken on basic functions of social integration.

> Bourgeois ideologies can assume a universalistic structure and appeal to generalizable interests because the property order has shed its political form and been converted into a relation of production that, it seems, can legitimate itself. The institution of the market can be founded on the justice inherent in the exchange of equivalents; and for this reason the bourgeois constitutional state finds its justification in the legitimate relations of production. This is the message of rational natural law since Locke.[14]

In contrast to traditional societies, the conflict potential of class opposition is transposed from the political into the economic sphere; legitimation no longer comes primarily 'from above' (from traditional world views) but 'from below' (from the inherent 'justice' of the market). Whereas the traditional form of appropriating a socially produced surplus product according to privilege is incompatible with universalistic modes of intercourse, the new form is compatible with universalistic value systems, in the guise, for examples of natural law theories and utilitarian ethics. In short, the class relationship is institutionalized through the labour market and therefore 'depoliticized'.

> Because the *social power* of the capitalist is institutionalized as an exchange relation in the form of the private labor contract, and the siphoning off of privately available surplus value has replaced *political dependency*, the market assumes, together with its cybernetic function, an ideological function. The class relationship can assume the anonymous, unpolitical form of wage dependency. In Marx, therefore, theoretical analysis of the value form has the double task of uncovering both the steering principle of commerce in a market economy and the basic ideology of bourgeois class society. The theory of value serves at the same time the functional analysis of the economic system and the critique of ideology of a class domination that can be unmasked, even for the bourgeois consciousness, through the proof that in the labor market equivalents are not exchanged.[15]

The type of crisis endemic to the liberal capitalist order is a function of this transposition of the conflict of class interests into the economic steering system: dangers to system integration (in the form of periodically recurring accumulation crises) are direct threats to social integration. 'Economic crisis is immediately transformed into social crisis; for in unmasking the opposition of social classes, it provides a practical critique of ideology of the market's pretension to be free of power'.[16] The displacement of conflicts of interest from the political to the economic sphere results in structurally insoluble problems (accumulation crises) that themselves bring to light the latent class antagonism. Thus Marx's critique of political economy could take the form of a systems analysis of the capitalist reproduction process that itself yielded action-theoretic assumptions for the theory of class conflict. His analysis of economic processes can be translated directly into an analysis of social processes. The liberal capitalist process of production is at the same time a 'dialectic of the moral life'.

Whatever its merits as an analysis of liberal capitalism – and Habermas holds them to be considerable – Marx's critique of political economy can no longer be applied to organized capitalism. There are a number of reasons for this, the primary among them being the changed relationship between the state and the economy; the latter no longer has the degree of autonomy that justified the exclusivity of Marx's focus. By means of global planning, the state regulates the economic cycle as a whole, and it creates and improves conditions for utilizing excess accumulated capital. Habermas is referring here to such phenomena as government credits, price guarantees, subsidies, loans, contracts, income redistribution, and labour policy through which adjustments are made between competing imperatives of steady growth, stability of the currency, full employment, and the balance of foreign trade; and to such phenomena as government organization of supra-national economic blocks, unproductive consumption (in armaments and space, for instance), improvement of the material and immaterial infrastructures (such as transportation, communication, health, housing, city planning, science, and research and development), improvement of the productivity of labour (through general education, vocational schools, training programmes and the like), and relief from the social costs of private production (by unemployment compensation, welfare, and ecological repair, for example) through which opportunities for capital investment are opened and improved and the productivity of labour is increased. As a result of this altered configuration of the economic and political-administrative sub-systems, a number of the presuppositions underlying the classical Marxian crisis arguments no longer hold true. I shall mention two of the most important: (1) Governmental activity has altered the form of the production of surplus value; by filling functional gaps in the market, the state intervenes in the process of capital accumulation. It heightens the productivity of labour through the production of 'collective commodities' (material and immaterial infrastructure) and through organizing the educational system in general, and scientific-technical progress in particular. The state

> now expends capital to purchase the *indirectly productive* labor power of scientists, engineers, teachers, etc. and to transform the products of their labor into cost-cutting commodities of the category referred to. If one holds fast to a dogmatic conceptual strategy and conceives of reflexive labor as unproductive labor (in the Marxian sense), the specific function of this labor for the realization process is overlooked. Reflexive labor is not productive in the sense of the direct production of surplus value . . . But it is also not unproductive; for then it would have no net effect on the production of surplus value . . . This reflection shows that the classical fundamental categories of the (Marxian) theory of value are insufficient for the analysis of governmental policy in education, technology and science. It also shows that it is an empirical question whether the new form of production of surplus value can compensate for the tendential fall in the rate of profit, that is, whether it can work against economic crisis.[17]

(2) In certain large sectors of the economy the mechanism of the market has been replaced by 'quasi-political compromise' between business and unions in determining the cost of labour power. Since the cost of labour power is the unit of measure in the Marxian calculation of value, this introduces a political dimension into the very foundations of value theory.

> Through the system of 'political' wages, negotiated on the basis of wage scales, it has been possible – above all in the capital- and growth-intensive sectors of the economy – to mitigate the opposition between wage labor and capital and to bring about a partial class compromise . . . Of course, one can again hold fast to a dogmatic conceptual strategy and equate by definition the average wage with the costs of the

reproduction of labor power. But in so doing one prejudices at the analytical level the (no doubt) empirically substantial question of whether the class struggle, organized politically and through unionization, has perhaps had a stabilizing effect only because it has been successful in an economic sense and has visibly altered the rate of exploitation to the advantage of the best organized parts of the working class.[18]

The relations of production have been repoliticized. Price setting, which replaces competition in oligopolistic markets, has its counterpart in the 'political price' that the commodity called labour receives. In Marxist terms, 'class compromise' of a sort has become part of the structure of advanced capitalism; the real income of the dependent workers depends not only on exchange relations in the market but on relations of political power as well.

The point of this line of argument is that the organizational principle of capitalism has changed. The 'unpolitical' relationship between wage labour and capital and the autonomy of the economic sphere vis-à-vis the political, have given way to a 'quasi-political' distribution of the social product and to the assumption by the state of market-complementing and market-replacing functions. Thus the Marxian theory of value and the crisis arguments formulated in terms of it are inadequate. This is not to say that economic crises cannot or will not occur. Rather the arguments for their inevitability have lost their cogency. In the present state of knowledge, there are no decisive arguments of a purely economic nature for the necessity of crisis. To the extent that what happens in the economy is a function of government activity, the examination of crisis tendencies in contemporary society has to take into account the nature and limits of administrative intervention.

In making good the functional weaknesses of the market and compensating for its politically intolerable consequences, the state apparatus is faced simultaneously with two tasks.

> On the one hand, it is supposed to raise the requisite amount of taxes by skimming off profits and income and to use the available taxes so rationally that crisis-ridden disturbances of growth can be avoided. On the other hand, the selective raising of taxes, the discernible pattern of priorities in their use, and the administrative performances themselves must be so constituted that the need for legitimation can be satisfied as it arises. If the state fails in the former task, there is a deficit in administrative rationality. If it fails in the latter task, a deficit in legitimation results.[19]

Accordingly Habermas moves next to an assessment of arguments for the inevitability of a 'rationality crisis' in advanced capitalism. This concept is modelled after that of the economic crisis; it is a form of system crisis in which a breakdown in steering performances (system integration) leads to a breakdown in social integration. However, the steering mechanism in question is no longer a self-regulating market but a state apparatus that has taken on market-replacing and market-complementing functions. A deficit in administrative rationality occurs when the state is unable to reconcile and fulfil imperatives issuing from the economic system. But although rationality crises are in this sense displaced economic crises, the terms of their development and possible resolution are markedly different: administrative planning and the exercise of political power do not have the same 'logic' as the market.

Habermas reviews several different arguments for this type of crisis, arguments based on the incompatibility of collective planning with the 'anarchistic' interests of private capital and other organized groups; arguments based on the permanent inflation and crisis in public finances that result from the government's assumption of the costs of a more and more socialized production (such as armaments, transportation, communication, research and development, housing, health care, social security, and so on) and the costs of its dysfunctional side-effects (among them, welfare, unemployment, ecological repair, and so forth); arguments based on the tension between the state's responsibility as a global planning authority and its need for immunization against demands that cripple the process of growth; and arguments based on the systematic propagation of elements incompatible with the economic system that results from government activity (for example politically oriented private investment policies, the proliferation of occupational spheres – planning bureaucracies, public service sectors, science and education – increasingly detached from the market mechanism and oriented to concrete goals, and the growth of the inactive proportion of the population that does not reproduce itself through the labour market).

Although these arguments do point out very real problems inherent in the present organization of society, they do not, Habermas argues, suffice to demonstrate the inevitability of a rationality crisis. The limits of administrative capacity to process such problems are unclear. It is difficult to specify, for example, the critical threshold of tolerance for disorganization and the extent to which it can be adapted to an increasingly disorganized environment. Nor are the limits of administrative negotiation and compromise with various interest groups and sectors of society by any means so clear as the controlling principles of the free market.

> Thus there exists no *logically necessary* incompatibility between interests in global capitalist planning and freedom of investment, need for planning and renunciation of intervention, and independence of the state apparatus and dependency on individual interests. The possibility that the administrative system might open a compromise path between competing claims that would allow a sufficient amount of organizational rationality, cannot be excluded from the start on logical grounds.[20]

Again this is not to say that an administrative system crisis cannot or will not occur. Rather the arguments for the inevitability of a rationality crisis are not decisive. Their cogency rests on the assumption of limits to planning capacity that cannot be reliably determined in the present state of knowledge.

There is, however, another side to the capacity of the political system to discharge the necessary planning functions: the need to secure legitimation for governmental activity. If the adequate level of mass loyalty and compliance cannot be maintained while the steering imperatives taken over from the economic system are carried through, there is the danger of a legitimation crisis. Although both rationality crises and legitimation crises arise in the political system, they are importantly different. The former are 'output' crises; they occur when the state apparatus cannot, under given boundary conditions, adequately steer the economic system. In this sense, a rationality crisis is a displaced economic crisis; the threat to system integration, in the form of a disorganization of steering performances, leads to a withdrawal of legitimation, a threat to social integration. By contrast, the legitimation crisis is not directly a system crisis, but an 'identity crisis', that is, a direct threat to social integration.

One would initially suppose that crisis arguments directed to the sphere of legitimation would be even more tenuous than those focusing on the political–administrative system. If the logic of government planning is such that hard and fast limits are difficult to determine, the logic of procuring and maintaining legitimation is, it seems, even less amenable to the drawing of precise boundaries. Nevertheless it is here that Habermas takes his stand. He deploys a two-sided argument, focusing first (and inconclusively) on the type of legitimations needed in organized capitalist society and then on the limits set them by certain aspects of socio-cultural development.

With the repoliticization of the relations of production, the ideology of fair exchange has lost its force. There is a general awareness that the distribution of social wealth depends in no small measure on governmental policies and the quasi-political negotiation of rewards and obligations. At the same time, if the capitalist principle of organization is to be maintained, economic growth has to be achieved in accord with priorities shaped by private goals of profit maximization. Since these priorities have lost the appearance of being 'natural', there is a need for legitimation. In this sense, the basic contradiction of organized capitalism remains the private appropriation of public wealth, and the class structure, although latent, is still behind the basic legitimation problem: how to distribute the social product inequitably and yet legitimately. Since the appeal to the inherent 'justice' of the market no long suffices, there is need for some 'substitute programme'.

> Recoupling the economic system to the political . . . creates an increased need for legitimation. The state apparatus no longer, as in liberal capitalism, merely secures the general conditions of production . . . but is now actively engaged in it. It must therefore . . . like the pre-capitalist state . . . be legitimated, although it can no longer rely on the residues of tradition that have been undermined and worn out during the development of capitalism. Moreover, through the universalistic value system of bourgeois ideology, civil rights – including the right to participate in political elections – have become established; and legitimation can be dissociated from the mechanism of elections only temporarily and under extraordinary conditions. The problem is resolved through a system of formal democracy. Genuine participation of citizens in processes of political will-formation, that is, substantive democracy, would bring to consciousness the contradiction between administratively socialized production and the continued private appropriation and use of surplus value. In order to keep this contradiction from being thematized, the administrative system must be sufficiently independent of legitimating will-formation.[21]

'Formally democratic' institutions and procedures ensure both a diffuse, generalized mass loyalty and the requisite independence of administrative decision making from the specific interests of the citizens. They are democratic in form but not in substance. The public realm, whose functions have been reduced largely to periodic plebiscites in which acclamation can be granted or withheld, is 'structurally depoliticized'.

Essential to this system is a widespread civil privatism – 'political abstinence combined with an orientation to career, leisure, and consumption' – which 'promotes the expectation of suitable rewards within the system (money, leisure, time, and security)'.[22] This involves a 'high output – low input' orientation of the citizenry vis-à-vis the government, an orientation that is reciprocated in the welfare state programme of the latter, and a 'familiar–vocational privatism' that consists in a 'family orientation with developed interests in consumption and leisure on the one hand, and in a career orientation suitable to status competition on the other', an orientation that corresponds to the competitive structures of the educational and occupational systems.[23] Furthermore the structural depoliticization of the public sphere is itself justified by democratic elite theories or by technocratic systems theories, which – like the classical doctrine of political economy – suggest the 'naturalness' of the existing organization of society.

According to Habermas, legitimation deficits arise in this system when civil privatism is undermined by the spread of administrative rationality itself:

A legitimation deficit means that it is not possible by administrative means to maintain effective normative structures to the extent required. During the course of capitalist development, the political system shifts its boundaries not only into the economic system, but also into the socio-cultural system. While organizational rationality spreads, cultural traditions are undermined and weakened. The residue of tradition, however, must escape the administrative grasp, for traditions important for legitimation cannot be regenerated administratively. Furthermore, administrative manipulation of cultural matters has the unintended side effect of causing meanings and norms previously fixed by tradition and belonging to the boundary conditions of the political system to be publicly thematized. In this way, the scope of discursive will-formation expands – a process that shakes the structures of the depoliticized public realm so important for the continued existence of the system.[24]

The expanded activity of the state produces an increase in the need for legitimation, for justification of government intervention into new areas of life. At the same time, the very process of subjecting sectors of social life to administrative planning produces the unintended side-effect of undermining traditional legitimations. 'Rationalization' destroys the unquestionable character of validity claims that were previously taken for granted; it stirs up matters that were previously settled by the cultural tradition in an unproblematic way; and thus it furthers the politicization of areas of life previously assigned to the private sphere. For example, educational (especially curriculum) planning, the planning of the health system, and family planning have the effect of publicizing and thematizing matters that were once culturally taken for granted. 'The end effect is a consciousness of the contingency, not only of the contents of tradition, but also of the techniques of tradition'.[25] And this development endangers the civil privatism essential to the depoliticized public realm. 'Efforts at participation and the plethora of alternative models . . . are indications of this danger, as is the increasing number of citizen's initiatives.'[26]

Attempts to compensate for ensuing legitimation deficits through conscious manipulation are faced with systematic limits, for the cultural system is 'peculiarly resistant' to administrative control. 'There is no administrative production of meaning. The commercial production and administrative planning of symbols exhausts the normative force of counterfactual validity claims. The procurement of legitimation is self-defeating as soon as the mode of procurement is seen through'.[27] Thus the effect of the administrative processing of economically conditioned crisis tendencies (that is, of the introduction of 'legitimate power' into the reproduction process) is an increased pressure for legitimation. This pressure issues not only from the need to secure acceptance of increased activity in new spheres but from the unavoidable side-effects of that activity as well; and it cannot be relieved by the 'administrative production of meaning'. If it cannot be otherwise relieved, legitimation deficits occur. 'The scope for action contracts precisely at those moments in which it needs to be drastically expanded.'[28]

These arguments, if valid, support the thesis that advanced capitalist societies encounter legitimation problems. But they are not sufficient to establish the insolubility of these problems and the necessity of crisis. For one thing, it is not at all certain that some acceptable trade-off between the ever scarcer resource 'meaning' and the more available resource 'value' cannot be managed. If the missing legitimation can be offset by rewards conforming to the system — money, success, leisure, security, and the like — then there is no reason why a legitimation crisis need occur. The welfare state is, after all, a relatively comfortable and secure abode: by historical standards it might appear to be palatial. Habermas acknowledges this point and passes accordingly to the last stage of his argument.

> This reflection supports my thesis that only a rigid socio-cultural system, incapable of being randomly functionalized for the needs of the administrative system, could explain a sharpening of legitimation difficulties into a legitimation crisis. A legitimation crisis can be predicted only if expectations that cannot be fulfilled either with the available quantity of value or, generally, with rewards conforming to the system, are systematically produced. A legitimation crisis must be based on a motivation crisis – that is, a discrepancy between the need for motives declared by the state, the educational and the occupational systems on the one hand, and the motivation supplied by the socio-cultural system on the other.[29]

Since he does not think it possible to predict shortages of the fiscally available quantity of value, he focuses now on the limits to procuring legitimation set by 'normative structures that no longer provide the economic–political system with ideological resources, but instead confront it with exorbitant demands.'[30]

It is evident that the arguments for a legitimation crisis and those for a motivation crisis are tightly intertwined. Both are concerned with socio-cultural rather than with economic or administrative crisis tendencies, with disturbances in the delicate complementarity between the requirements of the state apparatus and the occupational system on the one hand, and the interpreted needs and legitimate expectations of the members of society on the other. In fact the distinction between them is basically one of orientation: the former focuses on the increased need for legitimation that arises from changes in the political system (expanded state activity), the latter on changes in the socio-cultural system itself, changes that tendentially undermine the complementarity referred to above. The two can be regarded as different sides of a single argument for 'a legitimation crisis based on a motivation crisis'. The core of the second (motivational) strand of the argument is a demonstration that 'the socio-cultural system is changing in such a way that its output becomes dysfunctional for the state and the system of social labor.' Since the most important motivational patterns required for the continued stability of advanced capitalist society are the 'syndromes of civil and familial–vocational privatism' that sustain a formally democratic political order and an economy based on the private appropriation of socially produced wealth, the heart of this demonstration lies in showing that these 'syndromes' are being undermined.

Habermas's argument involves both systematic and historical considerations. The systematic considerations concern limitations arising from the form of socialization in which motivations for action are produced.

> I doubt whether it is possible to identify any psychological constants of human nature that limit the socializing process from within. I do, however, see a limitation in the kind of socialization through which social systems have until now produced their motivations for action. The process of socialization takes place within structures of linguistic inter-subjectivity; it determines an organization of behavior tied to norms requiring justification and to interpretive systems that secure identity. This communicative organization of behavior can become an obstacle to complex decision-making systems . . . As long as we have to do with a form of socialization that binds inner nature in a communicative organization of behavior, it is inconceivable that there should be a legitimation of any action norm that guarantees, even approximately, an acceptance of decisions without reasons. The motive for readiness to conform to a decision-making power still indeterminate in content is the expectation that this power will be exercised in accord with legitimate norms of action . . . These limits . . . could be broken through only if . . . the identity of socio-cultural systems [changed]. Only if motives for action no longer operated through norms requiring justification, and if personality systems no longer had to find their unity in identity-securing interpretive systems, could the acceptance of decisions without reasons become routine, that is, could the readiness to conform absolutely be produced to any desired degree.[31]

I shall return to this argument below. The historical considerations concern the erosion of traditions in which motivational patterns essential to capitalist society – especially civil and familial-vocational privatism – were produced and the concomitant spread of dysfunctional motivational structures.

Although Habermas stresses the importance of the ideology of fair exchange in liberal capitalism, he by no means considers it to have been the sole source of socio-cultural support for that system. 'Bourgeois culture as a whole ... was always dependent on motivationally effective supplementation by traditional world views' (for example, religion, a traditionalistic civil ethic, the vocational ethos of the middle class, the fatalism of the lower class) and on such 'specifically bourgeois value orientations' as possessive individualism and Benthamite utilitarianism.[32] But the process of capitalist development has itself undermined the 'remains of prebourgeois traditions' on which liberal capitalism 'parasitically fed'. Traditional world views proved to be socio-structurally incompatible with the expansion of the sphere of 'strategic-utilitarian action', that is, with the 'rationalization' (Weber) of areas of life once regulated by tradition; at the same time they proved to be cognitively incompatible with the growth of science and technology and the spread of scientific-technical modes of thought through universalized formal schooling. As a result, the remains of prebourgeois traditions, which fostered civil and familial-vocational privatism, are being 'non-renewably dismantled'.

On the other hand, core components of bourgeois ideology, such as possessive individualism and orientations to achievement and exchange value, are also being undermined by social change. The achievement ideology — the idea that social rewards should be distributed on the basis of individual achievement — becomes problematic to the extent that the market loses its credibility as a 'fair' mechanism for allocating these rewards; the education system fails as a replacement mechanism, either because of intrinsic inequities or because of the increasingly problematic connection between formal education and occupational success; increasingly fragmented and monotonous labour processes undermine intrinsic motivation to achieve; and extrinsic motivation to achieve (such as income) is undermined by the non-competitive structure of the labour market in organized sectors of the economy and the tendency toward equalization of the standards of living of lower income groups and those on welfare or unemployment. Possessive individualism becomes problematic to the extent that capitalist societies attain a level of social wealth at which the avoidance of basic risks and the satisfaction of basic needs are no longer the principal determinants of individual preference systems. The constant interpretation and reinterpretation of needs can — despite massive manipulation — lead to preference systems that are dysfunctional for the political-economic system. Moreover the 'quality of life' is increasingly dependent on 'collective commodities' (transportation, health care, education, and the like) that are less susceptible to differential demands and private appropriation. Finally orientation to exchange value is weakened by the growth of those segments of the population who do not reproduce their lives through the labour market and the proliferation of occupational spheres increasingly detached from the market mechanism and oriented to concrete goals. In addition, as leisure pursuits acquire increased importance, needs that cannot be satisfied monetarily expand.

These arguments, while suggestive, are clearly less than decisive. Whereas the erosion of traditional world views is a well-documented development, the erosion of the 'specifically bourgeois value elements' that foster civil privatism (political abstinence) and familial–vocational privatism (crystallized around the achievement motive) is a more recent and more ambiguous phenomenon. It is not at all clear that the motivational patterns associated with welfare-statism, the competitive structures of the educational and occupational spheres, and the orientation to consumption and leisure have been weakened to the extent that we could speak of a tendency to a motivation crisis. Moreover even if we grant that normative structures and motivational patterns are undergoing profound change, the question remains as to where these changes will lead. Might they not, for instance, issue in some altered constellation of passivity, privatism, and consumerism no less functional for the formally democratic welfare state?

This question brings us to the next step in Habermas's argument. He maintains that the elements of bourgeois culture that are still relevant for motive formation are dysfunctional; they prevent the formation of functional equivalents for civil and familial-vocational privatism. He is thinking here of scientism, modern art, and universal morality. (1) The 'authority of science' is ambiguous. We have seen that scientism, technocracy theories, and the like can fulfil ideological functions. But it is important also to see that this authority encompasses a broadly effective demand for discursive justification and critique of arbitrary structures of prejudice. Traditional attitudes of belief cannot withstand this kind of scrutiny. (2) The relationship of modern art to capitalist society is less ambiguous. Once it shed the aura of classical bourgeois art and proclaimed its radical autonomy from bourgeois society, modern art 'expresses not the promise, but the irretrievable sacrifice of bourgeois rationalization, the plainly incompatible experiences and not the esoteric fulfilment of withheld, but merely deferred, gratification'.[33] This development has produced a counter-culture that strengthens the divergence between the values fostered by the cultural system and those required by the political and economic systems. Clearly neither of these reflections possesses the force that Habermas requires for his crisis argument. And in fact, it is on (3), the development of universal morality, that he places the burden of proof. This brings us back to the systematic considerations concerning socialization and social evolution that were introduced above. It is here that the conceptual apparatus Habermas has developed is brought directly to bear.

His argument can be broken down into the following theses:

(1) The components of world-views that secure identity and are efficacious for social integration – that is, moral systems and their accompanying interpretations – follow with increasing complexity a pattern that has a parallel at the ontogenetic level in the logic of the development of moral consciousness. A collectively attained stage of moral consciousness can, as long as the continuity of tradition endures, just as little be forgotten as can collectively gained knowledge (which does not exclude regression).[34]

This thesis was discussed elsewhere; in the present state of knowledge it can claim the status only of a working hypothesis.

(2) There is a 'conspicuous asymmetry in the form of reproduction of social life . . . Because the mechanisms which cause developmental advances in normative structures are independent of the *logic* of their development, their exists *a fortiori* no guarantee that a development of the forces of production and an increase of steering capacity will release exactly those normative alterations that correspond to the steering imperatives of the social system . . . We cannot exclude the possibility that a strengthening of productive forces, which heightens the power of the system, can lead to changes in normative structures that simultaneously restrict the autonomy of the system because they bring forth new legitimacy claims and thereby constrict the range of variation of goal values.[35]

Although this thesis is formulated in terms of the theory of social evolution, it claims no more than the possibility of disproportionate political–economic and socio-cultural developments.

(3) Precisely this is happening in advanced capitalism: normative structures are changing in such a way that the complementarity between the requirements of the political—economic system and the legitimate expectations of society's members is breaking down. This of course is the heart of the argument. Restricted to the critical sphere of moral development it asserts:

(a) 'As long as we have to do with a form of socialization that binds inner nature in a communicative organization of behavior, it is inconceivable that there should be a legitimation of any action norm that guarantees, even approximately, an acceptance of decisions without reasons.'[36]

(b) Since liberal capitalism, the need for legitimation of norms can be met only through appeal to universalistic value systems.

(c) Today, the only form of universal morality capable of withstanding the destruction of tradition is a communicative ethics in which all politically significant decisions are tied to the formation of rational consensus in unrestricted discourse.

(d) The basic elements of a communicative ethics are today already influencing typical socialization processes in several social strata, that is, they have achieved 'motive-forming power'.

(e) As a result, the privatistic motivational patterns essential to formal democracy are threatened with disintegration, a threat that can be documented in the spread of withdrawal and protest syndromes.

Each of these assertions is certainly debatable, both on theoretical and on empirical grounds. Even if we grant the systematic points that moral systems follow a developmental logic and that communicative ethics represents the highest stage of this development, we are left with the demonstration that empirical mechanisms are today actually producing this structural alteration in patterns of motive and identity formation. This is clearly an immense undertaking, and Habermas's suggestions do little more than point the way. To mention only two — but two central — considerations: (1) the socio-psychological studies to which he specifically refers in developing the thesis that communicative ethics today has 'motive-forming power' are recent and limited in scope.[37] That they have the long-term and far-reaching implications that he wishes to draw from them is surely not yet established. He does argue more generally that a 'conventional' outcome of the adolescent crisis is becoming increasingly improbable because the expansion of the educational system makes possible an extended 'psychosocial moratorium' for a larger segment of the population, because improved formal schooling increases the probability of dissonance between proffered patterns of interpretation and perceived social reality, and because the spread of non-authoritarian child-rearing techniques, the loosening of sexual prohibitions, and the temporary liberation (for many) from directly economic pressures are transforming socialization processes.[38] But it is clearly too early to predict that these developments will lead to increased withdrawal and protest rather than to some more or less hedonistic accommodation with the system or to other equally functional motivational patterns. In short they seem to be much too ambiguous at present to carry the weight of Habermas's argument.[39]

(2) More generally the alternative posed in *Legitimation Crisis* between acceptance of decisions without reasons and acceptance of decisions as the expression of a rational consensus may well be too broad to capture actually effective motivations. One face of the growing 'cynicism of the bourgeois consciousness' to which Habermas frequently refers might be described as the willingness to accede to a political order *because* it provides an acceptable flow of system-conforming rewards. This too is a reason that can and does serve to legitimate political systems. The point here is not to side with the 'brave new world' theorists against Habermas but to introduce a middle ground: acceptance of decisions for the reason that nothing better seems practically possible in the given circumstances. Even supposing the stage of universal morality to be widespread and granting that natural law and utilitarian interpretations have lost their force, it is difficult to see why the justification of a political order on the grounds that it provides an acceptable (in an imperfect world) distribution of 'primary goods' (Rawls) could not be widely effective in sustaining that order. Appeals to the evident imperfections of the human condition, to the importance of the 'bird in the hand' as opposed to the 'two in the bush', to the advantages of a reformist as opposed to a revolutionary programme, and the like, do not seem to be ruled out either by Habermas's systematic considerations (they have, or could easily be given, a universalistic form) or by his empirical arguments (they seem at present to have at least as much 'motive-forming power' as communicative ethics and counter-cultural motifs) . . .

As the review of *Legitimation Crisis* made clear, Habermas

regards the repoliticization of the public sphere as the potentially most crisis-laden tendency in contemporary capitalist society. The 'syndrome of civil and familial–vocational privacy' is being undermined by (among other things) certain changes in the dominant mode of socialization, changes producing motivational patterns and value orientations that are incompatible with the requirements of the economic and political systems. Youth becomes politically relevant in this situation not as a social class but as a critical phase in the socialization process in which it is decided whether the adolescent crisis has a conventional outcome. Thus the focus is on the passage to adult status in contemporary society and on the factors promoting the formation of post-conventional identities, which are, from a systemic point of view, dysfunctional. But the politically important questions remain open:

> Can the new potentials for conflict and apathy, characterized by withdrawal of motivation and inclination toward protest, and supported by subcultures, lead to a refusal to perform assigned functions on such a scale as to endanger the system as a whole? Are the groups that place in question, possibly passively, the fulfilment of important system functions identical with the groups capable of conscious political action in a crisis situation? Is the process of erosion that can lead to the crumbling of functionally necessary legitimations of domination and motivations to achieve at the same time a process of politicization that creates potentials for action? . . . We have not yet developed sufficiently precise and testable hypotheses to be able to answer these questions empirically.[40]

If the repoliticization of the public sphere is the 'new conflict zone' in organized capitalism; if neither 'the old class antagonism' nor 'the new type of underprivilege' has the potential to 'activate this conflict zone'; and if 'the only protest potential that gravitates toward it' arises among groups whose capacity for conscious political action remains doubtful, critical theory finds itself in a familiar embarrassment; there is no organized social movement whose interests it might seek to articulate.[41] It is this, I believe, that is ultimately behind the generality of Habermas's crisis argument. In the absence of an identifiable 'agent of social transformation', he is forced to remain at the level of pointing out broad crisis tendencies intrinsic to the structure of advanced capitalism. His critique retains an anonymous character, addressed to 'mankind as such' and thus to no group in particular.

In this respect the initial situation of critical theory today is not unlike that in which the earlier members of the Frankfurt school found themselves after the emigration. Habermas's response to it, however, is less pessimistic than was theirs. He has concentrated his considerable energies on developing the positive side of critique and has found reason to believe that the 'total society' is not so 'seamless' after all. In support of this contention he has met the contemporary sciences of man on their own fields and shaped them into a critical consciousness of the age. No better example could be found for Bloch's dictum: 'reason cannot flourish without hope, hope cannot speak without reason.'

NOTES

1 Habermas, *Legitimation Crisis* (Boston, 1975), pp. 45ff.
2 Ibid, p. 49.
3 Ibid, p. 40.
4 Ibid.
5 Ibid, p. 93.
6 Cf. ibid, p. 117, pp. 141–2.
7 Ibid, p. 92.
8 Preface to ibid.
9 Ibid, p. 143. Cf. p. 33, where he writes: 'It is not easy to determine empirically the probability of boundary conditions under which the *possible* crisis tendencies *actually* set in and prevail. The empirical indicators we have at our disposal are as yet inadequate . . . It goes without saying that an argumentation sketch cannot replace empirical investigations, but can be at best a guide to them.'
10 Ibid, p. 2.
11 Ibid. Throughout the book Habermas makes rather free use of systems-theoretic terminology. On the other hand, he argues explicitly that the systems-theoretic approach is inadequate, that it must be integrated with the 'life-world' perspective. 'Both paradigms, life-world and system, are important. The problem is to demonstrate their interconnection' (p. 4). Although Habermas provides a number of suggestions as to how this might be done (cf. pp. 8–17), he has not (nor does he claim to have) yet worked out an integrated general theory. Nevertheless the argument in *Legitimation Crisis* is constructed with such a theory in view; aspects of both self-regulation and symbolic interaction figure essentially in it. One could argue, however, that the life-world perspective predominates, since the crisis argument depends on action-theoretic assumptions developed in the theory of communication.
12 Ibid, p. 4.
13 What follows is Habermas's interpretation, in his terminology.

14 Ibid, p. 22. This is not to say that the bourgeois ideology of the inherent justice of the market was effective in all social classes: 'The loyalty and subordination of the members of the new urban proletariat, recruited mainly from the ranks of peasants, were certainly maintained more through a mixture of traditionalistic ties, fatalistic willingness to follow, lack of perspective, and naked repression than through the convincing force of bourgeois ideologies' (p. 22).

15 Ibid, p. 26.

16 Ibid, p. 29.

17 Ibid, pp. 56–7.

18 Ibid, p. 57.

19 Ibid, p. 62.

20 Ibid, p. 64.

21 Ibid, p. 36.

22 Ibid, p. 37.

23 Ibid, p. 75.

24 Ibid, pp. 47–8. As he puts it in 'Legitimation problems in the modern state'. *Communication and the Evolution of Society*, pp. 178–204, the state is perceived as generally responsible for shortcomings and for their removal (pp. 194–5).

25 Ibid, p. 72.

26 Ibid, p. 72.

27 Ibid, p. 70.

28 Ibid, p. 69.

29 Ibid, pp. 74–5.

30 Ibid, p. 93.

31 Ibid, pp. 43–4. Habermas does not deny that 'whether legitimations are believed certainly depends on empirical motives'; he wants to insist, however, that the latter 'are not shaped independently of the reasons that can be mobilized'. *Legitimation Problems*, p. 183.

32 Ibid, p. 77.

33 Ibid, p. 85.

34 Ibid, p. 12. In *Legitimation Problems* he makes a related point in terms of a hierarchy of 'levels of justification', that is, of 'formal conditions for the acceptability of reasons that lend to legitimations their effectiveness, their power to produce consensus and shape motives', p. 184. The kind of reason effective at one level loses its power to convince at the next; at present he wants to argue, only the 'procedural type of legitimation', that is, the appeal to free agreement among equals, is effective.

35 Ibid, pp. 12–13.

36 Ibid, p. 43. The qualifying phrase 'as long as we have to do with' is an allusion to the 'end of the individual' thesis discussed in part III of ibid.

37 Cf. ibid, pp. 90ff.

38 Ibid, p. 90.

39 Habermas admits as much on p. 129 of ibid.

40 *Theory and Practice*, pp. 6–7. In the same passage he raises a series of

open questions concerning the potential for political action within the working class.

41 The terminology in quotation marks appears in 'Technology and science as "ideology"', *Toward a Rational Society* (Boston, 1970), p. 120. For Habermas's views on the student movement, see *Protestbewegung und Hochschulreform* (Frankfurt, 1969), parts of which were translated in chapters 1 to 3 of *Toward a Rational Society*. In general his position is that (a) the situation of organized capitalism is not 'revolutionary'; (b) 'radical reformism' is at present the only way to bring about conscious structural change; (c) for this a repoliticization of the public sphere is necessary; and (d) student protest can and did serve this end. Apart from this active role in politicizing the public sphere, student protest is important as a symptom of fundamental changes in the socialization process that are undermining the orientations to achievement and possessive individualism and eroding formal–democratic and technocratic legitimations. While Habermas developed both of these perspectives in his writings of the late sixties, his more recent writings stress the social–psychological potential rather than the active political role of youth.

8

On the 'Legitimation Crisis'

GEORGE KATEB

Is there a 'legitimation crisis' in the United States, as some say? There would be, if there were deep and widespread feelings and opinions marked by disaffection from or hostility to the constitutive principles and informing spirit of the country's political arrangements. It is true that other arrangements – other institutions and practices – may come within the scope of feelings and opinions concerning legitimacy. Indeed, there may be a legitimation crisis in non-political institutions without an effect on political institutions, just as the reverse may obtain. It is likely, however, that if there is a legitimation crisis at all, that crisis will affect many of society's arrangements and institutions, political and non-political, but attain its most visible and focused and therefore most vivid expression politically. Sooner or later the crisis will find its way into the political sphere, whether in the form of constitutional conflict or principled withdrawal or both. So it is not arbitrary or reductively 'politicist' – to adapt the notion of 'economism' – to begin with the crisis of basic political arrangements, if there is a legitimation crisis at all – or, at least, if theorists and analysts say there is. In any case, the natural home of the concept of legitimacy is politics despite the common usage concerning the status of children. The elementary fact is that the word is derived from the Latin word for law.

I realize that I am not using the phrase exactly as its originator, Jürgen Habermas, uses it. My belief, however, is that, if one is to examine the condition of legitimacy in a society, one must look first to the state of repair of its basic political principles before diagnosing specific ailments, no matter how severe they may appear to be. At the same time, a discussion of political principles must reach to questions of culture and personality.

Source: George Kateb, 'On the "legitimation crisis"', *Social Research* (Winter, 1979), reprinted with permission of *Social Research*.

IS THERE A CRISIS?

Is there, then, a legitimation crisis affecting constitutional representative democracy in the United States? The question is not really answerable. To put it abstractly, a legitimation crisis need not be a definite thing; it need not be a clearly manifested condition. It could exist without full explicitness, without people knowing how really disaffected or hostile they were. In the past, great political and social convulsions have sometimes come as a surprise to everyone, including the disaffected and the hostile. Some incident or opportunity, or some quick, sharp change in condition was needed to crystallize and then to energize the sentiments of crisis. Is the condition of the United States now such that some comparatively slight event or shift could lead to a revolutionary transformation? We cannot say with any certainty.

A plausible guess would be that the United States is not at all ripe for a thoroughgoing change in its basic political arrangements. It would seem, that is, that there are not deep and widespread feelings and opinions marked by disaffection from and hostility to constitutional representative democracy. It would seem, furthermore, that even some grave emergency – to leave aside nuclear war – would not detach the people from their present acceptance, commitments, and loyalties.

There are very few movements – and they are small and usually short-lived – that expressly proclaim their rejection of the principles and spirit of constitutional representative democracy. The conventional way of talking about these movements is in the vocabulary of psychopathology or social psychology, as if to say that the phenomenon was not one of reason, judgement, or self-interest, but rather of personal abnormality or mutilation or aggravated failure. That way of talking may be heartless; it may even be deceived by the distorted appearances of what may be genuinely human fears and needs. But that is nevertheless the prevalent way. If these movements were felt to be more threatening, some other more ample and nuanced way of talking might be found; or, alternatively, the desire to understand them might be extinguished by the much greater desire to resist and destroy them. At present, the Nazis, the Klan, the violent Black or White left are marginal; while groups that are not regularly political, like the People's Temple or the Manson family, but are political in part of their meaning and relevance, are episodic, evanescent – though we may be sure that groups like them will continue to emerge. We may be sure, if for no other reason than that such groups have always existed in American society.

But to mention the people (on the one hand) or minor radical groups (on the other hand) is not to dispose of the question as to whether there is a legitimation crisis in the United States. The fact is that there is significant, or potentially significant, disaffection from, and hostility to, constitutional, representative democracy among intellectuals. I refer to the authoritarian right-of-centre and to the radical left. I do not mean to pin labels on individuals. I do not mean to do an even worse thing, to locate moral and political truth in the centre, as if to say that, of course, where there seems to be an avoidance of extremism there must be moral and political truth, or that a commitment to the idea of constitutional, representative democracy is, necessarily, a commitment without extremism. That would be to make that idea into one of compromise, and thus not to understand it. On the contrary, in some important ways, there is commonality between right-of-centre and left that helps to define the uniqueness of constitutional democracy. I do mean, instead, to suggests that there may still be some convenient sense in using the old terms of left and right, even though, in our case, the right is not conservative; it is nearly as disaffected from and hostile to the established principles and spirit as the left is. At the same time, the substantial confinement of disaffection and hostility to some intellectuals is not, in itself, evidence of the lack of practical importance in their arguments. They may be simply more prescient, more sensitive to dangers, now or in the future; they may feel now what many others are bound to feel some day. Our concern must be with the merits of their arguments; and only a detailed examination can settle the matter of merits.

We cannot provide that detailed examination here. It must be sufficient to engage in some very incomplete itemization. First of all, we should distinguish, from all the itemized elements, the matter of secret official lawlessness, especially when it reaches to the violation of constitutional rights. We must assume that in the context of the national-security state, constitutional rights are in constant jeopardy, not because security requires occasional violation or steady attenuation, but because national security is a superb pretext for unnecessary violation or attenuation that officeholders seek for other reasons. These reasons include personal or partisan advantage; revulsion at dissent; a paranoid disposition; a casual lack of scruples on behalf of some policy; a passion to experiment on people for the sake of an unclean curiosity or at the behest of an urge to manipulate; a wish to provoke extreme action in order to have expensive enemies as well as to discourage the tamer dissidents; and so on. Secret official lawlessness, when discovered, may clothe itself in principles and arguments; but almost always they are rationalizations. They do not inspire behaviour; though, to be sure, they may subsequently inspire the behaviour of others. The phenomenon of secret official lawlessness is grave in its importance, in itself and as a display of present mentality and future possibility. But, for us here, the phenomenon is not part of the legitimation crisis, just because it is not principled. Our interest is in those intellectuals whose disaffection or hostility *is* principled.

Second, we should distinguish public and legal claims made by the government with regard to its own rightful powers. Sometimes these claims precede official behaviour; sometimes they come afterwards; sometimes they do not issue in behaviour, but are merely stated. What is at issue here is a willingness to take advantage of the silence or ambiguity of the Constitition or the laws to do, or to claim the right to do, deeds that seem to be anti-constitutional in their spirit. The motives need not be corrupt; rather, they tend to be a wish to get a job done no matter what, or to explore the permissions of the Constitution with the hope that they are broader than commonly assumed. Just to confine ourselves to the Carter administration, we can mention such matters as the now-abandoned intention to allow any government agency to make into a condition of employment the need to submit manuscripts written for publication for prior scrutiny; the prosecution of Snepp; the prosecution of *The Progressive* magazine; the use of financial support to claim ownership of cryptographically relevant research in mathematics, and thus to prevent its publication; and the manifold effort to achieve in a piecemeal way the substantial effects of an official secrets act, an official immunity act, and a recognition of an inherent executive power to engage in certain kinds of surveillance or preventive action. The most lurid gesture of all, perhaps, is supporting the claim that congressional aides, under cover of congressional immunity, may commit burglary or murder in the line of duty. All these occurrences have antecedents or precedents in earlier administrations, which also contain abundant examples of anti-constitutional claims now quiescent. Perhaps the most audacious of these is Nixon's assertion, in a brief, of the sovereignty of the office of the Presidency. To claim that the American government may assert sovereignty over the American people shatters the constitutional framework, as Hannah Arendt has most recently reminded us; but to claim that the President is the locus of such sovereignty in the government is a desperate stratagem of megalomania.

I do not mean that all actions undertaken by any branch of government that are later found unconstitutional by a court are animated by an anti-constitutional attitude. The boundaries of constitutional action are not always clear.

Principled and unprincipled anti-constitutional claims and conduct by the government are deeply disturbing. But as long as the will to resist them exists in the government itself and in the public, and the resistance is successful to some degree, we perhaps need not think that we are faced with a legitimation crisis. When we turn our attention to intellectuals and publicists, we encounter a genuine crisis. My attention will be critical. I only hope that, in preparing an itemization of feelings and opinions I find adversary to the principles and spirit of constitutional democracy, I am not myself guilty of inconsistency. I hope that I do not show an accusatory tendency of intolerance. Doubtless the accused can take care of themselves. Let us consider the right-of-centre first.

ATTRITION FROM THE RIGHT

Schematically put, the right-of-centre hates much of what is going on in America. In hating what goes on, these intellectuals and publicists actually hate the life and civilization of constitutional democracy, though they do not usually think that that is what they hate. Some believe, to the contrary, that there is a legitimation crisis among the people, a mass disaffection from or hostility to the principles of constitutional democracy. But their elaborated responses, inspired by their strong dislikes, show, I think, that a legitimation crisis exists among them.

The collective and undiscriminating name for the intellectuals and publicists on the right-of-centre is authoritarianism. Some forms of authoritarianism are anti-constitutional in emphasis; others are anti-democratic, though these forms blend into each other. It is by no means the case that those who are anti-constitutional are characteristically extreme majoritarians or even pro-democratic, or that those who are anti-democratic are characteristically pro-constitutional or extreme affirmers of individual rights and limited government. Whatever may have been the pattern in the past, anti-democratic and anti-constitutional sentiments and ideas are combined or appear compatible. That is to say, the anti-constitutionalists are not believers in the authority of the people and their representatives; and the anti-democrats are not believers in the authority of the principles of constitutionalism. The authoritarians believe in authority or authorities of different kinds.

There is variety among the anti-democratic authoritarians. Main aspects of their tendency are caught by Ralf Dahrendorf in his comments on the Trilateral Commission's report, *The Crisis of Democracy*. He says, in some gentle mockery, that democracies '. . . have to avoid the belief that a little more unemployment, a little less education, a little more deliberate discipline, and a little less freedom of expression would make the world a better place, in which it is possible to govern effectively'. He has in mind the authors of the report (Crozier, Huntington, and Watanuki), but not only them. In the background is the theory of democratic elitism, the theory of the irony of democracy, present as early as the forties. Democracy is best when it is not fully itself, when many do not participate, and most lack all passionate intensity. The true democrats are the few; upon them democracy rests. If the many had their way, democracy would not exist except in licentiousness or spasms of majoritarian intolerance. I know that is a rather crude caricature, but I do not think it betrays the underlying sentiment.

More recently, new strands have appeared: newly conceived or newly introduced or reintroduced into American discourse. If the theory of democratic elitism, in its unconscious way, already reflected a rather deep disaffection from the spirit of democracy but not its principles, other kinds of elitism challenge both spirit and principles. *The Crisis of Democracy* shows an authoritarianism of order. In his contribution, Samuel P. Huntington writes as if democracy were a form of government that left the very notion of governance unaffected. Thus democracy is one possible means for achieving the universal ends that other forms may also achieve. The ends are several, but the overarching end is preservation: preservation of the established order and of the country's place in international competition. Like other forms of government, democratic government governs, it rules; its citizens are subjects. Huntington never considers the possibility that rule itself, in the sense associated with all other forms of government, may be theoretically out of place in a democracy, or find a new place and hence a new meaning. The possibility is foreign to him and his colleagues. If democracy means self-rule by a people, then rule is not what it is elsewhere. Self-rule may be imperfect or even badly damaged by the concurrent existence of dissonant economic and social institutions and arrangements. Yet, in theory at least, democratic citizens rule themselves in a constitutional representative democracy.

The key point is that authority is attached only to offices; and to offices created by a popularly enacted and maintained constitution, filled by popularly decided contests, and held for limited purposes and periods. Authority exists on popular sufferance and by means of universal suffrage. It is granted by those over whom it is exercised. It cannot therefore be rule as non-democratic polities understand rule. It is ludicrous behaviourism to believe that government in the United States and the Soviet Union (for example) do the same things but in different ways under different names. The assimilation of democracy to other forms of government shows a pronounced authoritarian tendency, and therewith a terrific hostility to constitutional democracy. If large numbers of intellectuals and other people thought like Huntington and his colleagues, there would in truth be a widespread legitimation crisis.

Related to Huntington's kind of authoritarianism is that found in various presentations in the *Daedalus* volume, *Toward the Year 2000: Work in Progress* (1967), and in writings by Zbigniew Brzezinski and others. The authority affirmed here is that of experts, those with superior technical knowledge of diverse kinds. The stress is on the intractable complexity of social life where all is interdependent, the scale of everything is enlarged, all things are in constant motion and ferment, and the alternatives appear ever more to be chaos and regimented adaptation. A firm and knowing hand is needed if collapse is to be avoided. The people do not know what they need; and if they did they would not have the will or self-control to achieve it. Present in this tendency of thought is the belief that democracy has outlived its plausibility, though its death may proceed somewhat gradually. More and more, public policy is inevitably and rightly withdrawn from the judgement of the people. Thus the democracy is preparing for its own substantial supersession. This outlook incorporates an attitude that mixes adventurousness and slavishness. On the one hand, there is an overpowering appetite to exploit new human potencies, to push virtuosity to the limit, to construct and dismantle new realities, to redefine humanity by constantly demonstrating the illimitability of its creativeness. In truth, such adventurousness is entirely consonant with democratic life. On the other hand, however, there is submission to the apparent logic of the next step, to so-called 'technological imperatives', to the unstated and only dimly suspected maxim that anything that can be done should be done, or must be done, or will, perhaps, really be done in spite of what anyone wants. (There is a confusion of moods.) The slavishness vitiates the adventurousness. The result of this outlook is to disparage and condemn as obsolete the very idea of politics as the locus of human consciousness and purposiveness in common affairs. Theorists of expertise believe that the more politics respects a self-denying ordinance, the more it moves to resemble organization, the more it denatures itself, the better. Obviously, democratic politics least resembles organization, at least theoretically; while human potencies are, paradoxically, most encouraged and most developed in democratic societies. Thus the lesson that politics must reduce itself is learned hardest in democracies. The real lesson that the *Daedalus* participants want learned is: democracy must reduce itself in order to expand the role of the knowledgeable elite. Thus intoxication with the possibilities of technical action leads to disdain toward the arrangements that frame democratic political action. And the deepening attachment to the organizational model among technical and entrepreneurial intellectuals and semi-intellectuals — the disaffection from democracy, from the mass of citizens not initiated into the work of elaborating human technical potencies — increases. In the long run, this may be the most serious expression of the legitimation crisis.

The last kind of authoritarianism I would mention is that articulated by some of the students and admirers of Leo Strauss. This is an authoritarianism of moral elitism. In some of the essays in Strauss's *Liberalism Ancient and Modern* and elsewhere, Strauss gives voice to opinions that seem unfriendly to ordinary people, opinions that are illiberal in the sense of being ungenerous. Doubtless there are intimations of some larger scepticism toward the demos in the body of Strauss's work, explicitly counterbalanced only occasionally, as in the remarkable tribute he pays to Athenian democracy in the ninth section of his chapter on Thucydides in *The City and Man*. Be that as it may, one can find in, say, the collection of essays *On Civil Disobedience*, edited by Robert A. Goldwin, and containing contributions by Harry Jaffa and Herbert Storing, among others, an attitude that does not strike me as compatible with democratic sentiments. I think a suitable way of designating this kind of authoritarianism is to call it paternalist. The quasi-Madisonian supposition, never defended, is that officeholders, lawmakers, will tend to be wiser in moral knowledge than the people and, whatever appearances, will use their offices to codify and enforce almost the entire range of morality and thus instruct and restrain and altogether improve a hedonist and transgressive population. This attitude is anti-libertarian, of course; but it also rests on an untroubled but unjustified confidence concerning the moral life. What is involved is hardly a defence of moral absolutism against the ravages of relativism: after all, constitutional democracy itself is a political embodiment of a certain kind of moral absolutism, the absolute value of a number of rights acknowledged to belong indefeasibly to all universally, despite any utilitarian or prudential temptation to abridge or deny them. No, what is involved, instead, is a superstitious and perhaps residually Kantian belief that every moral question whatever has one and only one right answer, and that officeholders will tend to know it and try to get the rest to behave as if they knew it, too. The Law is divinized, and, by extension, the laws are reverenced.

The democratic understanding that laws are only 'memoranda' to the people, to use Emerson's concept, and that policies are only human responses to emergencies, problems, and opportunities, is abandoned. Replacing this understanding is the sense that the government should be an all-noticing and supremely confident moral tutor. Gone from this approach to the moral life is a willingness to distinguish between those few moral questions that have one and only one right answer from those that have a range of putatively right answers (including, sometimes, sharply contrasting ones); those that are indeterminate, open-ended, and amenable only to provisional or radically imprecise answers; and those that are not answerable at all. (There is likely to be dispute over which category some questions belong to.) If the latter three categories of moral questions are ignored or theorized out of existence, the raw material of democratic politics, its pretext if not its real reason for being, is theoretically suppressed. No place is left for the contests between those who are morally equal or nearly so: the contests over public policies and rules that are characteristically moral at bottom and morally problematic. We are left with, at best, a qualified and circumstantial acceptance of constitutional, representative democracy . . .

Just to stay with the authoritarian right-of-centre, for the moment, we can point to, first, the advocacy in the report of the Trilateral Commission of a return to a strong use by public officials of the law of libel in order to induce the press to show what the author calls more 'responsibility'. He does not use the phrase 'seditious libel', but he might just as well have. In *Twilight of Authority*, Robert Nisbet, a prominent authoritarian, relegates free speech to a lesser status than other rights, thus reversing the preferred-position doctrine; and by doing that, calling into question the *sine qua non* of constitutional democracy and therefore the moral necessity for constitutional democracy. He describes free speech as an individual right merely, as if all its exercises were private; and in a curious simile, he likens it to a circus – that is, a distraction from more important matters like the right to hold a job. There is also the position associated with Walter Berns (especially in *Freedom, Virtue and the First Amendment*), which holds that only persons worthy of free speech should have the right of free speech; and that what makes a person worthy is his espousal of ideas that are either compatible with the preservation of the Constitution as right-of-centre authoritarians interpret it or supportive of it. Ideas that are incompatible are deemed either subversive or incendiary; in either case, vicious or false; and as such liable to political regulation. Only truth has rights, and the truth is never in doubt. But the 'truth' here is not the view of truth associated with the theorists of freedom as the foundational value, as the essence of constitutional democracy. If Berns persuaded us to act on his principles, his writings would be the first to be suppressed.

Even this inventory of recent authoritarian thought – limited and reductive as it is, and inattentive to the abundant historical antecedents – can perhaps serve a purpose: that is, to show how much anti-democratic and anti-constitutional disaffection and hostility there is on the right-of-centre. A highly gifted segment of American intellectuals and publicists is engaged in a war of attrition with the form and spirit of constitutional, representative democracy. The government of the American Constitution is conceived as itself the crisis: the source of danger to order, world power, anticommunism, economic efficiency, technological greatness, virtue, and truth. Freedom is treated as, at most, one value in a cluster of values; and thus reduced by not being seen as both the morally indispensable precondition of attaining all other values and importantly constitutive of the persons who seek to attain all other values. The civilization of freedom is rejected. There would really be a legitimation crisis if these sentiments and opinions were widespread and reflexive. But so far they are not.

ATTACK FROM THE LEFT

On the radical left there is, *by definition*, disaffection and hostility. We cannot therefore be surprised. There would be cause for surprise only if radical left sentiments and opinions were widespread and reflexive. They are not, just as authoritarian sentiments and opinions are not. But authoritarian sentiments and opinions appear to be much closer to the principles of constitutional democracy, a shading of them, rather than wholly discontinuous. I do not think that the appearance is entirely faithful to the reality. Let us say, however, that some authoritarians of the right-of-centre have more moments when they seem wholly within the elastic and ample range of constitutional and democratic principles than do many on the radical left. At the same time, if America lapses, it is hugely more likely to fall into right-of-centre, or even right authoritarianism than left radicalism. So that a student of the prospects of constitutional democracy in America had better pay more attention to the right-of-centre than to the radical left if he is a pessimist.

Yet I am not mainly interested in presenting a thesis on the possible future of constitutional democracy. (I will touch on the matter briefly at the end.) Consequently, I would turn here to a very few aspects of the radical left disaffection and hostility in order to balance the inventory. The left is the source of the concept of legitimation crisis, but many distinctions must be made. One set of distinctions is between the revolutionary left, the reconstructionist left, and the disappointed left. Another distinction is between those who really want a new life that does not resemble that which grows up in a society committed, at least in theory, to the principles of constitutional democracy and those who are not entirely clear about the society they want and about what they would keep from the society of constitutional democracy and what they would throw out. Another distinction is between those whose critique is so conceptually foreign to the principles of constitutional democracy as to deny them the capacity to stimulate reformist sentiment and those whose radicalism, though considerable, still can challenge adherents of constitutional democracy to examine themselves without thinking that they must undergo a conversion before they can profit from the radicalism. Yet another distinction is between those who believe there is a legitimation crisis among the people and those who lament popular docility or co-optation.

I am not able to delineate the situation of the radical left with the care and subtlety it needs. Instead, I would flatten the necessary distinctions by saying, first, that just as an anti-democratic and anti-constitutional trust in authority seems to unify the divergent elements of the right-of-centre, so anticapitalism seems to unify the elements on the radical left. Howsoever those on the left may differ as regards the considerations I have just noticed, they join in rejecting modern corporate capitalism. Obviously there is, at first sight, an asymmetry between right and left: the right is directly political while the left appears to focus its critical energies on the economic system. But the matter is not settled by the appearance, even though the appearance is not deceiving. The attack on capitalism, as it unfolds, turns into an implicit attack on the form and spirit of constitutional democracy. This is not to say that an attack on any aspect of capitalism whatever is necessarily an attack on constitutional democracy. I am not even prepared to say outright that, in modern circumstances, constitutional democracy must coexist with corporate capitalism if it is to exist at all; though I think the preponderance of plausible conjecture is on the side of this assertion. Though, for a while, capitalism could get on without constitutional democracy, the reverse is much more dubious. The radical attack on capitalism is an attack on constitutional democracy because in its moral indictment of capitalism it repudiates certain attitudes toward the self that are protected and encouraged by capitalism. These attitudes, I believe, are necessary components of a larger conception of self that is at once peculiarly suited to constitutional democracy and represents its highest attainment – a self that needs and is needed for constitutional democracy. (Doubtless the authoritarian right-of-centre is at war with the self of constitutional democracy, but not as fundamentally.)

There is no constitutional democracy without the idea of 'the abstract individual', an idea frequently attacked by radical theorists under Marx's inspiration. Unless it is correct to posit the individual as the basic unit in the discourse of moral and political philosophy and in the deliberations of both everyday life and public policy, there is no constitutional democracy. Furthermore, general or abstract rights and duties must be seen as helping to constitute the individual self. The self must be envisaged, for the purpose of initial reflection, as demarcated, fenced in, distinct, besieged, claimant. The essence of these abstractions is the creation of moral distance between the self and everyone and every convention around it. The self must be taught to think of itself as a self in distinction from, in likely contrast to, in frequent opposition to, other selves, private and public. The negative capabilities, so to speak, must be cultivated, so that each self learns how to say no, how to dissent and disagree without shame, how to resist immersion of self, loss of self, in thoughtless, unthinking endeavours. Is there, in the circumstances of industrial civilization, any economic system other than capitalism that requires and fosters the sense of self as demarcated and besieged? I know of none, in practice or theory.

Closely related to this foregoing aspect of self is the attitude that one owns oneself, one has inalienable property in oneself, to employ Locke's notion. The benefit of this attitude is that society may avoid the condition in which individuals think of themselves as owned by others, by the rest, by the state dressed in the prestige of authority – authority that is pervasive and all-infecting, whether or not it is centralized or federated, coercive or manipulative, blatant or friendly. The sense of being owned, which the Russian emigré dissident Andrei Amalrik found dominant in the Soviet Union, is akin to a general servility. This manifests itself in the total enclosure of the individual in the role of member; and if all one is is a member, then one is merely a means to the ends of others. If all are members and, more terribly, members of one organization – if they live in society as if it were one organization – the maximum of servility has been achieved. The acceptance of victimage, the subtle assent to arbitrary treatment, the courageous but self-destructive reconciliation to unjust imprisonment and punishment, is simply the logical extension of this servility, as Nadezhda Mandelstam has so powerfully shown in Hope Against Hope. The sense spreads that one should have no purposes but common ones or external ones; that one has to live one's life as if one were repaying a debt and could repay that debt only by thinking one lived in order to do good to others constantly. One would always be living in the presence of and under the surveillance of others, transparent to others, unknown to oneself. The self would never emerge; there would be an inhuman loss of personal identity. There would not be a practised 'doubleness' within the self, the self watching the self to make sure it never loses itself to mindless activity, but preserves its independence. Once again, the self-owning self seems to accompany the institutions of capitalism in the modern age.

The self that is besieged and self-owning is the self suited to constitutional democracy, though it would be wrong to estimate a kind of self only because it met the requirements of a form of government. There is a reinforcing mutuality in the relationship. What makes the relationship all the richer is that the form of government, though not the end for which individuals live, is nevertheless itself not merely a means to the ends of policy but also a crystallization of moral relationships that are valuable apart from all policies.

Yet one must acknowledge that the self that is besieged and self-owning is also the acquisition and consumerist self: what C. B. Macpherson has called 'the possessive individual'. If capitalism seems the only economic system that preserves the self suited to constitutional democracy, it also damages the self by imprisoning it in economic fixations and fetishisms, and thus wasting its putative independence on an atomized competitiveness rather than encouraging its flow of energies into citizenship. That damage, someone like Macpherson can say, is much greater than any benefit for human character that could possibly be extracted from the capitalist economic system. I think that there is substance in this argument: the kind of stimulus to non-radical thought that some radical thought provides. Still, I would say that, great as the damage is, the benefit is inextricably intertwined with it; and that the benefit is so important to humanity as a whole that any cost must be paid to keep it alive, for the sake of those who have it, and to keep it present to human consciousness in all those places where it does not exist. After all, what is the legitimation crisis, as Habermas defines it, if not the continuous growth of the demand for an accounting, the growth of the expectation that authority will be rational and explicit and 'discursive', the growth of the demand for participation? He thinks that political authority in capitalist societies cannot cope with the rush of these demands, that the system will die from its very successes. He does not mean, in the Marxist sense, that the capitalist system furnishes its own grave-diggers by creating both an impoverished mass and the capitalistically unusable capacity to abolish poverty. No, rather, in Habermas's account, the people become ever *richer* – that is, morally and intellectually richer, at least from a rationalist perspective – and demand more of what they have grown to expect. These expectations are the fruit of the self that is besieged and self-owning. Such a self has grotesque wastes and distortions, just as the economic system that helps to engender that self has systemic wastes and distortions that are grotesque. But I do not believe there is an alternative.

Some radicals would say there is slight evidence, if any at all, of the self that answers to my description. The most sustained accusation of the selves we are and see around us is found, perhaps, in Marcuse's *One-Dimensional Man*. Marcuse achieves an internally coherent depiction, one that shows considerable quasi-literary powers of projection. But I do not think that American reality has borne him out. American society has more than once struck observers as, in Tocqueville's words, agitated and monotonous, as doomed to dance the same old dance while proclaiming its variety and independence. Yet how could a society without strong class distinctions ever appear to the observer steeped in old Europe to be anything but one-dimensional? In several senses, some ironic, the one-dimensional society is the classless society. If that perspective is abandoned, however, who would be prepared to see in the record of American experience the condition Marcuse posits? Of course, there is forfeiture of the opportunities of freedom in a capitalist society and their conversion into vulgarity, trash, perversion, shallow sociability, remote and automatic cruelty. That is only to say, again, that the costs of capitalism are immense, though capitalism is hardly the sole source of these human failures . . .

RADICAL HEROISM

To repeat the original contention: there is a legitimation crisis among numbers of intellectuals and publicists of the right-of-centre and the radical left in the United States. They combine in their abandonment of the spirit of constitutional, representative democracy. They want what that form of government and that distinctive civilization do not and cannot give. All the authoritarians want authority; they want the sovereign state of European practice and European political theory. Many radical Socialists want social control, social coherence, society or community, not as Europe has experienced these arrangements and institutions in practice and theory, but as European radicalism, rooted in spite of itself in European attitudes, has imagined them. The legitimation crisis results when intellectuals and publicisits look at America and fail to see either a state or a society as Europe has lived or conceptualized either of them. Failing to see what their theory predisposes them to want, they claim to see a legitimation crisis. The authoritarians see ungovernability or wasteful interference with technological logic or promiscuous self-indulgence. They do not see the moderated anarchy that has always constituted American life. Radical socialists see self-seeking or privatism or conformist cowardice or exploitation. They too do not see the moderated anarchy that has always constituted American life.

Correspondingly, the troubles, the failures and forfeitures, of America are not those of Europe. Iran seems to have had a genuine legitimation crisis; it may be that Italy and West Germany are now having one, and that France had one erupt in 1968. In all these cases, the prevailing arrangements were or are challenged by masses of people, and challenged on behalf of principles discontinuous with those of the prevailing arrangements. Iran seems to be saying, We do not want to become Americans. If one is to judge by some of the art and rhetoric of Germany, especially the films of Wim Wenders, the same thing is being said, left and right: 'We cannot be Americans; we do not know how; we turn into pigs if we try; we cannot abolish the old expectation that government will be sovereign and that society will be orderly and tight and stable and not convey that feeling of unreality that American society conveys. Only Americans know how to be American. We must go on living in the Old World.' That may be all to the good. But these sentiments are European; they are not suited to constitutional democracy in America. I really doubt whether they are suitable for constitutional democracy anywhere, if constitutional democracy is the name not only of a form of government but of a distinctive civilization, of a distinctive ensemble of human relationships that everywhere shows at least traces of the spirit of constitutional democracy. The legitimation crisis in the Old World may stem from basically reactionary feelings and opinions.

Habermas's characterization of the crisis may thus partly suit America and partly suit the Old World. The constant demand for rationality and explicitness in government is certainly present in America; but this demand has always aggressively existed, whatever the scope of government activity. If there is a crisis, it is the same crisis that has existed from the beginning. On the other hand, demand for greater government control of more and more aspects of life may be present in Europe and elsewhere; but this demand we have always associated with the Old World. If there is a crisis there now, it may be for the reasons implicit in Habermas: the loss of the psychological surety that grew out of the class system and a concomitant desire to have the state somehow make good the loss. In any case, seeing what they think they see and failing to see the continuity between the past and the present and thus failing to see the present, intellectuals and publicists also fail to glimpse the essential radical heroism of American life. That radical heroism emanates from the sense of self to which I have already referred. I have so far mentioned only its negative components: not blending into others, not being owned by others. The negative components are the precondition for something positive, for, precisely, a radical heroism. Of course, the heroism is not the aristocratic or great-man heroism of Europe but some other kind or kinds.

What then is the heroism of the civilization of constitutional democracy? What are the positive components of the sense of self that go with the negative components? Any answer must be prosaic, formulaic, and sound tired and hackneyed. Despite that, the theorists of the legitimation crisis (left and right) compel the flat utterance. Three components stand out under the pressure of left and right: first, the voluntary principle; second, the exploration of extremes; and third, the cultivation of a philosophical relation to reality. With the emergence of a society in which many selves attain, though in varying degrees, the negative ones first and then, climactically, the positive ones, the arrangements of constitutional democracy complete their vindication.

For the most ramified conceptualization of the voluntary principle we go to Tocqueville. He helps us to see what tens of thousands see without his conceptualization, without his coaching. The voluntary principle is, precisely, the substitute for the sovereign state and the traditionally ordered society of Europe. Relations are subject to consent, and are limited and maybe temporary. The arts of cooperation merge with the arts of interaction and elicit and reward energies, not all of them self-seeking. Unless reality is consciously created, it does not exist. The distinction between what is best in private life and what is best in public life is blurred, as each sphere of life is asked to show the influence of the other. Unless consent were the heart of the matter, the democratic fluidity of all relations, public and private, would not be possible. The contribution of the New Left to this moral idea was powerful and completely in accord with the best inherited American idealism.

We go to another foreigner for the best conceptualization of the idea that the American self is an explorer of extremes: D. H. Lawrence in his inexhaustibly rich book, *Studies in Classic American Literature* (1922). He shows how the absence of the European state and European society liberate the American from the middle world and send him into the recesses of the psyche and the unexplored mysteries of nature. The American characteristically seeks to experiment with himself and with natural reality, and thus touches the polar extremes of savagery and self-consciousness, rapacity and etherealization. Loneliness inevitably fills the adventurous self. Yet the sum of extreme experience added to the human record justifies the pain endured and inflicted. The American self enlarges humanity.

The philosophical relation to reality includes the voluntary principle and the will to be adventurous, and never loses all connection to the feeling of being besieged and the insistence on imagining oneself self-owned. But it goes beyond all these components to something higher; and that is expressed in related but individuated ways by Emerson, Thoreau, and Whitman. These three are the greatest theorists of the civilization of constitutional democracy because they are the greatest poets of the philosophical self — not the philosophical self simply, but the philosophical self that suits the form and spirit of constitutional democracy. Above everything, that self is able to talk about itself in sentences and leaves as little as possible to the heavy comfort of mute customs and traditions. The philosophical self never loses itself to experience but remains somewhat detached from it: 'Both in and out of the game and watching and wondering at it', in the great words of Whitman in 'Song of Myself'. These are indications of the self as master of its experience, master not of others and not of itself in a stoic or repressed grimness, but retrospective master, able and desirous to convert experience into words; and by incessant practice, influencing – gradually and to some degree – the ways in which the self experiences. The ideal is reached when the self is energized by its detachment and becomes fully serious because philosophically playful. It lives at home as if home were the open road. It is irrepressibly generous because of its reserve, its refusal to be serious as the world ordinarily understands seriousness. No pretence is made that all people, all the time, and with equal commitment, live out the promptings of the philosophical self. So much conspires to block the road, especially the fevers of money-making. But people have their moments and their longings. Even when possessed by money-making, they may betray a lightness that removes their behaviour from the reach of such a category as greed. In all activities Americans seem abstract: that is one of the most frequently recurrent judgements found in poetry and fiction about this country and in the best sociology. One has only to read, for example, Sennett and Cobb's *The Hidden Injuries of Class* to detect this peculiar dignity that consists in seeing oneself, seeing through oneself, seeing around one's situation, and thus prepared to talk self-consciously about one's life.

The American self is a loose-fitting self. Americans are characteristically unformed, restless, self-doubting, and constantly putting on some new aspect only to discard it as unfitting. The scene has its own aesthetic but it is not likely to satisfy the sensibility of old Europe. Europe and the whole Old World are built on roles: more roles than American society clearly has and consciously defines; roles that are more sharply differentiated from each other; roles that are more fully or more permanently enacted. Such a society is anti-universalist in its ethic, and may make for a more full-bodied array of character types and social types than American society does. But what of the insides? Where is the greater average richness, the greater average freely playing consciousness? Is it clear that the answer is, Not America? American thinness goes together with American wildness, and both conduce, it seems to me, to a greater reflectiveness in the average person. There must be greater reflectiveness because the effect of living in a constitutional democracy – one, from the start, as Tocqueville knew – is to encourage the question, Who am I? The Old World replies, 'Don't be silly. How could you not know? You are your gender, place, work, family, class, past.' The philosophical self declines the answer, and assumes the burden of making an identity. And in the process of making an identity it alters the nature of identity: every self is imagined as never finished, never exhausted by its failures and successes, encouraged to think that it has indefinite resources for change in the midst of changing experience. Of course, identity is a burden.

The right-of-centre and the radical left are blind to the glories of the self that suits constitutional democracy, or afraid of them. I know that it is not helpful to use this language of accusation. I also know that one does not have to be in either camp to worry a lot. The point is not to have a vested ideological interest in alarmist exaggeration, or to base one's worry on misperceptions of American historical experience. The real legitimation crisis would appear when the hitherto sympathetic are overcome by their worry; when large numbers of people feel that the life of constitutional democracy is too much, and that something safer and more comfortable should replace it. That day may come. The truth is that the heroism of constitutional democracy may not be endurable.

We must, once again, make some distinctions, as we think about prospects, and indulge our worry. (It would be churlish to deny that the right-of-centre and the left both offer some valuable clues.) First, the material preconditions of the American constitutional democracy may be seriously impaired. Second, certain democratic tendencies may threaten the continuation of constitutional democracy. Third, the inevitable pathologies of democratic civilization may threaten the continuation of constitutional democracy.

On the material preconditions, it would seem that nothing in American history and society could prepare the people to tolerate deep inequalities combined with serious scarcities in a static economy. There is nothing to give theoretical support to such a pattern of distribution: it would lack legitimacy. If there would not be class warfare, there would be, perhaps, an unmoderated anarchy like that which is matchlessly presented in Kubrick's film *A Clockwork Orange*, a work more pertinent to American life than Burgess's splendid novel. To render Kubrick's allegory: As long as there is recollection of some better standard of living, and some residual belief in endless possibility, scarcity amid deep inequality engenders resentment of a terrible kind. The energetic deprived act out of rage and do casual violence: they cannot understand why they should be permanently deprived, especially when others are not. Those with advantages do not understand that either: they are morally unprepared for their advantage, and turn to perversity, and await some reckoning. The rage of the deprived is vengeance on the excesses of the advantaged; but the deprived wish only to change places with the advantaged. There seems no way to make people content or to reconcile them to either advantage or disadvantage. They live a life without legitimacy; and all authority can do is engage in strategems of desperation: occasional terror, occasional therapy.

This is a tendentious rendering of a complex film; but I think the work stands there as one of the most plausible conjectures about the effects of a new scarcity that we have.

When, next, we speak of certain democratic tendencies that may threaten the continuation of constitutional democracy, we may mean that the democratization of everyday life may undermine the traits of character needed for the public politics of constitutional democracy. Is it possible that there is something self-defeating in, say, treating children too democratically? If strength of character depends on a more authoritarian upbringing than democratic people seem willing to provide, will not citizenship weaken publicly exactly to the degree it is strengthened in family life? Similarly, if the concern for women's rights spreads and intensifies — a concern that grows out of the democratization of the self — will family life weaken to the point that a dangerously large number of children will grow up feeling unwanted or abandoned, with a consequent growth of desolation?

And last, we must acknowledge that there are disturbances and pathologies of the self that is suited to constitutional democracy. We do not have to go as far as D. H. Lawrence when he said in his book on American literature that the 'essential American soul is hard, isolate, stoic, and a killer'. But the loose-fitting identity most certainly has its accompanying defects and menaces. The most fashionable complaint at this time is that America is a country of narcissists. We are all familiar with other terms of criticism and disparagement: a world-absorbing egoism; a lethally indifferent privatism; terrible confusion and drifting; a calculated spontaneity; an unconscious guile; a compulsive play-acting; an unappeasable wish to 'score'; a merely additive quest for unconnected experience; a search for novelty and sensations; a fickle mobility; and so on. Often these accusations mistake the democratic essence for a disturbance or a pathology; often the one resembles the other or is alloyed with the other. But just as often even the most ardent democrat will see disturbance or pathology, and see them as the unavoidable effluences of democracy itself.

The disturbances and pathologies are part of the cost. Will the cost be perceived by masses of people as too great? Will they want to be saved from themselves as well as from others? Will the revulsion grow, fed also by doubt concerning the truly democratic tendencies that seem self-defeating, and doubt concerning the democratic essence itself? Will the lines separating essence, self-defeating tendencies, and disturbances and pathologies become too faint? Or the will to see them weaken? Will there be a genuine legitimation crisis, at last, whether or not there is a new scarcity? No one knows, but my hope is that, if there is, some intellectuals and publicists will know how great the threatened loss is, and refuse any proferred consolation.

9

The Juridical Apparatus

MICHEL FOUCAULT

LECTURE I

I would say, that what has emerged in the course of the last 10 or 15 years is a sense of the increasing vulnerability to criticism of things, institutions, practices, discourses. A certain fragility has been discovered in the very bedrock of existence – even, and perhaps above all, in those aspects of it that are most familiar, most solid and most intimately related to our bodies and to our everyday behaviour. But together with this sense of instability and this amazing efficacy of discontinuous, particular and local criticism, one in fact also discovers something that perhaps was not initially foreseen, something one might describe as precisely the inhibiting effect of global, *totalitarian theories*. It is not that these global theories have not provided nor continue to provide in a fairly consistent fashion useful tools for local research: Marxism and psychoanalysis are proofs of this. But I believe these tools have only been provided on the condition that the theoretical unity of these discourses was in some sense put in abeyance, or at least curtailed, divided, overthrown, caricatured, theatricalised, or what you will. In each case, the attempt to think in terms of a totality has in fact proved a hindrance to research.

So, the main point to be gleaned from these events of the last fifteen years, their predominant feature, is the *local* character of criticism. That should not, I believe, be taken to mean that its qualities are those of an obtuse, naive or primitive empiricism; nor is it a soggy eclecticism, an opportunism that laps up any and every kind of theoretical approach; nor does it mean a self-imposed ascetism which, taken by itself, would reduce to the worst kind of theoretical impoverishment. I believe that what this essentially local character of criticism indicates in reality is an autonomous, non-

Source: Michel Foucault, 'Two lectures', in Colin Gordon (ed.) *Power/Knowledge* (New York: Pantheon Books, 1980), pp. 80–7, 92–108, reprinted by permission of Random House and Harvester Press.

202 The Juridical Apparatus

centralized kind of theoretical production, one that is to say whose validity is not dependent on the approval of the established regimes of thought.

It is here that we touch upon another feature of these events that has been manifest for some time now: it seems to me that this local criticism has proceeded by means of what one might term 'a return of knowledge'. What I mean by that phrase is this: it is a fact that we have repeatedly encountered, at least at a superficial level, in the course of most recent times, an entire thematic to the effect that it is not theory but life that matters, not knowledge but reality, not books but money, etc.; but it also seems to me that over and above, and arising out of this thematic, there is something else to which we are witness, and which we might describe as an *insurrection of subjugated knowledges*.

By subjugated knowledges I mean two things: on the one hand, I am referring to the historical contents that have been buried and disguised in a functionalist coherence or formal systemization. Concretely, it is not a semiology of the life of the asylum, it is not even a sociology of delinquency, that has made it possible to produce an effective criticism of the asylum and likewise of the prison, but rather the immediate emergence of historical contents. And this is simply because only the historical contents allow us to rediscover the ruptural effects of conflict and struggle that the order imposed by functionalist or systematizing thought is designed to mask. Subjugated knowledges are thus those blocks of historical knowledge which were present but disguised within the body of functionalist and systematizing theory and which criticism – which obviously draws upon scholarship – has been able to reveal.

On the other hand, I believe that by subjugated knowledges one should understand something else, something which in a sense is altogether different, namely, a whole set of knowledges that have been disqualified as inadequate to their task or insufficiently elaborated: naive knowledges, located low down on the hierarchy, beneath the required level of cognition or scientificity. I also believe that it is through the re-emergence of these low-ranking know-ledges, these unqualified, even directly disqualified knowledges (such as that of the psychiatric patient, of the ill person, of the nurse, of the doctor – parallel and marginal as they are to the knowledge of medicine – that of the delinquent etc.), and which involve what I would call a popular knowledge (*le savoir des gens*) though it is far from being a general commonsense knowledge, but is on the contrary a particular, local, regional knowledge, a differential knowledge incapable of unanimity and which owes its force only to the harshness with which it is opposed by everything surrounding it – that it is through the re-appearance of this knowledge, of these local popular knowledges, these disqualified knowledges, that criticism performs its work.

However, there is a strange kind of paradox in the desire to assign to this same category of subjugated knowledges what are on the one hand the products of meticulous, erudite, exact historical knowledge, and on the other hand local and specific knowledges which have no common meaning and which are in some fashion allowed to fall into disuse whenever they are not effectively and explicitly maintained in themselves. Well, it seems to me that our critical discourses of the last 15 years have in effect discovered their essential force in this association between the buried knowledges of erudition and those disqualified from the hierarchy of knowledges and sciences.

In the two cases – in the case of the erudite as in that of the disqualified knowledges – with what in fact were these buried, subjugated knowledges really concerned? They were concerned with a historical knowledge of struggles. In the specialized areas of erudition as in the disqualified, popular knowledge there lay the memory of hostile encounters which even up to this day have been confined to the margins of knowledge.

What emerges out of this is something one might call a genealogy, or rather a multiplicity of genealogical researches, a painstaking rediscovery of struggles together with the rude memory of their conflicts. And these genealogies, that are the combined product of an erudite knowledge and a popular knowledge, were not possible and could not even have been attempted except on one condition, namely that the tyranny of globalizing discourses with their hierarchy and all their privileges of a theoretical *avant garde* was eliminated.

Let us give the term genealogy to the union of erudite knowledge and local memories which allows us to establish a historical knowledge of struggles and to make use of this knowledge tactically today. This then will be a provisional definition of the genealogies which I have attempted to compile with you over the last few years.

You are well aware that this research activity, which one can thus call genealogical, has nothing at all to do with an opposition between the abstract unity of theory and the concrete multiplicity of facts. It has nothing at all to do with a disqualification of the speculative dimension which opposes to it, in the name of some kind of scientism, the rigour of well-established knowledges. It is not therefore via an empiricism that the genealogical project unfolds, nor even via a positivism in the ordinary sense of that term. What it really does is to entertain the claims to attention of local, discontinuous, disqualified, illegitimate knowledges against the claims of a unitary body of theory which would filter, hierarchize and order them in the name of some true knowledge and some arbitrary idea of what constitutes a science and its objects. Genealogies are therefore not positivistic returns to a more careful or exact form of science. They are precisely anti-sciences. Not that they vindicate a lyrical right to ignorance or non-knowledge: it is not that they are concerned to deny knowledge or that they esteem the virtues of direct cognition and base their practice upon an immediate experience that escapes encapsulation in knowledge. It is not that with which we are concerned. We are concerned, rather, with the insurrection of knowledges that are opposed primarily not to the contents, methods or concepts of a science, but to the effects of the centralizing powers which are linked to the institution and functioning of an organized scientific discourse within a society such as ours. Nor does it basically matter all that much that this institutionalization of scientific discourse is embodied in a university, or, more generally, in an educational apparatus, in a theoretical-commercial institution such as psychoanalysis or within the framework of reference that is provided by a political system such as Marxism; for it is really against the effects of the power of a discourse that is considered to be scientific that the genealogy must wage its struggle.

To be more precise, I would remind you how numerous have been those who for many years now, probably for more than half a century, have questioned whether Marxism was, or was not, a science. One might say that the same issue has been posed, and continues to be posed, in the case of psychoanalysis, or even worse, in that of the semiology of literary texts. But to all these demands of, 'Is it or is it not a science?', the genealogies or the genealogists would reply, 'If you really want to know, the fault lies in your very determination to make a science out of Marxism or psychoanalysis or this or that study.' If we have any objection against Marxism, it lies in the fact that it could effectively be a science. In more detailed terms, I would say that even before we can know the extent to which something such as Marxism or psychoanalysis can be compared to a scientific practice in its everyday functioning, its rules of construction, its working concepts, that even before we can pose the question of a formal and structural analogy between Marxist or psychoanalytic discourse, it is surely necessary to question ourselves about our aspirations to the kind of power that is presumed to accompany such a science. It is surely the following kinds of question that would need to be posed: What types of knowledge do you want to disqualify in the very instant of your demand, 'Is it a science?' Which speaking, discoursing subjects – which subjects of experience and knowledge – do you then want to 'diminish' when you say, 'I who conduct this discourse am conducting a scientific discourse, and I am a scientist'? Which theoretical-political *avant garde* do you want to enthrone in order to isolate it from all the discontinuous forms of knowledge that circulate about it? When I see you straining to establish the scientificity of Marxism I do not really think that you are demonstrating once and for all that Marxism has a rational structure and that therefore its propositions are the outcome of verifiable procedures; for me you are doing something altogether different, you are investing Marxist discourses and those who uphold them with the effects of a power which the West since medieval times has attributed to science and has reserved for those engaged in scientific discourse.

By comparison, then, and in contrast to the various projects which aim to inscribe knowledges in the hierarchical order of power associated with science, a genealogy should be seen as a kind of attempt to emancipate historical knowledges from that subjection, to render them, that is, capable of opposition and of struggle against the coercion of a theoretical, unitary, formal and scientific discourse. It is based on a reactivation of local knowledges – of minor knowledges, as Deleuze might call them – in opposition to the scientific hierarchization of knowledges and the effects intrinsic to their power: this, then, is the project of these disordered and fragmentary genealogies. If we were to characterize it in two terms, then 'archaeology' would be the appropriate methodology of this analysis of local discursivities, and 'genealogy' would be the tactics whereby, on the basis of the descriptions of these local discursivities, the subjected knowledges which were thus released would be brought into play.

So much can be said by way of establishing the nature of the project as a whole. I would have you consider all these fragments of research, all these discourses, which are simultaneously both superimposed and discontinuous, which I have continued obstinately to pursue for some four or five years now, as elements of these genealogies which have been composed – and by no means by myself alone – in the course of the last 15 years. At this point, however, a problem arises, and a question, Why not continue to pursue a theory which in its discontinuity is so attractive and plausible, albeit so little verifiable? Why not continue to settle upon some aspect of psychiatry or of the theory of sexuality etc? It is true, one could continue (and in a certain sense I shall try to do so) if it were not for a certain number of changes in the current situation. By this I mean that it could be that in the course of the last 5, 10 or even 15 years, things have assumed a different complexion – the contest could be said to present a different physiognomy. Is the relation of forces today still such as to allow these disinterred knowledges some kind of autonomous life? Can they be isolated by these means from every subjugating relationship? What force do they have taken in themselves? And, after all, is it not perhaps the case that these fragments of genealogies are no sooner brought to light, that the particular elements of the knowledge that one seeks to disinter are no sooner accredited and put into circulation, than they run the risk of re-codification, re-colonization? In fact, those unitary discourses, which first disqualified and then ignored them when they made their appearance, are, it seems, quite ready now to annex them, to take them back within the fold of their own discourse and to invest them with everything this implies in terms of their effects of knowledge and power. And if we want to protect these only lately liberated fragments are we not in danger of ourselves constructing, with our hands, that unitary discourse to which we are invited, perhaps to lure us into a trap, by those who say to us, 'All this is fine, but where are you heading? What kind of unity are you after?' The temptation, up to a certain point, is to reply, 'Well, we just go on, in a cumulative fashion; after all, the moment at which we risk colonization has not yet arrived.' One could even attempt to throw out a challenge, 'Just try to colonize us then!' Or one might say, for example, 'Has there been, from the time when anti-psychiatry or the genealogy of psychiatric institutions were launched – and it is now a good fifteen years ago – a single Marxist, or a single psychiatrist, who has gone over the same ground in his own terms and shown that these genealogies that we produced were false, inadequately elaborated, poorly articulated and ill-founded?' In fact, as things stand in reality, these collected fragments of a genealogy remain as they have always been, surrounded by a prudent silence. At most, the only arguments that we have heard against them have been of the kind I believe were voiced by Monsieur Juquin:[1] All this is all very well, but Soviet psychiatry nonetheless remains the foremost in the world.' To which I would reply, 'How right you are; Soviet psychiatry is indeed the foremost in the world and it is precisely that which one would hold against it.'

The silence, or rather the prudence, with which the unitary theories avoid the genealogy of knowledges might therefore be a good reason to continue to pursue it. Then at least one could proceed to multiply the genealogical fragments in the form of so many traps, demands, challenges, what you will. But in the long run, it is probably over-optimistic, if we are thinking in terms of a contest – that of knowledge against the effects of the power of scientific discourse – to regard the silence of one's adversaries as indicative of a fear we have inspired in them. For perhaps the silence of the enemy – and here at the very least we have a methodological or tactical principle that it is always useful to bear in mind – can also be the index of our failure to produce any such fear at all. At all events, we must proceed just as if we had not alarmed them at all, in which case it will be no part of our concern to provide a solid and homogeneous theoretical terrain for all these dispersed genealogies, nor to descend upon them from on high with some kind of halo of theory that would unite them. Our task, on the contrary, will be to expose and specify the issue at stake in this opposition, this struggle, this insurrection of knowledges against the institutions and against effects of the knowledge and power that invests scientific discourse . . .

Thus we have two schemes for the analysis of power. The contract–oppression schema, which is the juridical one, and the domination–repression or war–repression schema for which the pertinent opposition is not between the legitimate and illegitimate, as in the first schema, but between struggle and submission.

It is obvious that all my work in recent years has been couched in the schema of struggle–repression, and it is this – which I have hitherto been attempting to apply – which I have now been forced to reconsider, both because it is still insufficiently elaborated at a whole number of points, and because I believe that these two notions of repression and war must themselves be considerably modified if not ultimately abandoned. In any case, I believe that they must be submitted to closer scrutiny.

I have always been especially diffident of this notion of repression: it is precisely with reference to those genealogies of which I was speaking just now – of the history of penal right, of psychiatric power, of the control of infantile sexuality, etc. – that I have tried to demonstrate to you the extent to which the mechanisms that were brought into operation in these power formations were something quite other, or in any case something much more than repression. The need to investigate this notion of repression more thoroughly springs therefore from the impression I have that it is wholly inadequate to the analysis of the mechanisms and effects of power that it is so pervasively used to characterize today.

The course of study that I have been following until now – roughly since 1970/1 – has been concerned with the *how* of power. I have tried, that is, to relate its mechanisms to two points of reference, two limits: on the one hand, to the rules of right that provide a formal delimitation of power; on the other, to the effects of truth that this power produces and transmits, and which in their turn reproduce this power. Hence we have a triangle: power, right, truth.

Schematically, we can formulate the traditional question of political philosophy in the following terms: how is the discourse of truth, or quite simply, philosophy as that discourse which *par excellence* is concerned with truth, able to fix limits to the rights of power? That is the traditional question. The one I would prefer to pose is rather different. Compared to the traditional, noble and philosophic question it is much more down to earth and concrete. My problem is rather this: what rules of right are implemented by the relations of power in the production of discourses of truth? Or alternatively, what type of power is susceptible of producing discourses of truth that in a society such as ours are endowed with such potent effects? What I mean is this: in a society such as ours, but basically in any society, there are manifold relations of power which permeate, characterize and constitute the social body, and these relations of power cannot themselves be established, consolidated or implemented without the production, accumulation, circulation and functioning of a discourse. There can be no possible exercise of power without a certain economy of discourses of truth which operates through and on the basis of this association. We are subjected to the production of truth through power and we cannot exercise power except through the production of truth. This is the case for every society, but I believe that in ours the relationship between power, right and truth is organized in a highly specific fashion. If I were to characterize, not its mechanism itself, but its intensity and constancy, I would say that we are forced to produce the truth of power that our society demands, of which it has need, in order to function: we *must* speak the truth; we are constrained or condemned to confess or to discover the truth. Power never ceases its interrogation, its inquisition, its registration of truth: it institutionalizes, professionalizes and rewards its pursuit. In the last analysis, we must produce truth as we must produce wealth, indeed we must produce truth in order to produce wealth in the first place. In another way, we are also subjected to truth in the sense in which it is truth that makes the laws, that produces the true discourse which, at least partially, decides, transmits and itself extends upon the effects of power. In the end, we are judged, condemned, classified, determined in our undertakings, destined to a certain mode of living or dying, as a function of the true discourses which are the bearers of the specific effects of power.

So, it is the rules of right, the mechanisms of power, the effects of truth or if you like, the rules of power and the powers of true discourses, that can be said more or less to have formed the general terrain of my concern, even if, as I know full well, I have traversed it only partially and in a very zig-zag fashion. I should like to speak briefly about this course of research, about what I have considered as being its guiding principle and about the methodological imperatives and precautions which I have sought to adopt. As regards the general principle involved in a study of the relations between right and power, it seems to me that in Western societies since medieval times it has been royal power that has provided the essential focus around which legal thought has been elaborated. It is in response to the demands of royal power, for its profit and to serve as its instrument or justification, that the juridical edifice of our own society has been developed. Right in the West is the king's right. Naturally everyone is familiar with the famous, celebrated, repeatedly emphasized role of the jurists in the organization or royal power. We must not forget that the revitalization of Roman Law in the twelfth century was the major event around which, and on whose basis, the juridical edifice which had collapsed after the fall of the Roman Empire was reconstructed. This resurrection of Roman Law had in effect a technical and constitutive role to play in the establishment of the authoritarian, administrative, and, in the final analysis, absolute power of the monarchy. And when this legal edifice escapes in later centuries from the control of the monarch, when, more accurately, it is turned against that control, it is always the limits of this sovereign power that are put in question, its prerogatives that are challenged. In other words, I believe that the king remains the central personage in the whole legal edifice of the West. When it comes to the general organization of the legal system in the West, it is essentially with the King, his rights, his power and its eventual limitations, that one is dealing. Whether the jurists were the king's henchmen or his adversaries, it is of royal power that we are speaking in every case when we speak of these grandiose edifices of legal thought and knowledge.

There are two ways in which we do so speak. Either we do so in order to show the nature of the juridical armoury that invested royal power, to reveal the monarch as the effective embodiment of sovereignty, to demonstrate that his power, for all that it was absolute, was exactly that which befitted his fundamental right. Or, by contrast, we do so in order to show the necessity of imposing limits upon this sovereign power, of submitting it to certain rules of right, within whose confines it had to be exercised in order for it to remain legitimate. The essential role of the theory of right, from medieval times onwards, was to fix the legitimacy of power; that is the major problem around which the whole theory of right and sovereignty is organized.

When we say that sovereignty is the central problem of right in Western societies, what we mean basically is that the essential function of the discourse and techniques of right has been to efface the domination intrinsic to power in order to present the latter at the level of appearance under two different aspects: on the one hand, as the legitimate rights of sovereignty, and on the other, as the legal obligation to obey it. The system of right is centred entirely upon the king, and it is therefore designed to eliminate the fact of domination and its consequences.

My general project over the past few years has been, in essence, to reverse the mode of analysis followed by the entire discourse of right from the time of the Middle Ages. My aim, therefore, was to invert it, to give due weight, that is, to the fact of domination, to expose both its latent nature and its brutality. I then wanted to show not only how right is, in a general way, the instrument of this domination – which scarcely needs saying – but also to show the extent to which, and the forms in which, right (not simply the laws but the whole complex of apparatuses, institutions and regulations responsible for their application) transmits and puts in motion relations that are not relations of sovereignty, but of domination. Moreover, in speaking of domination I do not have in mind that solid and global kind of domination that one person exercises over others, or one group over another, but the manifold forms of domination that can be exercised within society. Not the domination of the king in his central position, therefore, but that of his subjects in their mutual relations: not the uniform edifice of sovereignty, but the multiple forms of subjugation that have a place and function within the social organism.

The system of right, the domain of the law, are permanent agents of these relations of domination, these polymorphous techniques of subjugation. Right should be viewed, I believe, not in terms of a legitimacy to be established, but in terms of the methods of subjugation that it instigates.

The problem for me is how to avoid this question, central to the theme of right, regarding sovereignty and the obedience of individual subjects in order that I may substitute the problem of domination and subjugation for that of sovereignty and obedience. Given that this was to be the general line of my analysis, there were a certain number of methodological precautions that seemed requisite to its pursuit. In the very first place, it seemed important to accept that the analysis in question should not concern itself with the regulated and legitimate forms of power in their central locations, with the general mechanisms through which they operate, and the continual effects of these. On the contrary, it should be concerned with power at its extremities, in its ultimate destinations, with those points where it becomes capillary, that is, in its more regional and local forms and institutions. Its paramount concern, in fact, should be with the point where power surmounts the rules of right which organize and delimit it and extends itself beyond them, invests itself in institutions, becomes embodied in techniques, and equips itself with instruments and eventually even violent means of material intervention. To give an example: rather than try to discover where and how the right of punishment is founded on sovereignty, how it is presented in the theory of monarchical right or in that of democratic right, I have tried to see in what ways punishment and the power of punishment are effectively embodied in a certain number of local, regional, material institutions, which are concerned with torture or imprisonment, and to place these in the climate – at once institutional and physical, regulated and violent – of the effective apparatuses of punishment. In other words, one should try to locate power at the extreme points of its exercise, where it is always less legal in character.

A second methodological precaution urged that the analysis should not concern itself with power at the level of conscious intention or decision; that it should not attempt to consider power from its internal point of view and that it should refrain from posing the labyrinthine and unanswerable question, 'Who then has power and what has he in mind? What is the aim of someone who possesses power?' Instead, it is a case of studying power at the point where its intention, if it has one, is completely invested in its real and effective practices. What is needed is a study of power in its external visage, at the point where it is in direct and immediate

212 The Juridical Apparatus

relationship with that which we can provisionally call its object, its target, its field of application, there − that is to say − where it installs itself and produces its real effects.

Let us not, therefore, ask why certain people want to dominate, what they seek, what is their overall strategy. Let us ask, instead, how things work at the level of ongoing subjugation, at the level of those continuous and uninterrupted processes which subject our bodies, govern our gestures, dictate our behaviours etc. In other words, rather than ask ourselves how the sovereign appears to us in his lofty isolation, we should try to discover how it is that subjects are gradually, progressively, really and materially constituted through a multiplicity of organisms, forces, energies, materials, desires, thoughts, etc. We should try to grasp subjection in its material instance as a constitution of subjects. This would be the exact opposite of Hobbes' project in *Leviathan*, and of that, I believe, of all jurists for whom the problem is the distillation of a single will − or rather, the constitution of a unitary, singular body animated by the spirit of sovereignty − from the particular wills of a multiplicity of individuals. Think of the scheme of Leviathan: insofar as he is a fabricated man, Leviathan is no other than the amalgamation of a certain number of separate individualities, who find themselves reunited by the complex of elements that go to compose the state; but at the heart of the state, or rather, at its head, there exists something which constitutes it as such, and this is sovereignty, which Hobbes says is precisely the spirit of Leviathan. Well, rather than worry about the problem of the central spirit, I believe that we must attempt to study the myriad bodies which are constituted as peripheral *subjects* as a result of the effects of power.

A third methodological precaution relates to the fact that power is not to be taken to be a phenomenon of one individual's consolidated and homogeneous domination over others, or that of one group or class over others. What, by contrast, should always be kept in mind is that power, if we do not take too distant a view of it, is not that which makes the difference between those who exclusively possess and retain it, and those who do not have it and submit to it. Power must be analysed as something which circulates, or rather as something which only functions in the form of a chain. It is never localized here or there, never in anybody's hands, never appropriated as a commodity or piece of wealth. Power is employed and exercised through a net-like organization. And not only do individuals circulate between its threads; they are always in the position of simultaneously undergoing and exercising this power. They are not only its inert or consenting target; they are always also the elements of its articulation. In other words, individuals are the vehicles of power, not its points of application.

The individual is not to be conceived as a sort of elementary nucleus, a primitive atom, a multiple and inert material on which power comes to fasten or against which it happens to strike, and in so doing subdues or crushes individuals. In fact, it is already one of the prime effects of power that certain bodies, certain gestures, certain discourses, certain desires, come to be identified and constituted as individuals. The individual, that is, is not the *vis-à-vis* of power; it is, I believe, one of its prime effects. The individual is an effect of power, and at the same time, or precisely to the extent to which it is that effect, it is the element of its articulation. The individual which power has constituted is at the same time its vehicle.

There is a fourth methodological precaution that follows from this: when I say that power establishes a network through which it freely circulates, this is true only up to a certain point. In much the same fashion we could say that therefore we all have a fascism in our heads, or, more profoundly, that we all have a power in our bodies. But I do not believe that one should conclude from that that power is the best distributed thing in the world, although in some sense that is indeed so. We are not dealing with a sort of democratic or anarchic distribution of power through bodies. That is to say, it seems to me — and this then would be the fourth methodological precaution — that the important thing is not to attempt some kind of deduction of power starting from its centre and aimed at the discovery of the extent to which it permeates into the base, of the degree to which it reproduces itself down to and including the most molecular elements of society. One must rather conduct an ascending analysis of power, starting, that is, from its infinitesimal mechanisms, which each have their own history, their own trajectory, their own techniques and tactics, and then see how these mechanisms of power have been — and continue to be — invested, colonized, utilized, involuted, transformed, displaced, extended, etc. by ever more general mechanisms and by forms of global domination. It is not that this global domination extends itself right to the base in a plurality of repercussions: I believe that the manner in which the phenomena, the techniques and the procedures of power enter into play at the most basic levels must be analysed, that the way in which these procedures are displaced, extended and altered must certainly be demonstrated; but above all what must be shown is the manner in which they are invested and annexed by more global phenomena and the subtle fashion in which more general powers or economic interests are able to engage with these technologies that are at once both relatively autonomous of power and act as its infinitesimal elements. In order to make this clearer, one might cite the example of madness. The descending type of analysis, the one of which I believe one ought to be wary, will say that the bourgeoisie has, since the sixteenth or seventeenth century, been the dominant class; from this premiss, it will then set out to deduce the internment of the insane. One can always make this deduction, it is always easily done and that is precisely what I would hold against it. It is in fact a simple matter to show that since lunatics are precisely those persons who are useless to industrial production, one is obliged to dispense with them. One could argue similarly in regard to infantile sexuality – and several thinkers, including Wilhelm Reich have indeed sought to do so up to a certain point. Given the domination of the bourgeois class, how can one understand the repression of infantile sexuality? Well, very simply – given that the human body had become essentially a force of production from the time of the seventeenth and eighteenth centuries, all the forms of its expenditure which did not lend themselves to the constitution of the productive forces – and were therefore exposed as redundant – were banned, excluded and repressed. These kinds of deduction are always possible. They are simultaneously correct and false. Above all they are too glib, because one can always do exactly the opposite and show, precisely by appeal to the principle of the dominance of the bourgeois class, that the forms of control of infantile sexuality could in no way have been predicted. On the contrary, it is equally plausible to suggest that what was needed was sexual training, the encouragement of a sexual precociousness, given that what was fundamentally at stake was the constitution of a labour force whose optimal state, as we well know, at least at the beginning of the nineteenth century, was to be infinite: the greater the labour force, the better able would the system of capitalist production have been to fulfil and improve its functions.

I believe that anything can be deduced from the general phenomenon of the domination of the bourgeois class. What needs to be done is something quite different. One needs to investigate historically, and beginning from the lowest level, how mechanisms of power have been able to function. In regard to the confinement of the insane, for example, or the repression and interdiction of sexuality, we need to see the manner in which, at the effective level of the family, of the immediate environment, of the cells and most basic units of society, these phenomena of repression or exclusion possessed their instruments and their logic, in response to a certain number of needs. We need to identify the agents responsible for them, their real agents (those who constituted the immediate social *entourage*, the family, parents, doctors etc.), and not be content to lump them under the formula of a generalized bourgeoisie. We need to see how these mechanisms of power, at a given moment, in a precise conjuncture and by means of a certain number of transformations, have begun to become economically advantageous and politically useful. I think that in this way one could easily manage to demonstrate that what the bourgeoisie needed, or that in which its system discovered its real interests, was not the exclusion of the mad or the surveillance and prohibition of infantile masturbation (for, to repeat, such a system can perfectly well tolerate quite opposite practices), but rather, the techniques and procedures themselves of such an exclusion. It is the mechanisms of that exclusion that are necessary, the apparatuses of surveillance, the medicalization of sexuality, of madness, of delinquency, all the micro-mechanisms of power, that came, from a certain moment in time, to represent the interests of the bourgeoisie. Or even better, we could say that to the extent to which this view of the bourgeoisie and of its interests appears to lack content, at least in regard to the problems with which we are here concerned, it reflects the fact that it was not the bourgeoisie itself which thought that madness had to be excluded or infantile sexuality repressed. What in fact happened instead was that the mechanisms of the exclusion of madness, and of the surveillance of infantile sexuality, began from a particular point in time, and for reasons which need to be studied, to reveal their political usefulness and to lend themselves to economic profit, and that as a natural consequence, all of a sudden, they came to be colonized and maintained by global mechanisms and the entire state system. It is only if we grasp these techniques of power and demonstrate the economic advantages or political utility that derive from them in a given context for specific reasons, that we can understand how these mechanisms come to be effectively incorporated into the social whole.

To put this somewhat differently: the bourgeoisie has never had any use for the insane; but the procedures it has employed to exclude them have revealed and realized – from the nineteenth century onwards, and again on the basis of certain transformations – a political advantage, on occasion even a certain economic utility, which have consolidated the system and contributed to its overall functioning. The bourgeoisie is interested in power, not in madness, in the system of control of infantile sexuality, not in that phenomenon itself. The bourgeoisie could not care less about delinquents, about their punishment and rehabilitation, which economically have little importance, but it is concerned about the complex of mechanisms with which delinquency is controlled, pursued, punished and reformed etc.

As for our fifth methodological precaution: it is quite possible that the major mechanisms of power have been accompanied by ideological productions. There has, for example, probably been an ideology of education, an ideology of the monarchy, an ideology of parliamentary democracy etc.; but basically I do not believe that what has taken place can be said to be ideological. It is both much more and much less than ideology. It is the production of effective instruments for the formation and accumulation of knowledge – methods of observation, techniques of registration, procedures for investigation and research, apparatuses of control. All this means that power, when it is exercised through these subtle mechanisms, cannot but evolve, organize and put into circulation a knowledge, or rather apparatuses of knowledge, which are not ideological constructs.

By way of summarizing these five methodological precautions, I would say that we should direct our researches on the nature of power not towards the juridical edifice of sovereignty, the state apparatuses and the ideologies which accompany them, but towards domination and the material operators of power, towards forms of subjection and the inflections and utilizations of their localized systems, and towards strategic apparatuses. We must eschew the model of Leviathan in the study of power. We must escape from the limited field of juridical sovereignty and state institutions, and instead base our analysis of power on the study of the techniques and tactics of domination.

This, in its general outline, is the methodological course that I believe must be followed, and which I have tried to pursue in the various researches that we have conducted over recent years on psychiatric power, on infantile sexuality, on political systems, etc. Now as one explores these fields of investigation, observing the methodological precautions I have mentioned, I believe that what then comes into view is a solid body of historical fact, which will ultimately bring us into confrontation with the problems of which I want to speak this year.

This solid, historical body of fact is the juridical-political theory of sovereignty of which I spoke a moment ago, a theory which has had four roles to play. In the first place, it has been used to refer to a mechanism of power that was effective under the feudal monarchy. In the second place, it has served as instrument and even as justification for the construction of the large-scale administrative monarchies. Again, from the time of the sixteenth century and more than ever from the seventeenth century onwards, but already at the time of the wars of religion, the theory of sovereignty has been a weapon which has circulated from one camp to another, which has been utilized in one sense or another, either to limit or else to reinforce royal power: we find it among Catholic monarchists and Protestant anti-monarchists, among Protestant and more-or-less liberal monarchists, but also among Catholic partisans of regicide or dynastic transformation. It functions both in the hands of aristocrats and in the hands of parliamentarians. It is found among the representatives of royal power and among the last feudatories. In short, it was the major instrument of political and theoretical struggle around systems of power of the sixteenth and seventeenth centuries. Finally, in the eighteenth century, it is again this same theory of sovereignty, re-activated through the doctrine of Roman Law, that we find in its essentials in Rousseau and his contemporaries, but now with a fourth role to play: now it is concerned with the construction, in opposition to the administrative, authoritarian and absolutist monarchies, of an alternative model, that of parliamentary democracy. And it is still this role that it plays at the moment of the Revolution.

Well, it seems to me that if we investigate these four roles there is a definite conclusion to be drawn: as long as a feudal type of society survived, the problems to which the theory of sovereignty was addressed were in effect confined to the general mechanisms of power, to the way in which its forms of existence at the higher level of society influenced its exercise at the lowest levels. In other words, the relationship of sovereignty, whether interpreted in a wider or a narrower sense, encompasses the totality of the social body. In effect, the mode in which power was exercised could be defined in its essentials in terms of the relationship sovereign – subject. But in the seventeenth and eighteenth centuries, we have the production of an important phenomenon, the emergence, or rather the invention, of a new mechanism of power possessed of highly specific procedural techniques, completely novel instruments, quite different apparatuses, and which is also, I believe, absolutely incompatible with the relations of sovereignty.

This new mechanism of power is more dependent upon bodies and what they do than upon the earth and its products. It is a mechanism of power which permits time and labour, rather than wealth and commodities, to be extracted from bodies. It is a type of power which is constantly exercised by means of surveillance rather than in a discontinuous manner by means of a system of levies or obligations distributed over time. It presupposes a tightly knit grid of material coercions rather than the physical existence of a sovereign. It is ultimately dependent upon the principle, which introduces a genuinely new economy of power, that one must be able simultaneously both to increase the subjected forces and to improve the force and efficacy of that which subjects them.

This type of power is in every aspect the antithesis of that mechanism of power which the theory of sovereignty described or sought to transcribe. The latter is linked to a form of power that is exercised over the earth and its products, much more than over human bodies and their operations. The theory of sovereignty is something which refers to the displacement and appropriation on the part of power, not of time and labour, but of goods and wealth. It allows discontinuous obligations distributed over time to be given legal expression but it does not allow for the codification of a continuous surveillance. It enables power to be founded in the physical existence of the sovereign, but not in continuous and permanent systems of surveillance. The theory of sovereignty permits the foundation of an absolute power in the absolute expenditure of power. It does not allow for a calculation of power in terms of the minimum expenditure for the maximum return.

This new type of power, which can no longer be formulated in terms of sovereignty, is, I believe, one of the great inventions of bourgeois society. It has been a fundamental instrument in the constitution of industrial capitalism and of the type of society that is its accompaniment. This non-sovereign power, which lies outside the form of sovereignty, is disciplinary power. Impossible to describe in the terminology of the theory of sovereignty from which it differs so radically, this disciplinary power ought by rights to have led to the disappearance of the grand juridical edifice created by that theory. But in reality, the theory of sovereignty has continued not only to exist as an ideology of right, but also to provide the organizing principle of the legal codes which Europe acquired in the nineteenth century, beginning with the Napoleonic Code.

Why has the theory of sovereignty persisted in this fashion as an ideology and an organizing principle of these major legal codes? For two reasons, I believe. On the one hand, it has been, in the eighteenth and again in the nineteenth century, a permanent instrument of criticism of the monarchy and of all the obstacles that can thwart the development of disciplinary society. But at the same time, the theory of sovereignty, and the organization of a legal code centred upon it, have allowed a system of right to be superimposed upon the mechanisms of discipline in such a way as to conceal its actual procedures, the element of domination inherent in its techniques, and to guarantee to everyone, by virtue of the sovereignty of the state, the exercise of his proper sovereign rights. The juridical systems – and this applies both to their codification and to their theorization – have enabled sovereignty to be democratized through the constitution of a public right articulated upon collective sovereignty, while at the same time this demo-cratization of sovereignty was fundamentally determined by and grounded in mechanisms of disciplinary coercion.

To put this in more rigorous terms, one might say that once it became necessary for disciplinary constraints to be exercised through mechanisms of domination and yet at the same time for their effective exercise of power to be disguised, a theory of sovereignty was required to make an appearance at the level of the legal apparatus, and to re-emerge in its codes. Modern society, then, from the nineteenth century up to our own day, has been characterized on the one hand, by a legislation, a discourse, an organization based on public right, whose principle of articulation is the social body and the delegative status of each citizen; and, on the other hand, by a closely linked grid of disciplinary coercions whose purpose is in fact to assure the cohesion of this same social body. Though a theory of right is a necessary companion to this grid, it cannot in any event provide the terms of its endorsement. Hence these two limits, a right of sovereignty and a mechanism of discipline, which define, I believe, the arena in which power is exercised. But these two limits are so heterogeneous that they cannot possibly be reduced to each other. The powers of modern society are exercised through, on the basis of, and by virtue of, this very heterogeneity between a public right of sovereignty and a polymorphous disciplinary mechanism. This is not to suggest that there is on the one hand an explicit and scholarly system of right which is that of sovereignty, and, on the other hand, obscure and unspoken disciplines which carry out their shadowy operations in the depths, and thus constitute the bedrock of the great mechanism of power. In reality, the disciplines have their own discourse. They engender, for the reasons of which we spoke earlier, apparatuses of knowledge (*savoir*) and a multiplicity of new domains of under-standing. They are extraordinarily inventive participants in the order of these knowledge-producing apparatuses. Disciplines are the bearers of a discourse, but this cannot be the discourse of right. The discourse of discipline has nothing in common with that of law, rule, or sovereign will. The disciplines may well be the carriers of a discourse that speaks of a rule, but this is not the juridical rule deriving from sovereignty, but a natural rule, a norm. The code they come to define is not that of law but that of normalization. Their reference is to a theoretical horizon which of necessity has nothing in common with the edifice of right. It is human science which constitutes their domain, and clinical knowledge their jurisprudence.

In short, what I have wanted to demonstrate in the course of the last few years is not the manner in which at the advance front of the exact sciences the uncertain, recalcitrant, confused dominion of human behaviour has little by little been annexed to science: it is not through some advancement in the rationality of the exact sciences that the human sciences are gradually constituted. I believe that the process which has really rendered the discourse of the human sciences possible is the juxtaposition, the encounter between two lines of approach, two mechanisms, two absolutely heterogeneous types of discourse: on the one hand there is the reorganization of right that invests sovereignty, and on the other, the mechanics of the coercive forces whose exercise takes a disciplinary form. And I believe that in our own times power is exercised simultaneously through this right and these techniques and that these techniques and these discourses, to which the disciplines give rise, invade the area of right so that the procedures of normalization come to be ever more constantly engaged in the colonization of those of law. I believe that all this can explain the global functioning of what I would call a *society of normalization*. I mean, more precisely, that disciplinary normalizations come into ever greater conflict with the juridical systems of sovereignty: their incompatibility with each other is ever more acutely felt and apparent; some kind of arbitrating discourse is made ever more necessary, a type of power and of knowledge that the sanctity of science would render neutral. It is precisely in the extension of medicine that we see, in some sense, not so much the linking as the perpetual exchange or encounter of mechanisms of discipline with the principle of right. The developments of medicine, the general medicalization of behaviours, conducts, discourses, desires, etc. take place at the point of intersection between the two heterogeneous levels of discipline and sovereignty. For this reason, against these usurpations by the disciplinary mechanisms, against this ascent of a power that is tied to scientific knowledge, we find that there is no solid recourse available to us today, such being our situation, except that which lies precisely in the return to a theory of right organized around sovereignty and articulated upon its ancient principle. When today one wants to object in some way to the disciplines and all the effects of power and knowledge that are linked to them, what is it that one does, concretely, in real life, what do the Magistrates Union[2] or other similar institutions do if not precisely appeal to this canon of right, this famous, formal right, that is said to be bourgeois, and which in reality is the right of sovereignty? But I believe that we find ourselves here in a kind of blind alley: it is not through recourse to sovereignty against discipline that the effects of disciplinary power can be limited, because sovereignty and disciplinary mechanisms are two absolutely integral constituents of the general mechanism of power in our society.

If one wants to look for a non-disciplinary form of power, or rather, to struggle against disciplines and disciplinary power, it is not towards the ancient right of sovereignty that one should turn, but towards the possibility of a new form of right, one which must indeed be anti-disciplinarian, but at the same time liberated from the principle of sovereignty. It is at this point that we once more come up against the notion of repression, whose use in this context I believe to be doubly unfortunate. On the one hand, it contains an obscure reference to a certain theory of sovereignty, the sovereignty of the sovereign rights of the individual, and on the other hand, its usage introduces a system of psychological reference points borrowed from the human sciences, that is to say, from discourses and practices that belong to the disciplinary realm. I believe that the notion of repression remains a juridical-disciplinary notion whatever the critical use one would make of it. To this extent the critical application of the notion of repression is found to be vitiated and nullified from the outset by the two-fold juridical and disciplinary reference it contains to sovereignty on the one hand and to normalization on the other.

NOTES

1 A deputy of the French Communist Party.
2 This Union, established after 1968, has adopted a radical line on civil rights, the law and the prisons.

10
The Dilemma of Legitimacy

WILLIAM CONNOLLY

> In our times we can neither endure our faults nor the means of correcting them.
>
> *Livy*

In a highly structured order, people tend to be pulled simultaneously by one wish to identify with established norms and another to evade or resist onerous claims made upon them. Some are drawn exclusively toward one of these poles, but many others are torn between them. The latter will endorse law and order belligerently and cheat on their income taxes, or express anarchistic impulses and raise their children to be lawyers, or insist that the government get off the backs of the people and support policies which extend surveillance over marginal constituencies. The tensions here are not merely psychological; they embody attempts to meet the claims of the self and the claims of order in a setting which makes it difficult to do both.

The classical doctrine of liberalism projected a vision of social life which honoured both sets of claims. Endorsing a general set of constitutional rules which all citizens were to obey, it entrusted a broad range of conduct to the impersonal control of the market and placed the remainder within a private sphere beyond the normal reach of direct public control. The liberal ideal never harmonized closely with the actual organization of private and public life, but the fit was close enough to allow its supporters to help define the form and limits of operative public authority.

The attraction of the liberal doctrine resided largely in its desire to acknowledge together the claims of public authority and private prerogative. But, as its conceptual resources have lagged behind changes in the structure of modern life, this attraction has faded.

Source: William Connolly, 'The dilemma of legitimacy', in John Nelson (ed.) *What Should Political Theory Be Now?* (Albany: State University of New York Press, 1983), pp. 307–37, reprinted with permission of the State University of New York Press.

The web of social life is now too tightly drawn to sustain this picture of public authority and private refuge. The current proclivity to characterize behaviour once thought to be eccentric as mental illness in need of medical care presents merely one sign of the penetration of public-private bureaucracies into the inner citadels of private life. Put another way, a broad range of private activities and social practices must today be co-ordinated (to use a neutral term) by public means; and a large number of people unable or unwilling to comply voluntarily with official expectations are now subjected to legal controls, therapeutic counsel, and incentive systems to bring their conduct in line with the limits of the order.

As the web of social discipline has tightened, other familiar doctrines of the nineteenth and twentieth centuries have also begun to seem vaguely disconnected from our current condition. Critics who appeal to a communitarian ideal of life or gesture toward anarchism illuminate features of our life otherwise left in the shadows, but the counter-ideals they pose lack specificity and credibility. Pressed very hard by communitarians or anarchists, most of us retreat toward liberal standards of citizenship, freedom, and privacy. And yet when the liberal, inflated by success in piercing these pretensions, attempts to woo us back to the liberal camp, we discern even more poignantly how the doctrine draws a veil of ignorance across the most disturbing features of contemporary life.

This condition can be generalized across the entire landscape of contemporary theoretical discourse. Dissident perspectives demystify features of the established order, but then condense into a light mist of lofty ideals; and the operative ideals, which retain some ability to set limits to the morally tolerable in the existing order, rest on assumptions and perceptions increasingly at odds with established realities. Political theorists thus find themselves wandering through the debris of old doctrines, searching for stray material from which to construct new understandings. These features of current political theory, I contend, are themselves symptoms of the dilemma of legitimacy which is beginning to emerge in our civilization.

How should we try to pick our way through this field? My own effort is informed by the following judgement: the categories supplied by a collectivist theory of legitimacy provide the most refined instruments with which to probe subterranean developments in our civilization, but these instruments themselves must be redesigned once that excavation is finished, once we begin digging our way out. In defending this perspective, I first delineate a collectivist conception of legitimacy which transcends the thin conception governing much current social theory, next define the contours of a dilemma of legitimacy which is beginning to take shape in American politics, then examine briefly two theories which are themselves symptoms of this development, and last confront an alternate perspective which might allow us to correct the repressive tendencies implicit within the collectivist problematic of legitimacy.

THE QUESTION OF LEGITIMACY

A thin theory of legitimacy continues to inform most accounts of current politics. It assumes that allegiance to the order is intact unless there is overt, widespread, and well-articulated opposition to it; that belief in the legitimacy of the order is equivalent to the order's legitimacy; that the beliefs most pivotal to the question of legitimacy are those concerning the constitutive principles of the political process; and that since the ends governing our civilization are inherently rational they could not themselves become illegitimate. Few theorists accept all of these provisions today. But a variety of recent theorists, representing diverse ideological positions, adopt one or more of them when posing questions about the legitimacy of the order.[1]

The thin conception of legitimacy misconstrues the way in which social relations and institutions are constituted. Misreading the constitutive dimensions of social life, it may be able to detect certain symptoms of a withdrawal of allegiance from the order, but it lacks the conceptual resources to comprehend its internal structure or to assess its potential import.

A healthy order, from the vantage-point of its participants, is a way of life which promotes the good we share in common; the limits it imposes are tolerable to most because they are thought to be necessary to the common good it fosters. To participate in such a way of life is to carry an enormous load of pre-judgements embodied in the common language and solidified in institutional practices. One's personal identity is intimately bound up with the larger way of life: it provides one with the density needed to maintain social relations, to form practical judgements, and to criticize specific features of the common life.

This is an incomplete picture of any way of life. (For instance, its structural dimension has been ignored.) But it is complete enough to allow us to relocate the question of legitimacy. First, if the pre-understandings implicit in social relations seriously misconstrue the range of possibilities inherent in the order, expressions of allegiance at one moment will rest upon a series of illusions which may become apparent at a future moment. The historical course of development actually open to the order may ensure that future generations will become disenchanted with it.

Second, a widespread commitment to the constitutional principles of the political order may be matched by distantiation from the role imperatives governing everyday life. In a highly structured order, the withdrawal of allegiance in this second sphere will carry profound implications for the performance of the economy, the tax levels required by the state, the scope of the state's police functions, and the ability of the state to bear the burdens imposed upon it. It may, in short, impair the state's ability to play its legitimate role in the current order of things.

Third, the ends and purposes fostered by an order can themselves become objects of disaffection. Hegel explored instances when a set of priorities which once gripped a populace lose their credibility as the negative dimensions in them become more fully visible to later generations. Such a contradictory tendency embodies a historical dimension whereby abstract goals inspire a populace at one moment but decline in their ability to secure reflective allegiance once their actual content becomes clear through cumulative experience. If the institutional complex sustaining these purposes has solidified, we might expect expressions of disaffection to be more symptomatic than articulate and more covert than overt. The lack of any sense of credible alternatives operates to limit the political definition of the new sense of disenchantment, but its emergence nonetheless affects the performance of the institutional complex.

But why such an emphasis on the symptomatic, the covert, the indirect, and the unarticulated when pursuing the question of legitimacy? Because, fourth, the identities of the participants are bound up with the institutions in which they are implicated. The modern individual, possessing the capacity for self-consciousness, is never exhausted by any particular set of roles. But one's sense of dignity, of self-identity, is intimately linked to one's ability to endorse the way of life one actually lives.

This relation between personal identity and institutional practice complicates the question of legitimacy. To become severely disaffected from that which one is called upon to do in work, family, and consumption is also to become disaffected from the self one has become. When the distance between what one is and what one does is great, one is likely to hold oneself in contempt. For one must now either appear to be unfree (acting only under duress) or appear deceitful (pretending to endorse roles experienced as hateful). In either case, one feels cast off from oneself, anxious and demoralized.

The situation is not helped if the experience is joined to the conviction that little can be done to remedy it through politics. One way to save appearances in such a setting is to reconnect rhetorically that which is disconnected in practice. Some politicians understand how difficult circumstances can foster collective self-deception or, better described, the careful cultivation of a shared innocence about the historical course a people is on. 'They want to believe, that is the point isn't it?' So Nixon whispered to Haldeman and the tape recorder when they were assessing his chances of overcoming the mass of evidence piling up against him. He understood the close relation between the quest for personal identity and the will to believe that all is right with the world.

Because these connections can be so intimate, a theory of legitimacy must probe the implicit, the unacknowledged, and the symptomatic as well as that which is acknowledged and articulated. And because it must do so, any particular account is bound to be controversial and problematic in some respects. This result resides more in the character of the object of inquiry than in the defective design of the theoretical perspective governing inquiry into it. The philosophical recognition of this feature of modern life carries political implications. It provides, as it were, philosophical space for politics. It identifies politics as the sphere of the unsettled, as the mode of social relations which properly emerges when issues require resolution and the available resources of reason and evidence are insufficient to settle them.

The question of legitimacy is important to us because we wish to live, to the extent possible in any complex, modern society, as free agents in an order which deserves our allegiance and is responsive to our deepest grievances and criticisms. It is also important because we sense that politics, in the best sense of that term, requires a background of public allegiance to the most basic principles governing the order. The thin conception of legitimacy appears to avoid a series of perplexing issues posed by acceptance of the alternate perspective. That is also its defect. It converts the concern behind the question of legitimacy into a set of more manageable and trivial questions.

PRODUCTIVITY AND LEGITIMACY

Two fundamental sets of priorities have governed the American civilization.[2] It seeks to sustain an economy of growth so that each generation can be more prosperous, secure, and comfortable than its predecessor. And it seeks to support a constitutional democracy in which the state is accountable to its citizens and the citizens have rights against the state. The first priority is expressed in the organization of work, profit, property, and consumption which typifies the society. These practices are constituted in part by the standards of efficiency, cost effectiveness, productivity, punctuality, and consumer satisfaction inherent in them. The second priority is reflected in our concern with human rights, freedom, the entitlements of citizenship, and competitive elections. Its constitution involves the readiness of participants to see themselves as citizens and to carry out the prerogatives of citizenship.

The legitimacy of the entire order involves, first, the ability of each set of priorities to retain the reflective allegiance of most citizens and, second, the continued ability of each priority to exist in harmony with the other.

I believe that the first set of institutions and priorities, the civilization of productivity, is progressively losing its credibility as its imperatives become more deeply entrenched. The decline in credibility involves a process of disillusionment in which the institutional pursuit of a set of ends once thought to be self-evident begins to appear more and more as self-defeating to new generations. In turn, the disillusionment adversely affects the ability of the institutions to promote these ends by non-coercive means. Since the institutional forms which constitute the order are now solidified, since they now form an interdependent structure in which none can be reconstituted very thoroughly without corollary shifts in the constitution of the others, this disaffection is not likely to find clear political expression. Its political articulation tends to be displaced. The disaffection does, though, take its toll in the civilization of productivity. It also increases the burdens imposed upon the welfare state, the one institution which is accountable to the electorate. The long-term effect strains the ability of the state to retain democratic accountability. The erosion of legitimacy in the one sphere eventually contaminates the legitimacy of the other.

What, more concretely, is involved in this experience of disillusionment? First, it becomes more apparent to consumers that the pursuit of universal private affluence, full of promise during its early stages, eventually generates a self-defeating dialectic. The economy may produce riches, but the good life contained within the ideal of 'affluence' seems to recede constantly into the horizon. Goods introduced initially as luxuries or conveniences later become necessary objects of consumption, and much of their initial charm is lost.

This conversion process is propelled partly by the changes in the social infrastructure of consumption which must accompany each significant change in the social composition of consumption goods.[3] The automobile, for example, brings with it an expensive public highway system, a complex apparatus for acquiring and refining oil, a military establishment to secure a steady supply of oil, changes in the location of stores, shopping centres, factories, recreational areas, and the entire redesign of cities. These changes in the infrastructure of consumption convert the initial luxury into an expensive necessity of consumption, they tend to reduce pleasure in the use of the vehicle, and they impose heavy costs of maintenance and support upon the state. Moreoover, many of the paradigmatic goods of the affluent society, because they are built around the assumption of private consumption, decline in value as they are extended to more people. Private resorts, technical education, suburban living, and (again) the automobile decline in value as they are universalized, partly because much of their initial value resided in the exclusivity of their possession and partly because the setting in which they are consumed normally deteriorates as they are universalized. If these goods (representing the paradigm goods of the affluent society) were to be restricted, the end of universal affluence which helps to legitimate the civilization of productivity would be jeopardized. But if they were indeed extended to everyone, the achievement of 'affluence' itself would contradict the hopes which inspired earlier generations to pursue it.

If the universalization of affluence is one of the ends which legitimize the role imperatives governing the civilization of productivity, and if that end is now seen by many to contain illusory expectations, everyday allegiance to role assignments will deteriorate. The reaction, experienced as growing scepticism about the system's ability to universalize the good life it pursues, does not expunge the desire for consumption goods, for to opt out of the expansionary process is to worsen one's own comparative position. But it does weaken the willingness to impose disciplines upon oneself at work, home, and school.

Suspicions arise in other areas as well. Institutions, standards, and norms which once seemed conducive to private welfare and public good now present a more ambiguous appearance. It begins to appear that the system of labour mobility, which promises to improve that standard of living for many in each generation, also operates over the long term to damage cherished ties of kinship and neighbourhood; that the stratification system needed to motivate people to fill the lowliest positions also operates persistently to close some segments of the society out of its paradigmatic rewards; that the massive exploitation of natural resources needed to fuel the economy of growth deepens the nation's dependence on resources located in foreign lands; that the established forms of investment, production, and work which generate abundance also render the natural environment less hospitable to future human habitation; that the pace of occupational change required to propel perpetual economic growth also renders each generation of workers obsolete just when it reaches the point in the life cycle where its members are most in need of the respect and dignity bestowed on those functionally important to the society; and that the intensification of managerial controls over the work process to increase productivity drains these role assignments of dignity and social significance. The suspicion forms that these are not dispensable 'side effects' to a common pursuit which can be carried out without them; rather they are intrinsic to the historical development of the civilization of productivity. They are part of its success, and any sustained effort to eliminate them would undermine the principal aims which the civilization of productivity can promote.

Other civilizations, of course, have faced difficulties in promoting the material welfare of their populations. But that is not the point here. For not many of these were constructed around the promise to universalize private affluence. I am not contending, either, that most people today have a 'lower standard of living' than people had two or three generations ago. The contention is rather that the orientation to the future is undergoing significant change. Nostalgia refers less to a past which is thought to have been richer and more secure and more to one which could believe in the future it was building. The nostalgia of today embodies a loss of innocence about the future we are building. As the feeling grows that the fulfilment of the American dream must always recede into the horizon, as it becomes clear that it might even become a nightmare for future generations, identification with the disciplines and sacrifices required to sustain the civilization of productivity is placed under severe strains. These strains in turn weaken the performance of the defining institutions of the civilization.

The relation between the state and the system of productivity works to deflect political articulation of this disillusionment, to increase the burdens imposed upon the state, to deplete the civic resources the state can draw upon in bearing these burdens, and to set up the welfare apparatus of the state as the screen upon which the disaffection is displayed. The welfare state looks in two directions at the same time. It is the agency of public accountability through competitive elections, and it is dependent upon the successful performance of the privately incorporated system of productivity. This dual accountability of the state discourages political articulation of the disillusionment with the civilization of productivity. For it must foster private productivity to generate tax revenues, and its successful accountability to the electorate depends upon its ability to generate those revenues.

The state is caught in a bind which its citizens actively help to create. Our cherished view of ourselves as free citizens depends upon the belief that the state, as the one institution of public accountability, has sufficient resources to promote common ends and purposes. Its capacity to act effectively is closely bound up with my understanding of myself as a free agent. I see myself as free if the roles I play are congruent with the principles and purposes I adopt upon reflection. If those rules or the purposes they serve were experienced as onerous and oppressive, and if individuals were unsuccessful in defining new ones, their sense of personal freedom would then depend on the ability of the state to reconstitute these established forms. If it could not act even if we wished it to and we were thoroughly disaffected from the drift of our private and public life, then we would have to see ourselves as unfree, as governed more by fate and necessity than by reason and decision. And our collective unfreedom would eventually become the unfreedom of particular individuals as well.

One way to preserve the desired appearance of collective and personal freedom is to define the troubles which grip us to fit within the range of options effectively available to the state in the current order. Victims of inflation, therefore, unable to alter the consumption priorities, shoddy products, expensive style changes, and price mark-ups in the corporate sector, demand what the state can give them: cuts in school budgets and welfare expenditures. They attack those proximate sources of inflation which are subject to public control. Workers in depressed areas, unable to stop runaway companies, call upon the state to expand unemployment benefits and to stimulate the production of new jobs. Citizens, unable to curb the processes which weaken kinship ties, call upon the state to care for the victims of this process (the elderly, the infirm, the mentally ill, and delinquents), even though state agencies cannot care for these dependent constituencies with the dignity needed.

The bind in which the corporate system and its citizens place the state is this: if state policies undermine economic expansion, it loses its economic basis for action; if it acts within these constraints, it increasingly absorbs the dependent constituencies and unprofitable tasks closed out of the privately incorporated economy. It is then unable to meet the standards of efficiency and profitability operative in the private economy or to hold its budget levels down; and it is held responsible for the failure to live up to these expectations.

The state is seen as accountable to the degree that it is seen to be capable of responding to our grievances in the established order. We see ourselves as free, free as a people, to the extent that we define our grievances to fall within the range of its capacity for action. The welfare state thus emerges from this historical process as a depository for clientele closed out of the system of productivity and programmes unable to resolve the troubles which it generated. The bloated welfare state is thus set up to be the visible target of public disaffection more deeply rooted in the priorities and practices of the civilization of productivity.

We publicly call upon the state to promote growth, eliminate superfluous public programmes, control inflation, and discipline those who siphon off public resources; and we resist privately the specific sacrifices it would impose upon us. The point in calling upon it in general to take those actions is that they fall within its orbit of legitimate action. The point in resisting the specific application of state policies to one's particular constituency flows from the conviction that the roles we bear in the civilization of productivity already constitute sacrifice enough. Anything more becomes unacceptable and unbearable. The cumulative result is a decline in allegiance to the welfare state and an increasing tolerance of state programmes designed to intimidate, control, and suppress its former clients. The decline in the legitimacy of the welfare state is joined to allegiance to an abstract idea of the American state in the civilization of productivity. The logic supporting such a combination is this: we are potentially free as long as the existing state bureaucracy is unnecessarily inept; it can be seen as unnecessarily inept as long as we can identify new courses of state action in the prevailing order which promise to transcend the policies of the discredited welfare state. This combination secures the appearance of collective freedom, but it does so by masking a deeper and rational disaffection from the institutional imperatives and priorities of the civilization of productivity.

The preceding summary leaves out themes which would have to be developed in a more complete presentation, but a more complete account would not prove convincing if this brief outline now appears incredible. The framework, I hope, is sufficiently clear to allow me to formulate the crucial elements in the dilemma (or perhaps dilemmas) of legitimacy.

First, the ends fostered by the civilizations of productivity no longer can command reflective allegiance of many who are implicated in those institutions, while the consolidation of these institutions into a structure of interdependencies makes it extremely difficult to recast the ends to be pursued. The institutional complex declines in its ability to secure the allegiance of its role bearers once its actual achievements have been experienced; but the practices of work, profit, international trade, consumption, and stratification have solidified into an interdependent structure resistant to serious reconstitution.

Second, it will become increasingly difficult to maintain the performance of the system of productivity, and the policies required to do so will further erode operational allegiance to its roles and priorities. These barriers emerge on two fronts. On the one side, the investment funds, disciplinary controls, and resources needed to promote the required rate of growth in an unfavourable environment will be generated by the imposition of austerity on large segments of the populace (if they are generated) and by a further retreat from environmental policies designed to protect the health of the populace. Maintenance of the system of productivity in adverse circumstances thus requires contraction of the paradigmatic benefits it promises to dispense. These selective reductions in affluence, security, and health will further deplete the allegiance of many who are expected to carry out role assignments within the system. On the other side, resistance to these impositions by those without effective market or political leverage (e.g. welfare recipients, workers in the market sector, low and middle level public employees, the mentally ill, delinquents, criminals) will encourage an extension of private and public modes of disciplinary control. The deterioration in the performance of the system of productivity, combined with the pressures to mobilize additional resources to maintain its performance, operates eventually to squeeze the space for democratic politics.

Third, if, as I claim, disenchantment with the civilization of productivity is based upon a growing experiential knowledge of illusions inside those pursuits, it is pertinent to ask, What constellation of ends, limits, imperatives, and priorities could a modern populace endorse today as worthy of its allegiance? If a reconstitution of the defining institutions were possible, what direction should the evolutionary changes take? What could replace or temper the ends of the civilization of productivity? The failure to answer this question, even at the level of theory, contributes to the gap between the covert symptoms of disaffection and the overt insistence on supporting established political priorities.[4] In the absence of credible alternatives, there is a certain rationality in holding on to illusions with which we are already familiar. One of the best ways to accomplish that is to cultivate a studied innocence about the historical course we are on.

The first two ingredients in the dilemma of legitimacy press most heavily on those who pretend that democracy and productivity can continue to cohere without undue strain. The third presses critics who believe that the future of democracy requires a reconstitution of the ends and imperatives governing the system of productivity. In what follows, I try to indicate how recent shifts within a variety of theoretical orientations provide indirect acknowledgement of the dilemma posed here; and I use the opportunity to ascertain how each orientation can, though not always intentionally, deepen our understanding of the character of this dilemma.

THE BIFURCATION OF LIBERALISM

Current liberalism cannot be defined merely through its commitment to freedom, rights, dissent, and justice. It must be understood, as well, through the institutional arrangements it endorses. Its unity grows out of the congruence between these ideals and their institutional supports. If the first principle of liberalism is liberty, the second is practicality. Liberal practicality involves the wish to support policies which appear attainable within the current order; it is the desire to be part of the action, to be 'in the middle' of things, to propose policies today which might be instituted tomorrow.

The priorities of liberty and practicality can be united as long as it is possible to believe that the welfare state in the privately incorporated economy of growth can be the vehicle of liberty and justice. Liberalism, so constituted, avoids the dilemma of legitimacy. But if such a dilemma is beginning to shake the ground underneath its feet, we should expect its proponents to acknowledge these shifts somehow, if only indirectly. I think this is happening. Liberalism is increasingly divided against itself. One constellation of liberals subordinates the commitment to practicality to preserve liberal ideals, and the other submerges the ideals to preserve practicality. Neither side acknowledges the dilemma of legitimacy. But the new division is a symptom of its emergence. The bifurcation of liberalism and the dilemma of legitimacy unfold together.

The first constellation, the beautiful souls of our day, strive to find space in the current order where the ideals of virtuous action, freedom, and justice can be preserved. Sometimes following the lead of Hannah Arendt, they strive to close the instrumentalities of labour, interest, profit, and consumption out of the political sphere. These practices and priorities are not to be treated as the materials of politics, properly understood. But because the virtues the new liberals support are increasingly at odds with the way of the world, and because they evade (treat as subordinate and secondary) the deep intrusion of these wordly concerns into political life, the commitment to liberal principles is increasingly matched by the disengagement from practical issues. The principles themselves tend to become more abstract, more difficult to articulate specifically or to link to particular questions.[5]

The gradual retreat from practicality is principled; the abstract voice of virtue does help to set the limits of the morally tolerable in the existing order. Its voice is not, therefore, to be demeaned or ridiculed. But this principled liberalism is neither at home in the civilization of productivity nor prepared to challenge its hegemony. Its protection of liberal principles, combined with the residual commitment to productivity, requires a retreat from practicality.

The other side of liberalism retains the commitment to practicality by sliding toward a technocratic conception of politics. It acknowledges indirectly the dilemma of legitimacy by insisting that significant areas of social life must be regulated increasingly through an elaborate set of incentives and coercive devices. Since these controls are thought only to do more consciously and coherently what traditional guides to conduct did unconsciously and unevenly, it can be concluded that they represent no real threat to liberty or democracy. By treating, first, widespread resistance to role expectations as a universal condition; second, the ends of the civilization as inherently rational; and, third, the enlarged sphere of social life in need of conscious co-ordination as merely a function of the greater complexity of the system of productivity, the technocrats retain both practicality and the semblance of concern for liberal freedoms. When the order is understood in this way, it is not an unjust infringement of freedom to do what is necessary to promote rational ends.

Charles Schultze, the last liberal intellectual to hold a position of importance in the government, represents this perspective when he reverses the traditional rationale for the market. If it was once thought to price goods rationally, to promote personal freedom, and to limit the effective hegemony of the state, it is now to become an instrument of state control. The idea is to introduce a system of incentives into the market so that it becomes more in the self-interest of workers, owners, and consumers to promote the imperatives of the civilization of productivity. This politicization of the market will work because it does not depend upon civic resources that are in scarce supply; it 'reduces the need for compassion, patriotism, brotherly love, and cultural solidarity as motivating forces behind social improvements'.[6]

This particular version of the theory contains serious defects. The introduction of these incentives will merely provide new motives and possibilities for evasion, unless the purposes they serve and the sacrifices they impose speak to the convictions of large segments of the populace. They enhance the space, for instance, for the growth of the 'underground economy'. Failing to understand the logic of this reaction, Schultze will be drawn into a negative dialectic whereby each new set of evasions must be met by a new set of incentives and controls. The dialectic of social dissolution thus moves in tandem with a corollary dialectic of regimentation. This, then is the version of the dilemma of legitimacy which emerges in the Schultzean theory, but it is not clearly recognized within the theory itself.

Schultze does faintly discern its outlines. For while he finds it unrealistic to promote public purposes without the institution of private incentives, he does ask how those incentives could be equitably introduced by democratic means. Confronting this issue, Schultze is forced to end 'rather lamely'. When we move from the regulation of private conduct to the question of forming the public will to establish those regulations, there turns out to be 'no instrumental solution to the dilemma'.[7] Exactly.

Schultze refuses to consider the next step. It is likely to be considered, though, by those technocrats who are no longer haunted by the ghost of liberal principles. The recent attraction of former liberals to the new theory of 'reindustrialization' is one index of how far the commitment to practicality can pull many proponents away from democratic convictions as the imperatives of the civilization of productivity make themselves felt more powerfully.[8] The dilemma of legitimacy produces a bifurcation in contemporary liberalism. When the two sides are brought into juxtaposition, we can see the dilemma at work in the background. For either liberal practicality or the belief in liberal ideals must be sacrificed by those who refuse to reconsider the priorities and standards governing the civilization of productivity.

THE RETREAT OF CRITICAL THEORY

The interpretation of the declining allegiance to the civilization of productivity advanced in this essay owes a considerable debt to the theories of 'legitimacy' and 'motivation' crisis developed earlier by Jürgen Habermas.[9] Habermas explores the ways in which the evolution of 'advanced capitalism' undermines its preconditions of healthy existence, depletes the motives needed to carry out the dictates of production, forces the state into the role of subsidizer and supporter of private production, and imposes new limits on the state's ability to meet the needs of constituencies to whom it is formally accountable.[10]

The theory deepens our comprehension of the problem of legitimacy in modern society. It helps us to understand why a range of practices which previously appeared to be co-ordinated through the impersonal market and unreflective tradition are now necessarily and visibly objects of conscious co-ordination by the state or private bureaucracies. Arrangements which previously appeared to be left to the market, such as income distribution, employment levels, comparative rates of development in different parts of the country, and the protection of the environment, are now the visible objects of political contestation; and those which previously appeared to be governed by unreflective tradition, such as the sexual division of labour, the treatment of old people, the composition of the school curriculum, the relations between parents and children, are now the visible objects of state policy. This means that the scope of policies and practices which must be legitimated explicitly to the citizenry has expanded. The question of legitimacy now encompasses an enlarged ensemble of social relations.

Habermas also shows us why it is no longer possible to aspire either to a democratic society in which citizens unreflectively identify with the way of life they share in common (the classic idea of civic virtue) or to one in which the citizenry has become highly privatized (the idea of civil liberty without civic virtue). Democratic politics today requires a combination of citizen self-consciousness and civic virtue. A relentless attempt to restore unreflective tradition today must issue in Fascist control; and the attempt to secure democratic order without civic virtue must founder against the imperative to co-ordinate by conscious means a wide variety of social practices and activities. To accept these two themes, though, is to establish both the primacy of the question of legitimacy and the difficulties in responding to it democratically.

Habermas does not seem to me to confront this last issue directly enough. Rather he acknowledges it indirectly by retreating to a metatheoretical question. He does not ask what reforms and new priorities could hope to be instituted and to attract the reflective allegiance of the populace. He asks instead how in principle could we decide whether a particular complex of understandings and practices is valid. The current question of legitimacy is translated into a universal problem of knowledge. The consensus theory of truth and morality emerge as the answer.

The theory can be criticized, even at the abstract level at which it is pitched. For example, if the conditions of ideal speech (e.g. the symmetrical distribution of chances to enter into dialogue, the effective opportunity to call any presupposition of established discourse into question, the suspension of all motives except the wish to reach the correct conclusion) are loosely defined, there is no assurance that one result could emerge from the discourse. And if the conditions are closely specified, it is always possible to claim that the specification itself is not neutral between alternate theoretical perspectives. The problem is that the expressive theory of language and discourse Habermas draws upon to construct his ideal of pure discourse contains within it the expectation that a discourse is unlikely to achieve the practical consensus to which Habermas aspires. Any consensus capable of generating specific courses of action will be based upon some set of pre-judgements which cannot be called into question during that discourse. Some set of pre-judgements must form the unreflective background of discourse while others are called into question, or the discourse will lack sufficient density to generate a conclusion. And if inquiry into a broader range of pre-judgements is encouraged, no free consensus is likely to emerge.

There is something apolitical in this ideal of a perfect consensus, even if it is situated outside the realm of historical probability. It understates the extent to which our limited resources of reason and evidence unavoidably generate a plurality of reasonable answers to perplexing practical questions. It thus fails to appreciate the creative role for politics in those persisting situations where public action must be taken and the resources of knowledge are insufficient to generate a single result. As an ideal, it aspires to take the heat out of the cauldron of contested interpretations and orientations to action. It is in this sense closer to a collectivization of administration than to the democratization of politics. In asking too much from legitimacy, it takes too much away from politics.

Yet apprehended from another angle. the construction of the ideal speech situation (and other versions of the consensus theory of practical judgement) can be seen to carry a political message. It is a symbol as well as a construct. It expresses the anxiety that the potential dilemma of legitimacy actually may be realized in history. It conveys the fear that the space for democratic discourse may become squeezed increasingly by the imperatives of the political economy. As a 'limiting case', unintended for full achievement, it helps to insulate thought from a world which threatens to become less hospitable to democratic ideals; it is an intellectual retreat which protects the idea of democracy by placing it beyond the reach of practical imperatives. The Habermas doctrine, failing as a theory of truth, succeeds as a symbol of the dilemma of legitimacy.

THE FOUCAULDIAN REVERSAL

Foucault would be unsurprised by the critique of the discourse theory of truth briefly outlined here. It is authorized by the 'episteme' governing modern discourse.[11] Whether defined as the implicit, the unconscious, the sedimented, the in-itself, the horizon, or the intersubjective background, theoretical discourse since the nineteenth century has been haunted by the unthought which provides the ground for its vaunted celebration of reflexivity or self-consciousness. Every philosophy which celebrates reflexivity also makes the material it works upon recede constantly into the darkness. Modern 'man' (as Foucault describes us) is endlessly pursued by a 'double', by 'the other that is not only a brother, but a twin', by an unshakeable 'shadow 'both exterior to him and indispensable to him'.[12]

This eternal regress in the relation between the thought and the unthought, between the subject and its other, makes reflexivity possible at the expense of rendering a valid political consensus impossible. It is always possible to dissent from any new interpretation of the previously unthought. 'For modern thought, no morality is possible ... As soon as [thought] functions it offends or reconciles, attracts or repels, breaks, dissociates, unites or reunites; it cannot help but liberate and enslave'.[13] My critique of Habermas, then, operates within the episteme which authorizes it. But it does not, Foucault would insist, pursue its own line to the limits. It fails to enunciate how the very problematic of legitimacy, with its associated concepts of the subject, freedom, reflexivity, allegiance, responsibility, and consent, is the juridical twin of the problematic of disciplinary order. The former is not, as it sees itself, the alternative to the latter; the two function together to produce the modern subject and to subject it to the dictates of the order. The critique, in Foucauldian terms, sets the stage for the reversal of the problematic of legitimacy.

In a perfectly legitimate order, the imperative becomes the indicative: the 'you must' assumes the form of 'we will'. All seems smooth and unruffled, but the voice of the body can still be detected beneath the whine of the socially produced soul. To extrapolate slightly, we might apply Foucault's documentary studies to an account of the relation between the theoretical perspective of Jean-Jacques Rousseau and the Marquis de Sade. For de Sade is not merely the adversary of Rousseau; the theorist of illicit desire is the double of the theorist of civic virtue. Rousseau's legitimate order invokes the free acceptance of self-restraint, the communal endorsement of self-censorship, the production of chaste, subordinate women. And the Sadean counter-order, perfect in its own way, treats these limits as invitations to transgressions: restraints are produced to be broken; censorship intensifies the will to pornography; and the women of virtue become the perfect objects of degradation.

By demanding self-restraint in pursuit of virtue, Rousseau's polity loads the counter-self with illicit desires. It doubles pleasure by adding the pleasure of transgression to the original desire, and the world of virtue produces perfect human objects for the realization of its intensified pleasures. Rousseau's vision of order through virtue thus contains virtue and an underground world of illlicit desire. He articulates one side of this polity, and de Sade articulates the other. Without the presence of the other to oppose and to provide the contrast against which virtue is defined, virtue could not emerge as an achievement; without the other embodied in specific figures of vice, virtue could not fend off the other in itself. But an order which constitutes vice in this way assures that the other will appear in a more aggressive form: it appears as those who take special pleasure in violating virtue. The struggle between vice and virtue is thus loaded in favour of vice, and the virtuous order thereby generates internal pressures to convert the other from the classical figure of vice into the modern object of medical treatment. The classical idea (or this version of it) sets up the modern order which medicalizes insanity, delinquency, sexual perversity, and abnormality. The new order subjects these newly defined figures to treatment; it strives thereby to dampen the pleasures that classical vice had experienced in its struggle with virtue. The old ideal prepares us for modern modes of treatment and discipline.

Individualization is the process by which the modern disciplinary self is produced. One part of the self endorses the rules of the order; it is the free, rational, responsible agent, worthy of punishment for breaking norms to which it freely consents. The second part represents the other which individuals seek to expunge in themselves and to treat when others manifest it in criminality, delinquency, madness, or perverse sexuality. The juridical apparatus and the disciplinary apparatus together constitute the subject and its other.

> In a system of discipline, the child is more individualized than the adult, the patient more than the healthy man, the madman and the delinquent more than the normal and non-delinquent. In each case, it is towards the first of these pairs that all the individualizing mechanisms are turned in our civilization; and when one wishes to individualize the healthy, moral and law-abiding adult, it is always by asking how much of the child he has in him, what fundamental crime he has dreamt of committing . . . All the sciences, analyses or practices employing the root 'psycho-' have their origin in this historical reversal of the procedures of individualization.[14]

Foucault's texts seek to document the multiple ways in which modern attempts to liberate sexuality, madness, and criminality from arbitrary and repressive controls entangle the self in a web of more insidious controls. The politics of liberation, in its radical and liberal guises, actually helps to produce the subject and to subjugate those other parts of the self which do not fit into this production. The reforms typically medicalize sexuality, delinquency, mental 'illness'. They enclose the objects of treatment in a web of 'insidious leniencies'.

Critical legitimists, of whom I am one, are generally eager to shrug off Foucault. We seek not to subjugate people in this order, but to imagine a counter-order which is worthy of their allegiance. But Foucault seems to identify us with our adversaries, and that could not be quite right. Besides, his vocabulary is inflated, and we speak more carefully.

But I do not think we (I) can be let off the hook so easily. Foucault's detailed archaeologies remind us how the dictates of a particular order and the conceptual resources of a particular episteme can soon appear barbaric to its successor (e.g. the way the ships of fools and torture as instruments of truth appear to us today). The history of unreason indirectly challenges the contemporary constitution of reason. Moreover, if Foucault's metaphors seem inflated to us, they challenge us to justify the mellow metaphors through which we characterize either the existing order or the one we would bring into being. In substituting 'surveillance' for 'observation', 'interrogate' for 'question', 'interrupt' for 'pause', and 'production' for 'emergence', he at once challenges the transparency of the mellow metaphors we adopt and claims to detect hidden violence within the discourse of the legitimist. In elaborating the microphysics of the modern subject as a disciplinary production, he is unmasking the denial of the body and how that denial functions. Legitimists are treated as participants in the cover-up. Our metaphors, slipped silently into our discourse, provide the medium through which our potential violence is disguised.

After Foucault, we can understand more clearly why Habermas struggled so valiantly to validate the principle of a free and rational consensus. For that would be a consensus which did not enslave while it liberated; it would create unity without subjugating the other. We can also understand why Foucault must read the project as a counter-tyranny of insidious leniency. For it constantly insists on assimilating material into its categories which can only be made to fit by force. It practises denial in the name of free discourse.

A case can be made, I think, in favour of the legitimist, particularly the dissident type, accepting Foucault as a double. The quest for legitimacy must open itself to the voice of the other; it must review itself from the vantage point of conceptualizations it finds alien, questions it tends to ignore, and answers it tends to exclude. It must confront three questions. What is to be done to, with, or 'for' the other which does not fit into the actual or ideal order? What is the justification for doing it? And what is the ground of the justification?

But can Foucault demand more? Must the quest for legitimacy itself be expunged because any answer given to it must tyrannize and subjugate? I think not. For Foucault is entangled in his own version of the dilemma of legitimacy. Consider the political strategy open to Foucault after the strategies of technocratic control, liberal reform, and radical liberation have been rejected. In his early work, Foucault sought to allow the 'voice of unreason' to speak for itself by historicizing the various relations to the other imposed by historical variations in the constitution of reason. His more recent stance is more overtly political; he now supports 'the insurrection of subjugated knowledges', and he is now more confident in his belief that the attempt to 'understand' the other within any established framework amounts to the attempt to control the other by insidious leniency.[15]

Yet Foucault is not, as he would characterize it, a naive anarchist of the nineteenth century. He does not seem to believe that an anarchistic order could be established. Order is unavoidable for social life; and any order, particularly any order in the modern world, necessarily implies limits.[16] Thus to oppose in principle the quest for legitimacy is to deny one postulate in the Foucauldian problematic. It is to subjugate one dimension of Foucauldian knowledge in the interest (the political interest) of allowing the other dimension to flourish. 'To imagine another system,' Foucault contends, 'is to extend our participation in the present system . . .; the 'whole of society' is precisely that which should not be considered except as something to be destroyed.'[17]

But if I am right, the exclusion of political imagination and affirmation emerges as the Foucauldian denial. Strategic considerations lead him to mask a dimension of his own theory, and the denial is fraught with political consequences dangerous to his own objectives. The release of subjugated knowledges may illuminate political imagination, but it does not release us from the enterprise. Because order implies limits, we must seek a set of limits which could deserve our allegiance. The dilemma of legitimacy inside Foucault's theory thus emerges starkly. It becomes a dilemma of order: social life requires order, but the order which does receive the allegiance of its subjects subjugates them, while the one which does not subjugates them too.[18]

The way to loosen the hold of this dilemma, at least at the level of theory, is to show that the circle of reflexivity is not as closed as Foucault pretends it must be. We may concede that the assimilation of the other to established dualities of reason/unreason, virtue/vice, sanity/insanity, and normality/abnormality always contains the elements of a political conquest. For Foucault's documentary histories do support the conclusion that standards and judgements which possessed hegemony at one historic moment appear arbitrary and closed from the perspective of another; and we can therefore suspect that those categories which now govern our thought and practice will assume such an appearance at a later date. Thus the view of reflexivity which assumes that we can listen to the other through our categories or that we can now broaden them enough to draw the other into their orbit without arbitrariness must now appear to be too narrow; the circle in which it moves is too tightly drawn. But what about a mode of reflexivity which profits from Foucault's histories of madness, criminality, and perversity and which acknowledges that it now lacks the resources to comprehend the other? What about a mode which reflexively acknowledges the limits to reflexive assimilation of the other? Such a view warrants a different response: it encourages us to find the space for the other to live and speak on the ground that we know enough to know that we cannot comprehend it. It supports, I want to say, an ideal of social order which can sustain itself without having to draw so much of the self into the orbit of social control.

This theoretic response contains implications for political conduct. If ours is an order which has 'dirt denying' tendencies; if we tend to sweep that which is out of place under the rug by pretending that we can assimilate it to established categories of rationality and treatment; if we medicalize, confine, and exclude the others who do not fit into the existing order of things, there have been other societies with a loose enough texture to be more 'dirt affirming'.[19] They could acknowledge the dirt that they themselves produce and thereby (though imperfectly or ambiguously) confront the limits of their own conceptual and political orders.

Tribal festivals of reversal had this quality. Seasonal festivals were enacted in which that which was forbidden was allowed and those who were normally subordinated (because their order necessitated it) were temporarily placed in a superior position. In these festivals, that which was officially circumscribed or denied was temporarily allowed and affirmed. The participants were able to glimpse the injustices implicit in their own necessities; they were encouraged to live these necessities with more humanity during the normal periods of the year. They acknowledged that some features of their own order, some of the dirt they produced, was mysterious to them. The reins of social co-ordination were not so tightly drawn that they had to pretend that they possessed sufficient categories to comprehend and eliminate the dirt in their order.

One criterion of comparative legitimacy suggested by the Foucauldian forays into the logic of unreason speaks to the differential capacity of regimes to acknowledge the dirt, the matter out of place, they themselves produce. The civilization of productivity, if its actual trajectory fits the course projected earlier in this essay, will be too constrained by the drive to mobilize its populace around the simultaneous pursuit of growth and austerity to nourish this capacity. To challenge the interdependent complexes of consumption, production, profit, and resource dependency which generate these imperatives is thus to challenge the preconditions of closure in the order. A margin of success on this terrain could help to maintain space for political dialogue. If, for instance, the infrastructure of consumption were reconstituted so that the intensification of consumption demands (or pleas) was not fuelled by the perpetual expansion of consumption needs, the imperative to impose growth and austerity together could be relaxed.[20] The effect would be the provision of needed slack in the order, allowing political engagement to be the medium through which we probe the ambiguities and cope with the limits of modern social life.

By 'slack in the order', I mean an order which does not have to co-ordinate so many aspects of our lives and relations to maintain itself; an order which can afford to let some forms of conduct be; an order which is not compelled by its own imperatives of co-ordination to convert eccentric, odd, strange behaviour into the categories of vice, delinquency, or abnormality. Such an order would require virtue among its citizens, but the space virtue must cover would not extend too broadly; a residual space would flourish in which neither the control of virtue nor coercion would be necessary. The provision of that space would itself allow virtue to displace coercive discipline in those areas where the order did require co-ordination to sustain itself.

This, at least, is the vision which seems to me to contain the most promise for responding to the dilemma of legitimacy. But slack in the order can only be produced if we can find ways to tame or relax the new imperatives which are generated by the civilization of productivity. And (again I express only an intuition) the relaxation of those imperatives can best be achieved if we reconstitute the infrastructure of consumption to reduce those consumption needs which now impel citizens to validate through the political process social disciplines and sacrifice which they themselves find onerous.

Perhaps there are other or better ways to promote slack in the order, but here I want to concentrate on the importance of the end rather than on the most appropriate means to it. For when the legitimist introduces the conception of slack into the problematic of legitimacy, we can hear the echo of an earlier liberal doctrine in the background. A theory which has been inspired by the wish to leave liberal notions of privacy, rights, tolerance, and diversity behind now redefines and reinstitutes them. The irony in this new vision contains the seeds of a renewed dialogue between liberals and radicals. For although the liberal appreciation of private space is acknowledged in this vision, it sees that established liberal programmes and priorities now erode both that space and the implicit allegiance of the populace to the order. Similarly, the radical appreciation of virtue is now endorsed as well as the understanding that an order must produce a double dialectic or regimentation and corruption when it loses the ability to sustain the affective allegiance of its participants. But the radical image is then modified by the admission that the ideal of virtue and legitimacy requires the provision of slack in the order. Slack is both a precondition of and limit to virtue in a modern polity.

Such a perspective is too abstract to resolve the dilemma of legitimacy. It does not define a common good which could at once reorient the priorities of the civilization of productivity, maintain contact with unavoidable parameters of modern life, and provide the slack needed for politics to flourish. Still, it does acknowledge the dilemma of legitimacy; and it establishes a direction to pursue in striving to loosen its grip.

NOTES

1 See Daniel Bell, *The Cultural Contradictions of Capitalism* (New York: Basic Books, 1976); James O'Connor, *The Fiscal Crisis of the State* (New York: St. Martin's Press, 1973); Theodore Lowi. *The End of Liberalism* (New York: W. W. Norton, 1968); George Kateb ('On the "legitimation crisis"'), *Social Research*, 46, 4 (Winter, 1979), pp. 695–727, and Erik Olin Wright, *Class, Crisis and the State* (London: New Left Books, 1978).

2 This section includes a radically abbreviated and modestly revised version of arguments I develop more fully in *Appearance and Reality in Politics* (Cambridge: Cambridge University Press, 1981). That text was not available when this paper was initially composed, and I think that this summary of its argument is still needed to set the stage for the new themes pursued in the remainder of the essay at hand.

3 This argument is most cogently developed in Fred Hirsch, *The Social Limits to Growth* (London: Routledge & Kegan Paul, 1977). An earlier version, more attuned to the implications for politics and less precise with respect to the self-defeating character of the universaliza-

tion of affluence, can be found in Michael Best and William Connolly, *The Politicized Economy* (Lexington, DC: Heath, 1976, 2nd, revised edition, 1982).

4 I am assuming that a shared commitment to constitutional democracy, while part of the answer, could not in principle provide a sufficient answer. I argue this point in chapter 4 of *Appearance and Reality in Politics*.

5 A good example of this principled liberalism can be found in Ronald Dworkin, 'Liberalism', in Stuart Hampshire (ed.), *Public and Private Morality* (Cambridge: Cambridge University Press, 1978, pp. 113–43). The essence of liberalism, says Dworkin, is not some particular conception of the good life or commitment to some particular set of institutional practices. It is to 'treat all its citizens with equal concern and respect'. This principle requires government to 'be neutral on what might be called the question of the good life'. But to conclude that established institutions meet this requirement, Dworkin is implicitly required to narrow the variety of 'conceptions of the good life' to those which fall within the range of tolerance of the established system of productivity. And if its tolerance becomes more restricted, his conceptions are likely to become more abstract. Similar tendencies can be found in George Kateb's challenging essay 'On the "legitimation crisis"', cited above. Kateb wants to preserve the open, exploratory conception of self encouraged by representative democracy. (That's the interesting part.) But he thinks the concentration on 'economic' issues tends to lose sight of that dimension of political life. I contend that we must politicize our understanding of economic life and seek ways to infuse these 'instrumentalities' with space for the open self. Failing that, the instrumentalities are likely to overwhelm the political sphere, as that sphere is understood by the beautiful souls. To them I must appear as an ugly duckling.

6 Charles Schultze, *The Public Use of Private Interest* (Washington, DC: The Brookings Institute, 1977, pp. 17–18).

7 Ibid.

8 *Business Week of* 30 June, 1980 is devoted to 'The Reindustrialization of America'. Amitai Etzioni claims to be one of the principal authors of this thesis. On p. 84, he claims that we ask too much of the American system of political system of political economy; we ask it to 'support an ever rising standard of living, create endless jobs; provide education, medical care, and housing for everyone; abolish poverty; rebuild the cities; restore the environment; satisfy the demands of Blacks, Hispanics, women, and other groups'. I would have thought those were among the defining ends and promises of the civilization of productivity, but they are now interpreted as excessive expectations on its behalf. To reindustrialize, we supposedly must give up these high expectations. We must: (1) shift from an emphasis on consumption to one of savings and investment; (2) shift within investment away from 'quality of life improvements' toward the 'production of capital goods'; (3) increase

state subsidies to business; (4) form a new social contract in which workers give 'management more help in improving productivity' and agree as well to decrease the rate of pay increases; (5) shift to coal and relax environmental constraints on its use; (6) introduce tax reforms to allow much higher depreciation allowances for business; (7) deregulate business to reduce impediments to growth and business costs of compliance; (8) increase military expenditures massively. With this in mind, my disagreement with the beautiful souls can be articulated more specifically. The reindustrializationists are approximately correct about what it would take to get the civilization of productivity rolling again: a progressive withdrawal from cherished liberal principles. Liberal principles are threatened if the system of productivity does not meet these imperatives, and they are threatened if it does. This 'deconstruction' of the beautiful soul is designed to bring out a certain beauty in its retreat and to open it to the possibility of reconsidering its residual commitment to the civilization of productivity.

9 See Jürgen Habermas, *Legitimation Crisis* (Boston: Beacon Press, 1973). My debt to and differences from Habermas are formulated in 'On the critical theory of Jürgen Habermas', *History and Theory*, 18, 3 (1979), pp. 397–417.

10 I prefer the (no doubt awkward) term 'civilization of productivity' for a variety of reasons. First, it refers to the fact that existing Socialist societies are also mobilized around the priorities of economic growth, rendering them inappropriate as contrast models. Second, it signals a refusal to organize a critique around the labour theory of value, thereby rejecting the idea that one technical analysis of the order can be supplanted by another. Third, it refers to the intersubjective dimension within the modes of work, consumption, and bureaucratic control constituting the system of productivity without losing sight of the ways in which those institutions form a complex structure. Fourth, it suggests the possibility that the priorities of productivity could overwhelm the practice of democracy. The squeeze on democratic politics could occur if the priorities are not met (i.e. intensified contestation over the limited economic pie could cast the democracy of compromise and equity into disarray); and it could occur if the priorities are met (i.e. forceful imposition of sacrifices on those without strategic market or political resources could close many out of effective citizenship).

11 An episteme is a temporally bounded set of rules which establish the space within which alternative theories can be articulated and contested. The episteme does not produce the hegemony of one discourse (ideology) over all others; it does produce the space in which alternative discourses can function. The episteme enables and confines theoretical discourse. It renders inoperative today, for instance, the theory of words as signs residing within the world conveying an eternal meaning to be interpreted by commentators; and it thereby renders the Renaissance comprehension of madness as meaningful text to be

deciphered inoperative. A 'discursive practice' functions inside the space provided by the episteme; it is a set of concepts, instruments, architectural structures, regulations, credentials, and rules of evidence which operate at a practical level. Penology and psychiatry are operative disciplines; prisons and asylums are among the media in which they function; delinquents, criminals, and a variety of mental patients are the objects they constitute and treat. These elements together form the discursive practices of criminology and psychiatry. The modern episteme allows these, but it does not uniquely determine them. It forecloses punishment as spectacle, for instance, because we cannot now think of the torture-confession complex as a sign of truth; but it allows the juridical conception of crime (rational agents who are responsible and guilty) to function alongside the treatment model. The shift in emphasis in the Foucauldian texts from archaeology to genealogy would need to be treated in a thorough discussion of his thought. I will not attempt that here.

12 Michel Foucault, '*The Order of Things*' (New York: Random House, 1970), p. 326.

13 Ibid., p. 328.

14 Michel Foucault, *Discipline and Punish* (tr.) Alan Sheridan (New York: Random House, 1977), p. 193.

15 Michel Foucault, *Power/Knowledge* (Brighton, Sussex: Harvester Press, 1980), p. 81. My reading of the earlier texts is supported on p. 108 of this more recent essay: 'it is not through recourse to sovereignty against discipline that the effects of disciplinary power can be limited because sovereignty and disciplinary mechanisms are two absolutely integral constituents of the general mechanisms of power in our society.'

16 Will the new episteme which is now beginning to tremble beneath our feet break this relation between life, order, and limits? We cannot now know. But it seems likely that the Foucauldian strategy of proliferating resistance and oppositions without affirmations rests upon a faith in the unknown possibilities residing in the next 'break'. The strategy seems designed to hasten its arrival. The insistence that radical breaks or ruptures divide the Renaissance from the classical age and the classical from the modern age (with its two giant regimes) is governed by this political intent. If those breaks were complete, maybe the next one will be too. I agree that the left needs a break, but there is no ground for such a faith. The strategy, in the order we now know, promises to tighten and extend reactive forces. A complete account would need to discuss this theory of breaks (it is exaggerated) and the reversal of the theory of the subject associated with it. Another defence of Foucauldian strategy rests upon the view that, since the forces of order are always with us, we need a counter-force unconfined by the need to affirm and, thereby, unconfined by the need to limit itself. But a reversal of the reversal is needed here: since the voice of order is always with us, we need to legitimize oppositional efforts through counter-

affirmations to gain leverage. My position depends on qualifying the theory of breaks, the reversal of the subject, and the denial of affirmation; and I think that advances in one of these areas will promote success in the others. At any rate, the Foucauldian schema itself is too mired in the present to authorize a strategy based upon faith in the break to come. Foucault says as much in the last paragraph (p. 387) of *The Order of Things*. 'If those arrangements were to disappear as they appeared, if some event of which we can at the moment do no more than sense the possibility . . . without knowing either what its forms will be or what it promises . . . were to cause them to crumble, as the ground of Classical thought did, at the end of the eighteenth century, then one can certainly wager that man could be erased, like a face drawn in sand at the edge of the sea.'

17 Michel Foucault, *Language, Counter Memory, Practice* (Oxford: Basil Blackwell, 1977), pp. 230, 233. It is possible, more than possible, that underlying the bravado about breaks and implicit in the restriction of oppositional discourse to resistance is the sense that the current order is beyond the reach of serious reconstitution.

18 On p. 96 of *Power/Knowledge*, Foucault declares: 'right should be viewed, I believe, not in terms of a legitimacy to be established, but in terms of the methods of subjugation it instigates.'

19 The terms are borrowed from Mary Douglas (who borrowed them from William James). See *Purity and Danger* (Baltimore: Penguin Books, 1966).

20 To change the infrastructure of consumption, it is necessary to revise also the modes of investment, profit, work, and state expenditures. These themes are developed in Best and Connolly, *The Politicized Economy*. I think the alternatives reduce to three: (1) refusing to support the imperatives of the system of productivity without modifying the institutions which produce them; (2) successfully imposing austerity on politically weakened constituencies to provide the basis for 'reindustrialization'; (3) reconstituting the established mode of consumption, etc. to curtail imperatives. Each of these strategies would face resistance, opposition, limits, setbacks, and so forth. But only one of them contains the promise to preserve space for democratic politics. That is also the one (3) which is unexplored within the established terms of political discourse.

11

The Political Paradox

PAUL RICOEUR

Many would maintain that the problem of political power in a Socialist economy is not fundamentally different from the same problem in a capitalist economy, that it offers comparable if not added possibilities for tyranny, and that it calls for equally if not more strict democratic controls. Yet this is precisely what is rejected by all those who do not subscribe to the relative autonomy of polity in comparison with the socio-economic history of societies.[1]

This autonomy of polity seems to consist of two contrasting features. On the one hand, polity works out a human relationship which is neither reducible to class conflicts, nor to socio-economic tensions of society in general. The state most noted for a ruling class is a state in that it expresses the fundamental will of the nation in its entirety. Hence it is not radically affected, as state, by changes which are nevertheless radical in the economic sphere. By means of this first feature, man's political existence displays a specific type of rationality which is irreducible to dialectics based upon economics.

On the other hand, politics fosters specific evils which are precisely political evils, evils of political power. These evils are irreducible to others, in particular to economic alienation. Thus, economic exploitation *may* disappear while political evil persists. Moreover, the means which the state employs in order to put an end to economic exploitation may be the occasion for the abuse of power, new in their expression and in their effects, but fundamentally identical in their passional incentive to those of past states.

Specific rationality, specific evil – such is the double and paradoxical originality of polity. It would seem to me that the task of political philosophy is to explicate this originality and to elucidate the paradox of it. For political evil can only be an outgrowth of the specific rationality of polity.

It is necessary to hold out against the temptation to oppose two

Source: Paul Ricouer, 'The political paradox', in Charles A. Kelbley (tr.) *History and Truth* (Evanston: Northwestern University Press, 1965), reprinted with permission of Northwestern University Press.

styles of political reflection, one which stresses the rationality of polity, drawing upon Aristotle, Rousseau, and Hegel, the other emphasizing the violence and untruth of power, following the Platonic critique of the 'tyrant', the Machiavellian apology of the 'prince', and the Marxist critique of 'political alienation'.

This paradox must be retained: that the greatest evil adheres to the greatest rationality, that there is political alienation *because* polity is relatively autonomous. Let us therefore now treat of the autonomy of polity.

THE AUTONOMY OF POLITY

What will always remain admirable in the political thought of the Greeks is that no philosopher among them – with the possible exception of Epicurus – ever resigned himself to the exclusion of politics from the domain of rationality. All or almost all knew that if politics were declared evil, foreign, and 'other', by comparison to reason and philosophical discourse, if politics were literally given over to the devil, then reason itself has capsized. For in that case, reason would no longer be of reality and in reality, at least not to the extent that human reality is political. If nothing is reasonable in man's political existence, then reason is not real, it is floating in the air, and philosophy becomes banished to the world of the ideal and duty. No great philosophy ever resigned itself to this, even (and especially) if it begins with the data of everyday existence and at first turns away from the world. Every great philosophy attempts to understand political reality in order to understand itself.

Now, politics discloses its meaning only if its aim – its *telos* – can be linked up with the fundamental intention of philosophy itself, with the Good and with Happiness. The Ancients did not understand how a Politics – a political philosophy – could possibly begin with something other than a teleology of the state, of the *res publica*, itself situated in relation to the final goal of mankind. Aristotle's *Politics* begins thus: 'Every State is a society of some kind, and every society, like all forms of association, is instituted with a view to some good; for mankind always acts for an end which is esteemed good. Now if all societies aim at some good, then the State, which is the highest of all societies, and which encompasses all the rest, aims at the highest and most perfect good.' The concept of the 'good life' mutually implicates politics and ethics.

Henceforth, to reflect on the autonomy of polity is to find in the teleology of the state its irreducible manner of contributing to the

humanity of man. The specific nature of polity can only be brought
to light by means of this teleology. It has the specific nature of an
aim, an intention. Through the political good, men pursue a good
which they could not otherwise attain and this good is a part of
reason and happiness. This pursuit and this *telos* constitute the
'nature' of the *Polis*. The nature of the state is its end, just as 'the
nature of each thing is its end'.[2]

From this standpoint, political philosophy is induced to determine how this meaning – which is the 'end' and 'nature' of the state
– resides in the State as a whole, as an entire body, hence how
humanity comes to man by means of the body politic. The
fundamental conviction of all political philosophy is that he 'who
by nature and not by mere accident can exist without a state would
be a despicable individual, either above or inferior to man . . . 'For
whoever has no need of society or is unable to live in society is
either a beast or a god. The social instinct is natural to all men.'[3] If
the destination of man passes through a corporate body, through a
whole, through a state defined by its 'sufficiency', then it is
forbidden to begin with the opposition between the state and the
citizen. The point of view of philosophy is, on the contrary, that
the individual becomes human only within this totality which is the
'universality of citizens'. The threshold of humanity is the threshold
of citizenship, and the citizen is a citizen only through the state.
Hence the movement of political philosophy starts with happiness,
which all men pursue, moves to the proper end of the state, then to
its nature as a self-sufficient totality, and from there to the citizen.
Because the 'State is the constant subject of politics and government', the movement of political thought proper proceeds from the
state to the citizen and not the inverse: 'A citizen is one who, in his
own country, has the power to take part in the deliberative or
judicial administration of the State.' Thus the citizen is characterized by the attribute of power: 'For according to our definition, the
citizen shares in the government of a state.'[4]

In its turn, citizenship fosters the 'virtues' peculiar to this
participation in public power. These are the 'virtues' which govern
the relationship of government to free men, virtues of obedience
distinct from servility, just as the authority of the state worthy of
this name is distinct from despotism. Hence, political thought
proceeds from the state, to citizenship, to civism, and not in the
reverse order.

Such is the disciplined thought proposed by the ancient model;
such also is the disciplined thought which ought to be indispensable
for any individual who wishes to gain the right to speak seriously

about political evils. A meditation on politics, which would begin with the opposition of the 'philosopher' and the 'tyrant' and which would reduce the whole exercise of power to the perversion of the will to power, would thereby forever enclose itself within nihilistic moralism. One of the first actions of political reflection should be to push the figure of the 'tyrant' off to the side, allowing it to emerge as the frightening possibility which cannot be coped with because men are evil. Still it should not be the object of political science: 'It is proper to mention in last place tyranny as the worst of all depravations and the least worthy of the name constitution. For this reason, we have kept it for the end' (Aristotle).

But the autonomy of polity is something more than this vague, communal destiny of the human animal, something more than the admission of man to humanity by means of citizenship. More precisely, it is the specific nature of the political bond as opposed to the economic bond. This second moment of reflection is basic to what follows; for political evil will be just as specific as this bond and the remedy for the evil as well.

It seems to me that one cannot undertake the critique of the authenticity of political life without having first demarcated the boundaries of the political sphere and acknowledging the validity of the distinction between polity and economics. Every critique presupposes this distinction and can by no means set it aside.

Now, no reflection is a better preparation for this recognition than that of Rousseau. To discover and reiterate within oneself the most profound motivation of the 'social contract' is, at the same time, to discover the meaning of polity as such. A return to Rousseau, linking up with the return to the Ancients – to Aristotle's *Politics* in particular – should provide the basis and the background for every critique of power which could not begin, in any case, with the individual.

The great, invincible idea of the *Social Contract* is that the body politic is born of a virtual act, of a consent which is not an historical event, but one which only comes out in reflection. This act is a pact: not a pact of one with another, not a pact of abstention in favour of a non-contracting third party, the sovereign, who, by not being part of the contract would be absolute. No – but it is a pact of each individual with all, a pact which constitutes the people as a people by constituting it as a state. This admirable idea, so criticized and so badly understood, is the basic equation of political philosophy: 'To find a form of association that will defend and protect with the whole common force the person and goods of each member, and in which each, while uniting himself with all, may still obey himself alone and remain just as free as before'.[5] Not the exchange of savage liberty for security, but the passage to civil existence through law which is given the consent of all.

One may well express dissatisfaction with the abstraction, idealism, and hypocrisy of this pact – and this is true in certain respects. But first one must recognize in this pact the founding act of the nation. This founding act cannot be engendered by any economic dialectics; it is this founding act which constitutes polity as such.

One might object that this pact has not taken place. Precisely. It is of the nature of political consent, which gives rise to the unity of the human community organized and oriented by the state, to be able to be recovered only in an act which has not taken place, in a contract which has not been contracted, in an implicit and tacit pact which appears only in political awareness, in retrospection, and in reflection.

Hence, untruth can very easily slip into polity; polity is prone to untruth because the political bond has the reality of ideality: this ideality is the equality of each before all others, 'for if each individual gives himself absolutely, the condition is equal for all; and, this being the case, then no one should have reason to make it onerous for others.'[6] But before being hypocrisy, behind which is hidden the exploitation of man by man, equality before the law, and the ideal equality of each before all, is the *truth* of polity. This is what constitutes the *reality* of the state. Inversely, the reality of the state, irreducible to class conflicts or to the dynamics of economic domination and alienation, is the advent of a legality which will never be completely reducible to the projection of the interests of the ruling class into the sphere of law. As soon as there is a state, a body politic, the organization of an historical community, there exists the reality of this ideality; and herein is contained a point of view of the state which may never completely coincide with the phenomenon of class domination. If the state is reduced to the ideal projection of the interests of the ruling class, then there is no longer a political state but despotic power. But even the most despotic state is still state in that something pertaining to the common good of the vast majority of citizens comes about through tyranny and therefore transcends the interests of one particular group or the dominant groups. Besides, only the original autonomy of polity can explain the hypocritical use of legality as a cloak for economic exploitation; for the ruling class would not experience the need to project its interests into juridical fiction if this juridical fiction were not first the condition of the real existence of the state. In order to become the state, a class must make its interests penetrate into the sphere of the universality of law; this law can mask the relation of force only in the measure that the power of the state itself flows from the ideality of the past.

I am aware of the difficulties related to the notion of general will, of sovereignty in Rousseau's writings. In the Geneva manuscript, Rousseau spoke even then of the 'abyss of politics in the constitution of the state' (just as, in the constitution of man, the action of the soul on the body is the abyss of philosophy). These difficulties are not the fault of Rousseau; they pertain to polity as such: a pact which is a virtual act and which founds a real community; an ideality of law which legitimizes the reality of force; a ready-made fiction to clothe the hypocrisy of a ruling class, but which, before giving rise to falsehood, founds the freedom of citizens, a freedom which ignores particular cases, the real differences of power, and the real conditions of persons, but which is nevertheless valuable because of its very abstraction – such is the peculiar labyrinth of polity.

Rousseau, at bottom, is Aristotle. The pact which engenders the body politic is, in voluntarist language and on the level of the virtual pact (of the 'as if'), the *telos* of the state referred to by the Greeks. Where Aristotle speaks of 'nature' and 'end', Rousseau uses 'pact' and 'general will'; but it is fundamentally the same thing; in both cases, the specific nature of polity is reflected in philosophical consciousness. Rousseau recognized the artificial act of an ideal subjectivity, of a 'public person', whereas Aristotle discerned an objective nature. But Rousseau's general will is objective and Aristotle's objective nature is that of man aiming toward happiness. The fundamental accord of these formulae comes out in their very reciprocity. In the two cases, with the *telos* of the state and the generating pact of the general will, it is a matter of manifesting the coincidence of an individual and passional will with the objective and political will, in short, of making man's humanity pass through legality and civil restraint.

Rousseau is Aristotle. Perhaps it should be noted that Hegel supports this view. It is important, since Marx, as we shall see, initiated the critique of the bourgeois state and, he thought, of every state, through the instrumentality of Hegel's *Philosophy of Right*. The whole of Western political thought, epitomized in such giants as Aristotle, Rousseau, and Hegel, is supposedly brought together in the Marxist critique.

When Hegel looks upon the state as reason realized in man, he is not thinking about a particular state, nor any state whatever, but rather about the reality which comes into being through empirical states and to which nations obtain access when they pass the threshold of organization as a modern state, along with differentiated organs, a constitution, an administration, etc., and reach the level of historical responsibility within the framework of international relationships. From this standpoint, the state appears as what is desired by individuals so as to realize their freedom: viz., a rational, universal organization of freedom. The most extreme, the most scandalous formulae of Hegel on the state, which Eric Weil recapitulated in his book *Hegel et l'état*,[7] should be taken as the limiting expression, as the advanced point of a thought determined to situate all its recriminations within the very interior of, and not outside of the fully recognized political reality. It is on the basis of this limiting expression that we must view all that can be said against the state and against the mad pretension which lays hold of its rational intention.

POWER AND EVIL

There is a specific political alienation because polity is autonomous. It is the other side of this paradox which must now be clarified.

The crux of the problem is that the state is will. One can stress as much as need be the rationality conferred upon history by polity – this is true. But if the state is rational in its intentions, it nevertheless advances through history by means of decisions. It is not possible to exclude from the definition of polity the idea of decisions of historic import, that is to say which change in abiding fashion the destiny of the human assemblage organized and directed by the state. Polity is rational organization, politics involves decisions: probable analysis of situations, probable projection as to the future. Polity necessarily involves politics.

Polity takes on meaning after the fact, in reflection, in 'retrospection'. Politics is pursued step by step, in 'prospection', in projects, that is to say both in an uncertain deciphering of contemporary events, and in the steadfastness of resolutions. Thus, if the political function, if polity, carries on without interruption, one can say in a sense that politics only exists in great moments, in 'crises', in the climactic and turning points of history.

But if it is impossible to define polity without including the voluntary moment of decision, neither is it possible to speak of political decisions without reflecting on power.

From polity to politics, we move from advent to events, from sovereignty to the sovereign, from the state to government, from historical reason to power.

It is in this fashion that the specific nature of polity becomes manifest within the specific qualities of the means of which it disposes. Considered from the point of view of politics, the state is the authority which holds a monopoly over lawful physical constraint. The adjective 'lawful' attests that the definition of the state, in terms of its specific means, refers to the definition of the same state in terms of its end and its form. But should the state ever manage by chance to become identified with its foundation of legitimacy – for example by becoming the authority of the law – this state would still be a monopoly of constraint; it would still be the power of a few over all; it would still cumulate a legitimacy, that is to say a moral power of exacting, and a violence without appeal, that is to say a physical power of constraining.

It is in this way that we reach the idea of the entire sweep of politics. Let us say that politics is the sum total of activities which have for their object the exercise of power, therefore also the conquest and preservation of power. Step by step, politics will encompass every activity whose goal or effect will be to influence the division of power.[8]

It is politics – politics defined by reference to power – which poses the problem of political evil. There is a problem of political evil because there is a specific problem of power. Not that power is evil. But power is one of the splendours of man that is eminently prone to evil. Perhaps in history it is the greatest occasion for and the most stupendous display of evil. The reason of course is that power is a very extraordinary phenomenon, since it is the vehicle of the historical rationality of the state. We must never lose sight of this paradox.

This specific evil of power has been recognized by the greatest of political thinkers with a signal unanimity. The prophets of Israel and the Socrates of the *Gorgias* concur unequivocally on this point. Machiavelli's *Prince*, Marx's *Critique of Hegel's Philosophy of Right*, Lenin's *State and Revolution* – and . . . the Khrushchev report, that extraordinary document on the evil in politics – are all in fundamental accord although certainly operating within radically different theoretical and philosophical contexts. This very concurrence attests to the stability of the political problematic throughout history and, thanks to this stability, we comprehend these texts as a truth valid for all time.

It is well worth noting that the earliest recorded Biblical prophecy, that of Amos, denounces political crimes and not individual faults.[9] Wherever one might be tempted to recognize a mere survival of the outdated notion of collective sin, previous to the individualization of punishment and fault, one must distinguish the denunciation of political evil as the evil of power. It is man's political existence that confers upon sin its historical dimension, its devastating power and, I would venture to say, its grandeur. The death of Jesus, like that of Socrates, resulted from a political act, a political trial. It was a political authority, the very one which, by its order and tranquillity, assured the historical success of *humanitas* and *universalitas*. It was Roman political power that raised the Cross: 'He suffered under Pontius Pilate.'

Hence sin manifests itself in power, and power unveils the true nature of sin, which is not pleasure but the pride of domination, the evil of possession and holding sway.

The *Gorgias* is certainly in accord with this. One can even say that the Socratic and Platonic philosophy springs in part from a reflection on the 'tyrant', that is to say on power without law and without consent on the part of subjects. How is the tyrant – the inverse of the philosopher – possible? This question cuts to the quick of philosophy, for tyranny is not possible without a falsification of the word, that is to say of this power, human *par excellence*, of *expressing* things and of communicating with men. The whole of Plato's argument in the *Gorgias* is based upon the conjunction between the perversion of philosophy, represented by sophistry, and the perversion of politics, represented by tyranny. Tyranny and sophistry form a monstrous pair. Hence Plato ferrets out one aspect of political evil, different from power but intimately linked to it: 'flattery', the art of inducing persuasion by means other than the truth. In this way, he brings to light the connection between politics and untruth. The point of his argument is quite important, if it is true that the word is the milieu, the fundamental element of mankind, the *logos* which unifies mankind and founds communication. Thus the lie, flattery, and untruth – political evils *par excellence* – corrupt man's primordial state, which is word, discourse, and reason.

Here, then, we have the elements of a meditation on the pride of power and on untruth, a meditation which shows these two phenomena to be evils linked to the essence of politics. We may rediscover this double meditation within these two great works of political philosophy: Machiavelli's *Prince* and Lenin's *State and Revolution*, both of which attest to the permanence of the problematic of power amid the various forms of governments, amid the evolution of technics and the transformations of social and economic conditionings. The question of power, of its exercise, its conquest, its defence and extension, has an astonishing stability which would make us apt to believe in a certain continuity of human nature.

Much has been said of the evil of 'Machiavellism'. But should we take the *Prince* seriously, as it must be, then we shall discover that it is by no means easy to evade its problem: how to establish a new power, a new state. The *Prince* evinces the implacable logic of political action: the logic of means, the pure and simple techniques of acquiring and preserving power. The technique is wholly dominated by the essential political relationship between the friend and the enemy: the enemy may be exterior or interior, a nation, nobility, an army, or a counsellor; and every friend may turn into an enemy and vice versa. The technique plays upon a vast keyboard ranging from military power to the sentiments of fear and gratitude, of vengeance and loyalty. The *Prince*, conscious of all the ramifications of power, the immensity, the variety, and the manifold measure of its keyboard, will be equipped with the abilities of the strategist and the psychologist, lion and fox. And so Machiavelli raised the true problem of political violence, not that of ineffectual violence, of arbitrary or frenetic violence, but that of calculated and limited violence designed to establish a stable state. Of course, one can say that by means of this calculation, inceptive violence places itself under the judgement of established legality; but this established legality, this 'republic', is marked from its inception by violence which was successful. All nations, all powers, and all regimes are born in this way. Their violent birth then becomes resorbed in the new legitimacy which they foster and consolidate. But this new legitimacy always retains a note of contingency, something strictly historical which its violent birth never ceases to confer upon it. Machiavelli has therefore elucidated the relationship between politics and violence. Herein lies his probity and his veracity.

Several centuries later, Marx and Lenin returned to a theme which can be called Platonic, the problem of the 'false consciousness'. It seems to me that what is most worthy of note in the Marxist critique of politics and the Hegelian state is not its explication of the state by means of the power relations among classes, which would therefore be the reduction of political evil to socio-economic evil, but rather the description of this evil as the specific evil of politics. I believe that the great error which assails the whole of Marxism–Leninism and which weighs upon the regimes engendered by Marxism is this reduction of political evil to economic evil. From this springs the illusion that a society liberated from the contradictions of the bourgeois society would also be freed of political alienation. But the essential point of Marx's critique[10] is that the state is not and cannot be what it claims to be. What does it claim to be? If Hegel is right, the state is conciliation, the conciliation, in a higher sphere, of interests and individuals which are irreconcilable at the level of what Hegel calls civil society, which is what we would call the socio-economic level. The incoherent world of private relationships is arbitrated and rationalized by the higher authority of the state. The state is a mediator and therefore reason. And each of us attains his freedom and rights by means of the authority of the state. I am free insofar as I am political. It is in this sense that Hegel maintains that the state is representative: it exists in representation and man is represented in it. The essence of Marx's critique lies in exposing the illusion in this pretension. The state is not the true world of man but rather another and unreal world; it resolves real contradictions only in virtue of a fictive law which is, in turn, in contradiction with the real relationships between men.

It is on the basis of this essential untruth, of this discordance between the pretension of the state and the true state of affairs, that Marx meets with the problem of violence. For sovereignty, not being the achievement of the people in its concrete reality, but being another, visionary world, is forced to look for support in a real, concrete, empirical sovereign. The idealism of right is maintained throughout the course of history only by means of the caprice of the prince. Thus the political sphere is divided between the ideal of sovereignty and the reality of power, between sovereignty and the sovereign, between the constitution and the government, or the police. It matters little that Marx was familiar only with constitutional monarchy, for the split between the constitution and the monarch, between law and caprice, is a contradiction internal to all political power. This also holds true in the Republic. Notice how recently our right to referendum was usurped by clever politicians who twisted *de facto* power against the sovereignty of the electoral body. This is of the essence of political evil. No state exists without a government, an administration, a police force; consequently, the phenomenon of political alienation traverses all regimes and is found within all constitutional forms. Political society involves this external contradiction between an ideal sphere of legal relations and a real sphere of communal relations – and this internal contradiction between sovereignty and the sovereign, between the constitution and power or, in the extreme, the police. We aspire to attain a state wherein the radical contradiction which exists between a universality pursued by the state and the particularity and caprice which it evinces in reality would be resolved. The evil is that this aspiration is not within our reach.

Unfortunately, Marx did not perceive the absolute character of this contradiction; he viewed it as a mere superstructure, that is to say the transposition on to a superadded plane of the contradictions pertaining to the inferior plane of capitalist society and, in the last analysis, an effect of class opposition. The state, then, is but the instrument of class violence, even though the state may possibly always envisage a scheme or project transcending disparate class interests. Oddly enough, it would seem that the evil peculiar to the state is its very opposition to this grandiose scheme. When the state is thus conceived of as the organized power of the ruling class for oppressing another, then the illusion of the state being universal conciliation is nothing but a particular instance of the vice of bourgeois societies, showing them unable to offset their own deficiency or to resolve their contradictions except by taking flight into the phantom of right.

I believe it must be maintained, against Marx and Lenin, that political alienation is not reducible to another, but is constitutive of human existence, and, in this sense, that the political mode of existence entails the breach between the citizen's abstract life and the concrete life of the family and of work. I think too that thereby we retain what is best in the Marxist critique, which interrelates with the Machiavellian, Platonic, and Biblical critique of power.

I should like to adduce the Khrushchev report alone as proof. The fundamental fact would seem to be that the criticism of Stalin has meaning only if the alienation of politics is an absolute alienation, irreducible to that of economic society. If it were not, then how is it possible to censure Stalin while continuing to sanction the socialist form of economy and the Soviet regime? The Khrushchev report is inconceivable without a critique of power and the vices of power. But since Marxism does not allow for an autonomous problematic of power, it falls back upon fable and moralizing criticism. Togliatti was somewhat incautious the day he declared that the explanations of the Khrushchev report did not satisfy him, wondering as he did how the phenomenon of Stalin had been possible in a socialist regime. The reply could not be given to him because it can only flow from a critique of socialist power, something which up to now has not been made and which, perhaps, could not be achieved within the compass of Marxism, at least in so far as Marxism reduces all alienations to economic and social alienation.

I should like to make it quite clear once and for all that the theme of political evil, which I have just set forth, by no means constitutes a political 'pessimism' and does not warrant any political 'defeatism'. Besides, the pessimist and optimist labels are to be banned from philosophical reflection; pessimism and optimism are but moods and only concern characterology, which is to say that no use may be made of them here. Yet it is quite important that we should acquire a lucidity with respect to the evil of power, for this is something which could not be divorced from a thoroughgoing reflection on polity. This reflection reveals that politics can be the seat of the greatest evil only because of its prominent place within human existence. The enormity of political evil is commensurate with man's political existence. More than any other, a meditation which would parallel political evil with radical evil, making of it the closest approximation of radical evil, ought to remain inseparable from a meditation on the radical significance of politics. Every condemnation of politics as corrupt is itself deceitful, malevolent, and infamous, at least if it neglects to situate this description within the dimension of the political animal. The analysis of polity, as the progress of man's rationality, is not abolished but constantly presupposed by meditation on political evil. On the contrary, political evil is serious only because it is the evil of man's rationality, the specific evil of the splendour of man.

In particular, the Marxist critique of the state does not suppress the analysis of sovereignty, from Rousseau to Hegel, but rather presupposes the truth of this analysis. If there is no truth in the general will (Rousseau), if there is no teleology of history amid 'unsocial sociability' and by means of this 'ruse of reason' which is political rationality (Kant), if the state is not 'representative' of man's humanity, then political evil is not grave. It is precisely because the state is a certain expression of the rationality of history, a triumph over the passions of the individual man, over 'civil' interests, and even over class interests, that it is the most exposed and most threatened aspect of man's grandeur, the most prone to evil. Political 'evil' is, in the literal sense, the madness of grandeur, that is to say the madness of what is great – grandeur and culpability of power!

Henceforth, man cannot evade politics under penalty of evading his humanity. Throughout history, and by means of politics, man is faced with *his* grandeur and *his* culpability.

One could not infer a political 'defeatism' on the basis of this lucidity. Such a reflection leads rather to a political vigilance. It is here that reflection, ending its long detour, comes back to actuality and moves from critique to praxis.

THE PROBLEM OF POWER IN SOCIALIST REGIMES

If our analysis of the paradox of power is correct, if the state is at once more rational and more passional than the individual, the great problem of democracy concerns the control of the state by the people. The problem of the control of the state, like that of its rationality, is equally irreducible to socio-economic history, as is its evilness irreducible to class contradictions. The problem of the control of the state consists in this: to devise institutional techniques especially designed to render possible the exercise of power and render its abuse impossible. The notion of 'control' derives directly from the central paradox of man's political existence; it is the practical resolution of this paradox. To be sure, it is, of course, necessary that the state *be* but that it not be too much. It must direct, organize, and make decisions so that the political animal himself might be; but it must not lead to the tyrant.

Only a political philosophy which has perceived the specific nature of polity – the specific nature of its function and the specific nature of its evil – is in a position to pose correctly the problem of political control.

Thus the reduction of political alienation to economic alienation would seem to be the weak point in the political thought of Marxism. This reduction of political alienation has, in effect, led Marxism–Leninism to substitute another problem for the problem of state control, that of the withering away of the State. This substitution seems disastrous to me; it grounds the end of the iniquity of the state upon an indefinite future, whereas the true, practical political problem pertains to the limitation of this evil in the present. An eschatology of innocence takes the place of an ethic of limited violence. At one and the same time, the thesis of the withering away of the state, by promising too much for the future, equally tolerates too much in the present. The thesis of the future withering away of the state serves as a cloak and an alibi for the perpetuation of terrorism. By means of a sinister paradox, the thesis of the provisory character of the state turns into the best justification for the endless prolongation of the dictatorship of the proletariat and forms the essence of totalitarianism.

It is quite necessary to realize that the theory of the withering away of the state is a logical consequence of the reduction of political alienation to economic alienation. If the state is merely an organ of repression, which springs from class antagonisms and expresses the domination of one class, then the state will disappear along with all the after-effects of the division of society into classes.

But the question is whether the end of the private appropriation of the means of production can bring about the end of all alienations. Perhaps appropriation itself is but one privileged form of the power of man over man; perhaps money itself is but one means of domination among others; perhaps the same spirit of domination is given expression in various forms: in economic exploitation, in bureaucratic tyranny, in intellectual dictatorship, and in clericalism.

Our concern here is not the hidden unity of all alienations. In any case, the reduction of the political form to the economic form is indirectly responsible for the myth of the withering away of the state.

It is true that Marx, Engels, and Lenin have attempted to elaborate this theory on the basis of experience. They interpreted the Paris Commune as the guarantee and the commencement of the experimental verification of the thesis of the withering away of the state; for them it demonstrated that the dictatorship of the proletariat may be something quite different from the mere transfer of the state's power into other hands, but indeed the overthrow of the state machine as the 'special force' of repression. If the armed populace is substituted for the permanent army, if the police force is subject to dismissal at any moment, if bureaucracy is dismantled as an organized body and reduced to the lowest paid condition, then the general force of the majority of the people replaces the special force of repression found in the bourgeois state, and the beginning of the withering away of the state coincides with the dictatorship of the proletariat. As Lenin says, 'it is impossible to pass from capitalism to socialism without a certain return to a primitive form of democracy.' The withering away of the state is therefore contemporaneous with the dictatorship of the proletariat, in the measure that the latter is a truly popular revolution which smashes the repressive organs of the bourgeois state. Marx could even say, 'The Commune was no longer a State in the literal sense of the word.'

In the thought of Marx and Lenin, the thesis of the withering away of the State was therefore not a hypocritical thesis but a sincere one. To be sure, few men have demanded so little of the state as the great Marxists: 'So long as the proletariat still has need of a state,' reads the letter to Bebel, 'it is not in order to secure freedom but to put down its adversaries; and the day when it becomes possible to speak of freedom, the State will cease to exist as such.'

But if the withering away of the state is the critical test for the dictatorship of the proletariat, then the crucial question is posed: why has the withering away of the state not in fact coincided with the dictatorship of the proletariat? Why, in fact, has the Socialist state reinforced the power of the state to the point of confirming the axiom which Marx believed to be applicable only to bourgeois revolutions: 'All revolutions have only served to perfect this machine instead of smashing it.'[11] The attempt to reply to this question is at the same time to provide the missing link to the Khrushchev report, for it is to explain how the phenomenon of Stalin was possible in the midst of a Socialist regime.

My working hypothesis, such as is suggested by the preceding reflection, is that Stalin was possible because there was no recognition of the permanence of the problematic of power in the transition from the old to the new society, because it was believed that the end of economic exploitation necessarily implied the end of political repression, because it was believed that the state is provisory, because one had substituted the problem of the withering away of the state for that of its control. In short, my working hypothesis is that the state cannot wither away and that, not being able to wither away, it must be controlled by a special institutional form of government.

Furthermore, it would seem that the Socialist state, more than the bourgeois state, requires a vigilant, popular control precisely because its rationality is greater, because it enlarges its sphere of analyses and forecasts so as to encompass sectors of human existence which elsewhere and in former times were given over to chance and improvisation. The rationality of a Socialist state, striving as it does to suppress class antagonisms and even aspiring to put an end to the division of society into classes, is certainly greater. But you see at once that its scope of power is also greater as well as the possibilities for tyranny.

It would seem that the task of a critique of Socialist power should be to articulate lucidly and faithfully the new possibilities of political alienation, that is to say those which are opened up by the very battle against economic alienation as well as by the reinforcement of state power which this battle entails.

Here are some avenues of approach which might be pursued by an investigation of power in Socialist regimes:

(1) We should first have to determine in what measure 'the administration of things' necessarily involves a 'governing of persons' and in what measure the progress in the administration of things gives rise to an augmentation of political power of man over man.

For example, planning implies a choice of an economic character concerning the order of priority in the satisfaction of needs and the employment of means of production; but this choice is from the very outset more than a matter of economics. It is the function of a general politics, that is to say of a long-term project concerning the orientation of the human community engaged in the experience of planning. The proportion of the part reinvested and the part consumed, the proportion of cultural and material goods in the general equilibrium of the plan, spring from a 'global strategic vision' in which economics is woven into politics. A plan is a technique serving a global project, a civilizing project animated by implicit values, in short, a project which in the last analysis pertains to man's very nature. Hence, insofar as it gives expression to will and power, polity is the soul of economics.

Thus the administration of things may not be substituted for the governing of persons, since the rational technique of ordering man's needs and activities on the macroscopic scale of the state cannot extricate itself from all ethico-cultural contexts. Consequently, in the last analysis, political power unites scales of value and technological possibilities, the latent aspirations of the human community, and the means unleashed by knowledge of economic laws. The connection between ethics and technics in the 'task' of planning is the fundamental reason why the administration of things implies the governing of persons.

(2) Next, we should have to determine how the reinforcement of state power, which is intimately linked to the expansion of the jurisdiction of the Socialist state in comparison with the bourgeois state, fosters abuses which are inherent to it in virtue of its nature as a Socialist state. This would constitute the elucidation of the idea mentioned earlier, that the most rational state possesses the most opportunities for being passional.

Engels points out in *Anti-Dühring* that the organization of production will remain authoritarian and repressive, even after the expropriation of expropriators, so long as there is a perpetuation of the old division of work and the other aliena-tions which make working a burden and not a joy. When it is not spontaneous, the division of work still arises from constraint, and this constraint is precisely connected to the passage from hazard to rationality.

The temptation toward forced labour therefore becomes one of the major temptations of the Socialist state. But it can easily be seen that the Socialist state is the least protected against this temptation, since its method of global planning also endows it with the economic monopoly over psychological constraint (culture, the press, and propaganda are encompassed within the plan and are therefore economically determined by the state). Hence, the Socialist state will have a whole arsenal of means at its disposal, including psychological means ranging from inducements and competition to deportation.

In addition to these opportunities for abuse provided by the organization of the means of production, there is the temptation to overcome irrational resistances by more expeditious means than those of education or discussion. In effect, the rational state encounters resistances of all kinds; some of these result from residual phenomena (described quite well by Chinese Marxists, in particular, and previously by Lenin in the *Infantile Disorder of Communism*). These resistances are typical of the peasantry and the lower middle class, demonstrating that the psychology of workers is not on the same plane as that of technocrats, but remains adapted to long-standing situations. Thus we find resistances of a psychological character which do not spring from considerations of the general welfare of the people but from the habituation to outdated economic conditions. Yet all resistances are not subject to this explanation by backward mentalities. The Socialist state has a more remote and more vast project than the individual whose interests are more immediate, limited to the horizon of his death or at the very most of that of his children. In the meantime, the state calculates by generations; since the state and the individual are not on the same wavelength, the individual develops interests which are not naturally in accord with those of the state. We are familiar with at least two manifestations of this variance between the goal of the state and that of the individual: one concerns the division between investment and immediate consumption, the other the determination of standards and the rate of production. The micro-interests of individuals and the macro-decisions of power are in a state of constant tension, fostering a dialectic of individual demands and state constraint which is an occasion for abuse.

Thus we find tensions and contradictions which are not the

remedies for the private appropriation of the means of production. Certain of these tensions and contradictions even derive
from the new power of the state.

Lastly, the Socialist state is more ideological than the 'liberal'
state. It may attribute to itself the ancient dreams of unifying
the realm of truth within an orthodoxy encompassing all the
manifestations of knowledge and all the expressions of the
human word. Under the pretext of revolutionary discipline and
technocratic efficacity, it can justify an entire militarization of
minds; it can do it, that is to say, it has the temptation and the
means to do so since it possesses the monopoly of provisions.

All of these reflections converge toward the same conclusion:
if the Socialist state does not abolish but rather revives the
problematic of the state – if it serves to further its rationality
while intensifying opportunities for perversion – the problem of
the democratic control of the state is still more pressing in
Socialist regimes than in capitalistic regimes, and the myth of the
withering away of the state stands in the way of a systematic
treatment of this problem.

(3) The third task of a critique of power in Socialist regimes
would then consist of coming back to the critique of the liberal
state in light of this idea of democratic control. This would
enable it to determine which institutional features of the liberal
state were independent of the phenomenon of class domination
and specifically adapted to the limitation of the abuse of power.
No doubt this critique could not be carried out within the
specifically critical phase of socialism; the liberal state had to
appear almost inevitably as a hypocritical means of perpetuating
economic exploitation. Yet today it is indispensable to discern
between the instrument of class domination and democratic
control in general, at least after the bitter experience of
Stalinism. Perhaps it is the case that Marxism in itself embodies
the ingredients for this revision when it propounds that a class in
its ascending phase pursues a universal function. In giving
expression to the problem of democratic controls, the 'philosophers' of the eighteenth century devised the true liberalism
which no doubt goes beyond the destiny of the bourgeoisie. It
does not follow that just because the bourgeoisie had need of
these controls in order to draw limits to monarchic and feudal
power and to facilitate its own ascension, that these controls
therefore exhaust their abiding significance within their provisory usage. In its profound intention, liberal politics comprised an

element of universality, for it was adjusted to the universal problematic of the state, beyond the form of the bourgeois state. This explains how a return to liberal politics is possible within a Socialist context.

I should like to cite a few examples of this discernment applied to the structures of the liberal state, examples of the division between the 'universal' aspects and the 'bourgeois' aspects of these structures. I shall present them in a problematic manner since we are practically at the end of a critique of Socialist power of which the first postulates are scarcely certain:

(a) Is not the independence of the 'judge' the very first condition of permanent legal remedy against the abuse of power? It seems to me that the judge is a personage who must be voluntarily placed, by the consent of all, on the fringes of the fundamental conflicts of society.

The independence of the judge, it will be objected, is an abstraction. Quite so. Society requires for its human respiration an 'ideal' function, a deliberate, concerted abstraction in which it projects the ideal of legality that legitimates the reality of power. Without this projection, in which the state represents itself as legitimate, the individual is at the mercy of the state and power itself, without protection against its arbitrariness. It stands to reason that the proceedings of Moscow, of Budapest, of Prague, and elsewhere, were possible because the independence of the judge was not technically assured nor ideologically founded in a theory of the judge as a man above class, as an abstraction of human proportions, as the embodiment of law. Stalin was possible because there were always judges to judge in accordance with his decree.

(b) The second condition of permanent legal remedy against the abuse of power is the citizen's free access to sources of information, knowledge, and science, independent of those of the state. As we have seen, the modern state determines the way of living since it orients economically all of man's choices by its macro-decisions, its global planning; but this power will become more and more indistinguishable from totalitarian power if the citizens are not able to form, by themselves, an opinion concerning the nature and the stakes involved in these macro-decisions.

More than any other, the Socialist state requires the counterpart of public opinion in the strict sense of the word, that is to say, a public which has opinions and an opinion which is given public expression. It is quite plain what this involves: a press that belongs to its readers and not to the state, and a press whose freedom of information and of expression is constitutionally and economically guaranteed. Stalin was possible because no public opinion could launch a critique of him. But then again, the post-Stalin state alone has dared to utter that Stalin was evil, not the people.

The independent exercise of justice and the independent formation of opinion are the two lungs of a politically sound state. Without these, there is asphyxiation.

These two notions are so important that it was in virtue of them that the overthrow of Stalinism was accomplished; the notions of justice and truth gave birth to the revolt. This explains the role of intellectuals in the abortive revolution of Hungary and in the successful revolution of Poland. If intellectuals, writers, and artists played a decisive role in these events, it is because the stakes at issue were not economic and social, notwithstanding misery and low wages; the stakes were strictly political, or to be more precise, they were the new political 'alienation' infecting Socialist power. But the problem of political alienation, as we are well aware of since Plato's *Gorgias*, is the problem of untruth. We have also learned of this through the Marxist critique of the bourgeois state, situated, as it is, entirely upon the terrain of untruth, of being and appearance, of mystification, and of falsehood. It is just here that the intellectual as such becomes involved in politics. The intellectual is driven to the fore of a revolution, and not merely within its ranks, as soon as the incentive for this revolution is more political than economic, as soon as it touches upon the relation of power with truth and justice.

(c) Next, it would seem to me that the democracy of work requires a certain dialectic between the state and labour councils. As we have seen, the long-term interests of the state, even apart from the consideration of money, do not immediately coincide with those of workers; this stands to reason in a Socialist period, in the precise sense of the word, that is to say in a phase of inequality of wages, wherein professional specialization is in opposition to unskilled and skilled labourers, directors, and intellectuals; this also stands to reason in a period of rapid or even forced industrialization. Consequently, only a network of liaisons between the state and associations representing the diverse interests of workers can consolidate the groping quests for a viable equilibrium, that is to say at once economically sound and humanly tolerable. The right to strike, in particular, would seem to be the sole recourse of workers against the state, even against the state of workers. The postulate of the immediate coincidence of the will of the Socialist state with all interests of all workers seems to me to be a pernicious illusion and a dangerous alibi for the abuse of state power.

(d) Lastly, the key problem is that of the control of the state by the people, by the democratically organized foundation. At this point, the reflections and experiences of the Yugoslavian and Polish Communists ought to be consulted and analysed very closely. The question is whether the pluralism of parties, the practice of 'free elections', and the parliamentary form of government derive from this 'universalism' of the liberal state, or whether they irremediably pertain to the bourgeois period of the liberal state. We must not have any preconceived ideas: neither for nor against; neither for Occidental custom, nor for radical criticism; we need not be in a hurry to answer. It is certain that planning techniques require that the Socialist form of production not be given over to the hazard of popular vote; that it be irrevocable, as is the republican form of our government. The execution of the plan calls for full powers, a government of long continuance, a long-term budget. Yet our parliamentary techniques, our manner of interchanging the majorities in power, would not appear very compatible with the modern rationality of the state. And yet, on the other hand, it is just as certain that discussion is a vital necessity for the state; through discussion it is given orientation and impetus; discussion curbs its tendency to abuse power. Democracy is discussion. Thus it is necessary that this discussion be organized in one way or another. Here we encounter the question concerning parties or the unique party. What may argue in favour of the pluralism of parties is that this system has not only reflected tensions between social groups, determined by the division of society into classes, but it has also invested political discussion as such with organization, and it has therefore had a 'universal' and not merely a 'bourgeois' significance. An analysis of the notion of 'party', on the sole basis of the socio-economic criterion, therefore seems to me dangerously inadequate and liable to encourage tyranny. This is why it is necessary to judge the theory of multiple parties and the theory of a single party not only from the standpoint of class dynamics, but equally from the viewpoint of the techniques of controlling the state. Only a critique of power in Socialist regimes could further advance this question. Yet this critique has hardly been launched.

I do not know whether the term political 'liberalism' can be saved from falling into disrepute. Perhaps its affinity with economic liberalism has compromised it once and for all, although of late the label 'liberal' tends to constitute a misdemeanour in the eyes of social Fascists in Algeria and in Paris, and thus recovers its bygone freshness.

If the term could be saved, it would state rather well what ought to be said: that the central problem of politics is freedom: whether the state founds freedom by means of its rationality, or whether freedom limits the passions of power through its resistance.

NOTES

1 Throughout this essay, particularly in the second section, the author contrasts polity (*le politique*) with politics (*la politique*). By polity, the author intends the ideal sphere of political organization and historical rationality; by politics, the empirical and concrete manifestations of this ideal sphere, the sum total of the means employed to implement the ideal sphere of polity. – Trans.
2 Aristotle, Politics, I, 2 (1252 b 32), tr.
3 Ibid (1253 a 2–3, 28–30), tr.
4 Ibid, III, 1 (1275 a-b), tr.
5 J.-J. Rousseau, *Contrat social* (Paris: Garnier, 1960), p. 243, (tr.)
6 Ibid, pp. 243–4 (tr.)
7 'If, then, society is the foundation, the by no means formless matter of the State, the conscious reason of self is wholly on the side of the State: outside of it there may be concrete morality, tradition, work, abstract right, sentiment, virtue, but there can be no reason. Only the State thinks, only the State can be totally thought', *Hegel et l'état* (Paris: Vrin, 1950), p. 68. For the definition of the state. cf. p. 45.
8 Max Weber calls politics 'the sum total of efforts with a view to participating in power, or of influencing the division of power either within the State or between States', *Politik als Beruf* (Munich, 1926).
9 *Amos*, 1:3–15: '. . . since they have crushed Galaad . . . since they have taken a large number of captives and delivered them to Edom . . . since they have hunted down their own brother at the sword's point without compassion . . . since they so coveted Galaad's land that they would rip open the womb of pregnant women, I shall not recall the sentence I have pronounced.'
10 Cf. J. Y. Calvez, *La Pensée de Karl Marx*, in the chapter on political alienation.
11 Marx, *The Eighteenth Brumaire of Louis Bonaparte*.

Index

achievement and rewards, 149–50
Adams, H., 105
administrative staff *see* bureaucracy
affluence/consumption, 227–9, 249
agency theory of state, 143–4
allegiance to order, withdrawal of,
   224–5
   see also disillusionment
Amalrik, A., 192
Amos, prophet, 257, 272
anthropological balance crisis, 141
anti-science, genealogies as, 204
Arendt, H., 108, 111, 118, 122,
   183, 234
'argumentation sketch', 158
Aristotle, 65, 251–3, 255
arms race, 142
art, 152–3, 172
artificiality of order, 113–14
association of 'estates', 36–7
associational life, 118–19
Augustine, St., 65
Australia, 89
Austria, 92, 94–6
authoritarianism, 184–90
authority
   humanly meaningful, 123–7
   leadership, 34–8, 50–9, 109–10,
     125
   loss of, 104–7, 112–13, 118–19
   of office-holders, 186–8
   Weber on, 8, 79, 104–5
   see also charismatic; discipline;
    domination; power
autonomy
   of polity, 251–6

of process, 119

Bacon, F., 23, 67, 115
banality, 122
Belgium, 89
belief in legitimacy, 108–10
Benjamin, W., 153
Bentham, J., 171
Berns, W., 189
bifurcation of liberalism, 17, 233–6
bourgeoisie
   decline of, 152, 172, 175
   ideologies of, 160, 171, 178
   and political hero, 77
   power and, 214–18
   reform and, 21–4, 28
Britain/England
   church in, 93
   monarch in, 62, 89
   pauperism in, 22–6
   politics in, 45, 94, 98
   stability of, 91
Brzezinski, Z., 186
budget, government, 144–5
bureaucracy and administrative
   system, 10, 39–50
   characteristics of, 39–42
   crisis avoidance, 144
   economic and social
    consequences of, 45–7
   epistemology, 119–22
   independence, 146–8
   in late capitalism, 137–8
   official, position of, 42–5
   power of, 47–50
   rationality and, 118–32